Chinese Pure Land Buddhism

Pure Land Buddhist Studies
a publication of the Institute of Buddhist Studies
at the Graduate Theological Union

PURE LAND BUDDHIST STUDIES

Chinese Pure Land Buddhism

Understanding a Tradition of Practice

Charles B. Jones

HAWAI'I

University of Hawaiʻi Press / Honolulu

Paperback edition 2020

Printed in the United States of America

25 24 23 22 21 20 6 5 4 3 2 1

Library of Congress Cataloging-in-Publication Data

Names: Jones, Charles Brewer, author.
Title: Chinese Pure Land Buddhism : understanding a tradition of practice / Charles B. Jones.
Other titles: Pure Land Buddhist studies.
Description: Honolulu : University of Hawaiʻi Press, [2019] | Series: Pure Land Buddhist studies | Includes bibliographical references and index.
Identifiers: LCCN 2019001148 | ISBN 9780824879716 (cloth ; alk. paper)
Subjects: LCSH: Pure Land Buddhism—China.
Classification: LCC BQ8512.9.C5 J66 2019 | DDC 294.3/9260951—dc23
LC record available at https://lccn.loc.gov/2019001148

ISBN 978-0-8248-8841-1 (pbk.)

The Pure Land Buddhist Studies series publishes scholarly works on all aspects of the Pure Land Buddhist tradition. Historically, this includes studies of the origins of the tradition in India, its transmission into a variety of religious cultures, and its continuity into the present. Methodologically, the series is committed to providing a venue for a diversity of approaches, including, but not limited to, anthropological, sociological, historical, textual, biographical, philosophical, and interpretive, as well as translations of primary and secondary works. The series will also seek to reprint important works so that they may continue to be available to the scholarly and lay communities. The series is made possible through the generosity of the Buddhist Churches of America's Fraternal Benefit Association. We wish to express our deep appreciation for its support to the Institute of Buddhist Studies.

University of Hawaiʻi Press books are printed on acid-free paper and meet the guidelines for permanence and durability of the Council on Library Resources.

Cover photo: Kumarajiva Temple at Wuwei, Gansu Province. Photo by author.

Dedicated to the memory of
Roger Jonathan Tashi Corless
1938–2007
Friend and Mentor

Contents

Series Editor's Preface

The study of Pure Land Buddhism in China has seen some significant contestation. Charles Jones' volume settles many of the controversies that have inhibited the field from developing as fully as it should. The recent history of the contestation follows several long-standing misconceptions and questionable categorizations. Perhaps the most enduring controversial issue is the normative role that the Pure Land sect of Hōnen has played in defining Pure Land Buddhism. Following that is the characterization of Pure Land as a version of Protestant Christianity and the ensuing question of whether Pure Land—defined by Hōnen's Jōdoshū and often described in terms parallel to Protestantism—is a form of Buddhism at all.

An additional problematic characterization was created by the application of a religious sociology based on Christianity to Buddhism. The familiar institutional categories of church, sect, and cult, which date back to the origins of the sociology of religion, have been unreflectively sublated as universally applicable. Consequently, Pure Land was expected to exist as a church, as a sect, or as a cult. Of course the term "church" is not used in the study of Buddhism; instead, "school" is generally used with much the same function and connotation. Still, attempts to identify a Pure Land school in China, inaccurately based on lineages propounded by Japanese Pure Land schools, failed, leading some scholars to propose that such an entity never existed.

The importance of lineage demonstrates further how Buddhist categories do not map well onto those commonly accepted by the sociology of religion. Initiatory lineages establish a practitioner's identity not only in connection to the initiating teacher in the present, but also in continuity back to Śākyamuni Buddha (or to another buddha such as Amitābha or Vairocana). In addition, initiation authorizes engaging in a practice whose efficacy is upheld by the continuity of the lineage itself. Lineages of practice are far from identical with other kinds of Buddhist institutions, and Buddhism has not typically promoted exclusive adherence.

For the vast majority of East Asian Buddhist history, a practitioner has been free to receive multiple initiations; practice has been the main purpose, not exclusive commitment to an institution.

Practice is also more central than doctrine for most Buddhists. In this volume, Jones refers to Pure Land Buddhism as a "tradition of practice." So, the history of defining this religious tradition by doctrine is revealed to be another distortion, an unreflective imposition of Protestant Christian conceptions to the study of Buddhism. This does not mean that there was no explanatory discourse supporting and justifying the practices of Pure Land Buddhism, nor that there were not proponents who argued strongly for its superiority. However, in Buddhist thought generally, while wrong views may impede awakening, proper belief (orthodoxy) is not in itself conducive to awakening. Proper views are beneficial mainly in guiding proper practice (orthopraxy). Furthermore, Jones argues that the lineage's *sine qua non,* an idea formed by Shandao and maintained by Japanese Pure Land thinkers, is that ordinary practitioners can attain awakening without accumulating vast stores of merit over many thousands of lifetimes.

To forward our perceptions of East Asian Pure Land Buddhism, we need to consider its unique characteristics, its complex network of concepts and practices, teachers and texts, continuities and changes, rather than looking for an East Asian version of a church. Jones' work has long moved in that direction, and the Pure Land Buddhist Studies series is happy that this volume brings that scholarship to a focus.

Preface

I've told this story before, but it bears repeating. In 1992, I moved to Taiwan for two and a half years of language study and dissertation research. During that time, I went regularly to a Buddhist temple near the town of San-hsia (*Sānxiá* 三峽) called the Pure Garden of the Western Lotus (*Xīlián jìngyuàn* 西蓮淨苑), a place that proclaimed itself a haven of Pure Land practice. I do not remember precisely when it happened, but I clearly recall the incident that led me to realize that the practices and teachings I observed there did not correspond to anything I had learned about Pure Land Buddhism in my graduate program.

I was at the temple during a three-day buddha-recitation retreat (called a "Buddha Three" or *fó sān* 佛三). The guest prefect (*zhīkè* 知客) accompanied me as I peeped into the main shrine hall to see the participants seated on meditation cushions chanting the name of Amitābha Buddha. I asked him if they were doing the buddha-recitation *kōan* (*niànfó gōng'àn* 念佛公案), a form of Chan–Pure Land dual practice (*chán-jìng shuāngxiū* 禪淨雙修) as recommended by the late Ming dynasty figure Yunqi Zhuhong (*Yúnqī Zhūhóng* 雲棲袾宏, 1535–1615). He replied with some impatience that this temple was strictly a place of Pure Land practice; it was *not* a Chan temple in any way. The participants were reciting the name of the Buddha in hopes of gaining rebirth in his western Pure Land after they died, and perhaps a vision of him in this life. It seemed that Pure Land had maintained a distinct identity and had not gone along with the Chan–Pure Land "syncretism" that, as I had learned, marked a significant development in the history of Chinese Buddhism.

I also noticed that Chinese Pure Land differed from the Japanese Pure Land schools of Jōdo Shū 淨土宗 and Jōdo Shinshū 淨土新宗 in many important respects. Most notably, the practitioners I observed and the texts I read in Taiwan drew no hard and fast distinction between "self-power" (*zìlì* 自力; J. *jiriki*) and "other-power" (*tālì* 他力; J. *tariki*). It was not immediately clear to me how the two related, but I got a clue from the title of an essay in one of the abbot's books: "The Two Powers of Self and Other" (*zì tā èr lì* 自他二力). Unfortunately, I lost that book many years ago, but I have other books by him in which he references this concept, and a modern Chinese Pure Land teacher, Ven. Daan (*Dàān* 大安, b. 1959) also uses this term. He notes that the inclusion of both Lushan Huiyuan, a proponent of the "two powers," and Shandao, a champion of "other-power," in the list of Pure Land "patriarchs" gave the Chinese a pair of live options, not a stark choice (Dàān 2006, 25–26, 142).

In addition, the practitioners did not seem to regard themselves as belonging exclusively to a distinct Buddhist institution. While they gave their practice the same name as the Japanese Jōdo Shū, *Jìngtǔ zōng* 淨土宗, the term seemed to be a Japanese import, and it was better to understand the word *zōng* 宗 as "tradition" rather than as "school" or "sect." Pure Land seemed to be the common property of *all* Chinese Buddhists. They all wore a small rosary (*niànzhū* 念珠) around their wrist as a marker of their Buddhist identity; they all replaced "hello" and "goodbye" with the name of Amitābha Buddha (*Āmítuófó* 阿彌陀佛) when addressing one another as Buddhists. They recited the Buddha's name to supplement whatever other practices they might have adopted.

In sum, it appeared evident that there was more work to do if western scholars were to understand the Chinese Pure Land tradition properly. My perception that our understanding had been somewhat distorted by the dominance of Japanese secondary scholarship was ratified by Kenneth Tanaka, who argued this point rather forcefully (1990, xv–xvi). In response, I embarked on this study, provisionally leaving aside the usual Japanese scholarly sources and going directly to the primary texts with fresh eyes. Because the impetus for this study was an encounter with the modern practice of Pure Land, I began with the modern period and worked backwards. The Xilian Temple took the modern figure Yinguang (*Yìnguāng* 印光, 1861–1940) as its main authority and inspiration, so I began with him. I then inquired into his sources and inspirations, and in this manner I settled into a study of Pure Land in the late Ming dynasty (1368–1644), focusing on the two figures of Yunqi Zhuhong and the layman and literatus Yuan Hongdao (*Yuán Hóngdào* 袁宏道, 1568–1610).

The result was a string of articles, mostly published in the late 1990s and early 2000s, examining various aspects of Chinese Pure Land Buddhism, especially in the late imperial period. I then left the subject for a while and followed some other lines of research. I have now returned to it, resulting in a couple of chapters that appear here for the first time. Because many of the previously published articles had become rather dated, and because the availability of electronic sources such as the Chinese Buddhist Electronic Text Association and my own continued study and reflection had made much more material accessible, I have taken the opportunity to significantly expand and revise all of these pieces.

I have had much help on this journey. Dr. Richard Payne of the Institute of Buddhist Studies and editor of *Pacific World* has been a longtime collaborator in this and given me much support and encouragement. Ven. Huimin 惠敏法師, vice-abbot of the Xilian Temple during the period of my dissertation research and now abbot and provost of Dharma Drum Mountain Institute of Buddhist Studies, gave me a great deal of access and leeway during my visits to the temple and has continued to help and encourage my studies. My dissertation director, Dr. Paul Groner, has always been there for conversation and feedback, and I continue to cherish his friendship as the years go on and I realize just how well trained I really was. My doctoral student, Mr. Michael Markovich, has been invaluable in helping locate sources and batting around many of the ideas that appear in these pages. Ms. Liu Yan 劉焱, another graduate student, introduced me to the wonders of WeChat as a way of finding out about Pure Land in mainland China. I owe a great deal as well to the collective entity known as the Scholars of Buddhist Studies Facebook group. Last but certainly not least, the late Dr. Roger J. Corless of Duke University was a mentor when I needed one, and it is no exaggeration to say that without his influence I would not have entered the academic life at all. The fact that he also studied Chinese Pure Land Buddhism is no coincidence. I dedicate this volume to his memory.

Abbreviations

CBETA	Chinese Buddhist Electronic Text Association
CBETA X	The CBETA version of texts from the *Xu zang jing* 續藏經
d.u.	dates unknown
DDB	Digital Dictionary of Buddhism
Rpt.	reprint
T.	*Taishō Shinshū Daizōkyō* 大正新脩大藏經. Ed. Takakusu Junjirō 高楠順次郎. 100 vols. Tokyo: Daizō shuppan kai, 1922–1933.
XZJ	*Xu zang jing* 續藏經. 750 vols. in 150 cases. Kyōto: Zōkyō Shoin, 1905–1912. Rpt.: 151 vols. Taipei: Xinwenfeng, 1993.

Titles of Texts

Amitābha Sutra = *Fó shuō Āmítuó jīng* 佛說阿彌陀經, T.366
Biographies of Eminent Monks = *Gāosēng zhuàn* 高僧傳, T.2059
Contemplation Sutra = *Fó shuō guān wúliàngshòu fó jīng* 佛說觀無量壽佛經, T.365
Larger Sutra = *Fó shuō wúliàngshòu jīng* 佛說無量壽經, T.360
Lotus Sutra = *Miàofǎ liánhuá jīng* 妙法蓮華經, T.262
Nirvana Sutra = *Dàbān nièpán jīng* 大般涅槃經, T.374
Platform Sutra = *Liù zǔ dàshī fǎbǎo tán jīng* 六祖大師法寶壇經, T.2008
Pratyutpanna-samādhi-sūtra = *Bānzhōu sānmèi jīng* 般舟三昧經, T.418
Vimalakīrti Sutra = *Wéimójí suǒshuō jīng* 維摩詰所說經, T.475
Wangsheng lun zhu = *Wúliàngshòu jīng yōupótíshè yuànshēng jié zhù* 無量壽經優婆提舍願生偈註, T.1819

Chapter 1

Introduction

Throughout China, Taiwan, Hong Kong, and sites where diaspora Chinese live, one may encounter Buddhist clerics and laypeople who wear a rosary (*niànzhū* 念珠) as a public sign of their Buddhist identity. While these strings of beads have other religious uses, they are mainly associated with the practice of *nianfo* (*niànfó* 念佛), or "buddha-recitation/contemplation," a practice wherein, at its simplest, the devotee recites the name of the Buddha Amitābha (*Āmítuófó* 阿彌陀佛) in the expectation of gaining rebirth in the western Pure Land (*xīfāng jìngtǔ* 西方淨土) called Sukhāvatī after they die. For those who doubt that they can achieve complete liberation and buddhahood in the present life (and this includes almost all Buddhists), this practice is the expression of a hope that while dwelling in this buddha's land and receiving his direct instruction, they will finally escape all future suffering. More than that, they will become buddhas and establish their own Pure Lands as bases from which to aid other suffering beings.

Westerners who know something about Buddhism have difficulty understanding this practice (Fujita 1996, p. 3). In university courses, popular books and magazines, and western-oriented practice centers, they learn that Buddhism is a religion of self-reliance. One studies the doctrines and engages in the practices, and by one's own efforts purifies the mind and realizes the truth leading to liberation. Upon hearing of "Pure Land Buddhism," usually in the Japanese formulation that emphasizes the helplessness of human beings in the present age of defilement and counsels complete reliance on the "other-power" (*tālì* 他力; J. *tariki*) of Amitābha, they frequently ask how anyone could consider such a teaching Buddhist at all. One scholar, writing in the 1980s, sought to establish on philosophical grounds that Pure Land Buddhism was not really Buddhism, as it represented such a departure from early Buddhism that it would be best to consider it a new religious formulation altogether (Steadman 1987). As Alfred Bloom once reported in a popular Buddhist magazine,

> Christmas Humphreys, a noted early English Buddhist scholar and proponent of Zen, once declared Shin "a form of Buddhism which on the face of it discards three-quarters of Buddhism. Compared with the teaching of the Pāli Canon it is but Buddhism and water." In fact, Shin Buddhism is often portrayed this way by those who believe meditation practice constitutes the core teaching of Buddhism. (Bloom 1995, p. 58)

This is not just a problem for westerners. As the reader will discover in chapter 6, many Buddhists in late imperial China also wondered whether Pure Land represented a distortion of the pure buddha-dharma, and the Chinese Pure Land tradition is all the more interesting for its sophisticated and witty responses to such attacks and the way it defended its position as an orthodox Buddhist tradition. The reader will see how Chinese Buddhist authors handled this in due course. Here let us simply note that such suspicions have resulted in a distinct lack of interest in Pure Land among western scholars and practitioners, at least until very recent times.

Another impediment to understanding the Chinese tradition in particular arose from the historical development of western scholarship on Chinese Buddhism. As recently as my days as a doctoral student in the early 1990s, scholars specializing in East Asian Buddhism generally learned literary Chinese for reading primary source texts, modern Japanese for reading secondary scholarship, but not modern spoken or written Chinese. I would hear that the Chinese did not produce scholarship worth consulting, and that the Japanese were thorough and insightful interpreters of the Buddhist traditions. As a result, what western scholarship existed on Chinese Pure Land Buddhism at the time based itself largely on Chinese primary sources and Japanese secondary literature. This resulted in western works on Chinese Pure Land Buddhism that imported the Japanese interpretive framework into their presentations. For example, a series of doctoral dissertations produced in the 1970s and early 1980s focused on Tanluan (*Tánluán* 曇鸞), Daochuo (*Dàochuò* 道綽), and Shandao (*Shàndǎo* 善導), figures prominent in the Japanese Pure Land patriarchal lineage but not reflected in any of the Chinese lineages, in which neither Tanluan nor Daochuo appear (see appendix).

Over the years, I have come to think that something else has also been discouraging western scholars from researching this tradition. While we have a few studies of isolated events or figures, we have lacked a general orientation to the tradition. As the next chapter will show, several prominent scholars have argued either that there is no such tradition or that it is so diffused throughout all of Chinese Buddhism that it cannot be isolated as a particular area of study. Thus, my purpose in assembling and revising past essays and composing some new ones is to present the reader with a broad overview that first defines Pure Land as a distinctive and bounded part of Chinese Buddhism and then follows out some of its major themes. To accomplish this, every chapter has had to bring together a great deal of material from various points in history. This is not a book of miniatures, but of landscapes.

One other methodological issue requires the reader's attention before proceeding to the individual chapters. Aside from the broad sweep of the chapters in time and space, my own approach to the topic has influenced the presentation. As narrated in the preface, my first encounter with Chinese Pure Land Buddhism was in a modern manifestation, and from there I proceeded backwards in history to see how this modern practice had come about. This means that the chapters to follow examine the topic from a retrospective angle. That is to say, I look at even the earliest materials from the Tang dynasty (618–907) and before in light of the later tradition that claimed them, not as precursors or harbingers, but as part of itself. This may give rise to some qualms. To ask, as the title of chapter 8 does, whether or not Lushan Huiyuan was a Pure Land Buddhist might be like asking whether Augustine of Hippo was a Presbyterian. If one is interested in understanding Augustine within his own historical, cultural, and religious moment, the question may well be inappropriate. However, if one's object of study is not Augustine but the Reformed Protestant tradition that claims him, then it is surely of great interest to know how that tradition understood Augustine's role and contribution. Likewise, chapter 8 asks not only what exactly Huiyuan believed about the Buddha Amitābha and the land of Sukhāvatī, but also traces the development of his image as the tradition incorporated him as its first "patriarch."

Chapter 2 revisits an old problem that fell into abeyance many years ago without resolution: What do we mean when we talk about Pure Land in China? The question is not easy to answer, as many scriptures, people, and texts refer to the Buddha Amitābha and the means of gaining rebirth in his Pure Land without falling within the purview of "Pure Land Buddhism," and it is very difficult to identify a bounded group of people that would qualify as a "school" or a "sect." I will contend that we can, indeed we must, identify a "Pure Land tradition" in China that achieved a coherent shape, however porous. We will then be in a position to affirm that this tradition is Buddhist and that it occupies a distinct place within Buddhism.

Chapter 3 will show how the idea of the Pure Land itself grew from the simple idea of a buddha-field to a richly variegated range of domains over which a buddha may preside. Chapter 4 will lay out the distinctive way that Chinese Pure Land authors defined the relationship between "self-power" and "other-power," adumbrating the way in which the individual practitioner's efforts at morality and practice interacted with the power of the Buddha Amitābha to advance him or her toward the goals of rebirth in the Pure Land and buddhahood. Chapter 5 will follow into the question of *why* the practitioner should put forth any effort at all, given that the power of the Buddha could accomplish these goals without the practitioner expending any effort. Chapter 6 will move to an examination of the ways in which Pure Land adherents defended their tradition's thought and practice against a number of accusations of laziness, selfishness, ineffectiveness, and infidelity to Buddhist principles. In chapter 7, we will examine *nianfo,* a word that points to the primary practice of the Pure Land tradition. However, we will see that it is a very open and multivalent term covering a considerable variety of practices that served a number of different purposes. Chapter 8 takes a fresh look at the figure of Lushan Huiyuan (*Lúshān Huìyuǎn* 廬山慧遠, 334–416), conventionally regarded as the first "patriarch" (*zǔ* 祖) of the tradition. This chapter asks about his status as a Pure Land Buddhist and the nature of his understanding of Pure Land practice, and then traces the centuries-long process through which he evolved into a Pure Land figure. The appendix will describe the process by which the widely accepted list of 13 Pure Land "patriarchs" evolved.

While this is not intended to be a complete history of Chinese Pure Land Buddhism, it is my hope that the reader who works through the essays that follow will finish this book with a clearer idea about the genesis, shape, and ethos of the Chinese Pure Land tradition, and a greater appreciation for its depth and sophistication.

Chapter 2

What Is the Chinese Pure Land Tradition?

And I think there's a sort of a something which is called a wallaboo . . .
—A. A. Milne, "At the Zoo"

As noted in the introduction, this is primarily a collection of thematic essays on the Chinese Pure Land tradition. Before exploring any individual theme, however, we need a paradigm for the phenomenon to which the chapters pertain. This has proven a difficult task because previous scholarship provides very little help or guidance. Most studies presume that "Pure Land Buddhism" and related terms point to something self-evident in Chinese history, so they provide no definition of it. A few studies argue that there actually is nothing there, and that "Chinese Pure Land" is an empty name whose referent disappears under analysis. Others define it so broadly that it becomes coextensive with all of Chinese Buddhism, leading in a different way to its dissolution. Nevertheless, when one approaches the matter through primary sources, one cannot escape the impression that, in the words of A. A. Milne, a "sort of a something" remains and stubbornly resists scholarly efforts to dissolve it. Because of this, the essays that follow presume the presence within Chinese Buddhism of a discrete tradition called "Pure Land" that has several features that distinguish it from other parts of the Buddhist landscape. Without this real presence, the remaining essays lack a subject and merely perpetuate an illusion. Therefore, this chapter will describe the Chinese Pure Land tradition's mode of presence and define its features. To do this, I will need to review and evaluate past studies, then make use of new criteria and methods in order to identify our subject.

Why the Object Eludes Us

It is commonly recognized that western academics were introduced to the Chinese Pure Land tradition largely through the writings of Japanese scholars who often worked in sectarian Buddhist universities. These scholars brought their own and their institutions' religious concerns and categories to bear in organizing the subject matter. To give one example, Mochizuki Shinkō's *Chūgoku jōdo kyōrishi* 中国浄土教理史 (Pure Land Buddhism in China: A doctrinal history) was written from the perspective of Mochizuki's Jōdo Shū 淨土宗 affiliation. Daniel Getz argues that his clerical standing in the Jōdo Shū was a determinative factor in his scholarship (in Mochizuki 2016, p. 2:2). For example, Mochizuki criticized the early Pure Land figure Jiacai (*Jiācái* 迦才, d.u.) for teaching that advanced bodhisattvas attain rebirth in the Pure Land while ordinary beings do not (1942, p. 178). One could cite other instances in which he judges Chinese figures according to Jōdo Shū standards.

The two dominant schools of Pure Land Buddhism in Japan, the Jōdo Shū 淨土宗 and the Jōdo Shinshū 淨土真宗 have institutional self-consciousness, autonomy, governing structures, membership rolls, and continuous lineages of teachers. Scholars from these schools tended to retroject these features onto their Chinese precursors, and western scholars followed suit. Kenneth Ch'en's 1964 *Buddhism in China: A Historical Survey* is often cited as an example of western dependence upon Japanese research on Pure Land, with occasional further mention of a series of doctoral dissertations produced in the United States in the 1970s and 1980s that focused on Chinese Pure Land figures who were known to the Japanese tradition as patriarchs but were not necessarily important to the Chinese. (See Marchman 2015, p. 12–14, 22, 25–26, and 66–67 for more discussion of specific manifestations of Japanese influence.)

This set up the foil against which subsequent scholarship later argued. As western researchers began to engage the primary sources for themselves, the earlier model began to unravel. Robert Sharf questioned whether Pure Land in China constituted a "school," a "tradition," or had any other kind of institutional identity (Sharf 2002a). Daniel Getz concluded that, with the possible exception of a few movements in North China during the sixth and seventh centuries, Pure Land had never displayed any of the marks of an independent institution (1999). Because of the work of these and other researchers, western scholars now agree that we should not consider Pure Land Buddhism in China as a "school" or identify it as a Japanese-style *shū* 宗.

Nevertheless, one still runs into signs that Chinese Buddhists identified something in their religious environment that they designated "Pure Land" (*jìngtǔ* 淨土) or an equivalent term such as "Lotus School" (*liánzōng* 蓮宗). In response to this, Getz asserted that the Chinese themselves created confusion by using institutional language, for example by drawing up lists of patriarchs (*zǔ* 祖; Getz 1999, p. 477; 2003, p. 68–70). He speculated that during the Song dynasty (960–1279) the leaders of this tradition were mainly associated with the Tiantai (*Tiāntái* 天台) school, a Buddhist institution that had its own list of chronologically contiguous patriarchs and exhibited a clearer corporate nature. These figures transferred their language of organization and patriarchate on to their Pure Land societies as a way of maintaining leadership, but in the end, this misled later followers and distorts current scholarship. For both Sharf and Getz, Pure Land simply melts into the ocean of Chinese Buddhism.

Another way that scholars submerge the Pure Land tradition into the wider field of Chinese Buddhism is to agree that there is such a tradition, but to define it so broadly that it once again recedes from view. Jan Nattier, for example, in her excellent study of the cult of Akṣobhya Buddha and early expressions of desire for rebirth in his buddha-land Abhirati, suggested that we broaden our definition of the Pure Land tradition to include any Buddhist practice aimed at rebirth in any buddha-field (2000, p. 74). This definition extends the range so much that almost everywhere one looks within Chinese Buddhism one will find Pure Land. Scholars would have to include any figure who ever commented on a "Pure Land sutra," recommended a practice for gaining rebirth in a buddha-land, formulated and used deathbed rituals for rebirth, or recounted rebirth stories within the tradition.

Studies such as these have been useful for removing past misconceptions, but they pose significant methodological problems for efforts to say more positively what Chinese Pure Land is. First, methods that aim solely to correct distortions engendered by the use of inappropriate categories cannot lead to a positive characterization of the object under scrutiny. For instance, if one believes that a patriarchal lineage must consist of individuals with direct master-disciple relations as in Chan and Esoteric Buddhism, then the Chinese Pure Land patriarchate will appear confusing and be dismissed from further consideration. However, faulting the Chinese for adding to *our* present misunderstanding means that we are not paying attention to what *they* meant by "patriarch." It replicates the difficulty that we imputed to the application of Japanese categories to the materials, only this time the misleading categories are ours. It is better to assume that those who formulated the extant patriarchal lists did so for their own purposes. Understanding *those* purposes should be the scholar's task. We will return to this point below.

Second, previous studies failed to find a clear Pure Land tradition in China because they addressed only the early period without pursuing the tradition past the Song and on to the late imperial and Republican periods. This restriction decreased the likelihood of discovering the Pure Land tradition because religious movements in the premodern world never arose fully formed within short periods of time. Most scholars now agree, for instance, that Mahayana Buddhism took shape slowly as a number of disparate trends and movements coalesced and achieved a degree of unity and self-consciousness over the span of a few centuries. A study that asked whether Mahayana actually existed as a category while looking only at material prior to the third century CE would have trouble finding it. Similarly, Pure Land in China grew over time out of a number of interests and discussions that did not yield unity or achieve self-consciousness until much later. Looking just at early materials, one will see only the "churn" of proposals and interpretations that would settle into a pattern later; one will not see the pattern. The knowledge that there would indeed be a Pure Land tradition by the Song and Ming dynasties is what leads us to look back in time to discover its sources; it does not follow that we will find Pure Land in any consistent or readily identifiable form in the early period.

In a similar manner, adopting a definition of Pure Land so broad and overdetermined that the object may be found virtually anywhere does not lead to a positive characterization either. Casting a wide net for the roots of the tradition, while useful for helping us to locate the early sources out of which the tradition grew, does not lead us to a precise understanding of Pure Land. For example, while Pure Land no doubt grew from general reflections about rebirth in buddha-lands, later proponents in China sought actively to exclude practices directed at other buddhas or bodhisattvas (such as Akṣobhya or Maitreya) dwelling in other lands from the tradition. In this and other ways, many Chinese thinkers over the course of centuries came to define a Pure Land tradition that they considered a part of orthodox Chinese Buddhism, but a distinct part.

In this chapter, I wish to use a different method to arrive at a different paradigm. I will grant the conclusions already established and not rehearse again the reasons why Japanese scholarly categories do not apply cleanly to Chinese Pure Land Buddhism. I will bracket that discussion and focus instead on looking afresh at the Chinese sources to see what *is* there rather than what is *not* there. To do this, I will refer especially (1) to terms frequently used for this tradition, and (2) literature in which Buddhist leaders concerned to promote Pure Land thought and practice gave their own accounts of the tradition. This literature comprises catechetic and apologetic texts, often in question-and-answer format. Within such texts, thinkers such as pseudo-Zhiyi (*Zhìyǐ* 智顗), Huaigan (*Huáigǎn* 懷感, d. 699), Tianru Weize (*Tiānrú Wéizé* 天如惟則, 1286?–1354), Yunqi Zhuhong (*Yúnqī Zhūhóng* 雲棲袾宏, 1535–1615), Yuan Hongdao (*Yuán Hóngdào* 袁宏道, 1568–1610), and Yinguang (*Yìnguāng* 印光, 1861–1940) explained and defended what they clearly considered an identifiable and separate tradition within Chinese Buddhism.

Institutional Markers: *Zōng* 宗 and *Zǔ* 祖

Following Japanese usage, scholars today refer to Chinese Pure Land, whether as an institution or as a set of doctrines and practices, as the "Pure Land *zōng*" (*jìngtǔ zōng* 淨土宗). Therefore, we shall begin by examining this term. The Chinese word *zōng* 宗 began as a kinship term. According to the *Hanyu dacidian* 漢語大詞典, the term can refer to an ancestral temple (*zǔmiào* 祖廟), ancestors in general (*zǔxiān* 祖先), or a clan (*zōngzú* 宗族); it is thus possible that the term *jìngtǔ zōng* 淨土宗 could point metaphorically to a grouping of people. However, a search of Chinese Buddhist texts in CBETA reveals just over fifty occurrences of the term *jìngtǔ zōng* 淨土宗, and in every case, the word *zōng* occurs in tandem with another character to create a compound meaning, a central principle, or cardinal teaching. For example, the Tang dynasty *Jìngtǔ lùn* 淨土論 (T.1963) by Jiacai (*Jiācái* 迦才, d.u.) uses the term this way: "Thus we know that the central intention of the Pure Land (*jìngtǔ zōngyì* 淨土宗意) is fundamentally as much for the sake of ordinary beings as for sages" (T.1963.47:90c17–c18). In other passages and other texts, the terms *zōngyào* 宗要 (essential doctrines), *zōngcī* 宗恉 (cardinal meaning), and *zōngzhǐ* 宗旨 (primary meaning) appear after the term "Pure Land." In no instance does the term *jìngtǔ zōng* 淨土宗 indicate an institutional or social formation.

We may take it as established, then, that there is no concept of a Pure Land "clan" in China, though we will need to ask what it means for something called "Pure Land" to have a "cardinal meaning" or an "essential doctrine." It is not until the late nineteenth century that I begin to find the term *jìngtǔ zōng* 淨土宗 used to indicate a "school" in the Japanese sense. For example, Chen Yangjiong's 陈扬炯 general history of Pure Land in China is entitled *Zhōngguó jìngtǔ zōng tōngshǐ* 中国净土宗通史. Another example would be a series of anthologies of articles about Pure Land Buddhism edited by Zhang Mantao 張曼濤, which all incorporate the term into their titles (e.g., *Jìngtǔ zōng gàilùn* 淨土宗概論). Even in these cases, though, the term is ambiguous; the term "school" might be used in its institutional sense, but it also might indicate a "school of thought."

The term usually translated as patriarch, *zǔ* 祖, requires more explanation because both Sharf and Getz make it central to their arguments about Pure Land's lack of institutional presence. Both authors note that the list of patriarchs accepted within the tradition since the Song dynasty (960–1279) was constructed for certain institutional purposes. Various versions of the list include figures that occupy adjacent places on the list but do not overlap chronologically. It also includes figures who apparently contributed nothing to the tradition (Getz 2003).

It is true that several figures that are adjacent to each other on the list were too separated geographically and/or chronologically to have had direct contact, but those who compiled these lists were well aware of that fact and ascribed no importance to it. For example, Zongxiao (*Zōngxiǎo* 宗曉, 1151–1214), who published his list of "Five Great Patriarchs Who Carried on the Lotus Society" (*Liánshè jìzǔ wǔ dàfǎshī* 蓮社繼祖五大法師) in 1199, explicitly noted that his list comprised only six figures whose lives spanned eight centuries. It is thus impossible that direct master-disciple links mattered to him (T.1969A.47:192c19–c20; see appendix). It may be that previous studies have read too much into the fact that the term *zǔ* was borrowed from the language of kinship, or that the term was used to describe figures in Chan and Esoteric lineages whose status as carriers of their traditions depended upon direct master-disciple transmission. However, the Pure Land patriarchal lists do not depend upon direct contact between contiguous figures for any ideological purpose. It would also be well to note that the *Hanyu da cidian* 漢語大詞典 defines the word *zǔ* in a number of ways, including that of "a prior teacher, one whose words, deeds, and achievements are admired by later generations." It seems clear that the compilers of patriarchal lists in China used the term *zǔ* in this sense.

In the early twentieth century, Taixu (*Tàixū* 太虛, 1890–1947) put the matter this way: "People were generally recognized as patriarchal masters of the Pure Land School on the basis of their accomplishments in spreading its teachings. It was not a matter of direct transmission from one to the other." (Taixu, *Chán tái xián liú guī jìngtǔ xíng* 禪台賢流歸淨土行, Complete works, n.p., n.d.) The modern-day scholar Chen Chienhuang 陳劍鍠 echoes this in an article detailing the process whereby the current list of thirteen patriarchs came into being:

> This list of thirteen patriarchs has never consisted of figures with master-disciple relations. For instance, the second patriarch Shandao 善導 is separated from the first patriarch Huiyuan 慧遠 by some two hundred years [. . .] The seventh patriarch Shengchang 省常 passed away in 1020, while the eighth patriarch Lianchi 蓮池 was not even born until 1532, meaning that there is a five hundred year gap between them. From this we can see that the purpose of the list of patriarchs was to honor the merit of great past masters and enable people in later times to give them due reverence and receive encouragement in their own progress. Thus, the significance of succession in this list differs from that of other schools (such as Chan and Tiantai). (Chen Chienhuang 2015, p. 33)

Finally, the following personal exchange also exemplifies the currency of this interpretation: I once posed the question "What is a patriarch?" to the abbot of a temple famous as a Pure Land *dàochǎng* 道場. His answer was that a patriarch is one who "had the Way and virtue" (*yǒu dào yǒu dé* 有道有德). He explained that a patriarch was one who deeply understood the Pure Land path and exemplified virtue.

Ascription of patriarchal status thus never needed to involve evidence of direct transmission from a previous patriarch; it was simply a status granted by acclamation.

Practical Markers: *Fǎmén* 法門 and *Zōng* 宗 (redux)

While I have not found any indication that Pure Land in China was ever conceived as a denomination-style institution, text after text and author after author refer to something most commonly referred to as the "Pure Land dharma-gate" (*jìngtǔ fǎmén* 淨土法門). Perhaps the key to discovering the way in which the Chinese themselves conceived of Pure Land is to determine what a dharma-gate is.

We may begin by observing that the word "gate" (*mén* 門) occurs in many compounds that indicate a certain religious practice and its doctrinal justifications. For example, one frequently encounters the term *xíngmén* 行門 as a general term covering all methods of Buddhist self-cultivation. In the Pure Land context, we see this term used by Huaigan in his *Shì jìngtǔ qúnyí lùn* 釋淨土群疑論 (Treatise explaining a number of doubts about Pure Land, T.1960): "As the sutras say, there is not just one special gate of practice that leads to rebirth in the Pure Land, and the nine grades of people who attain rebirth are distinct" (T.1960.47:36b21–b22). The word "gate" may also be suffixed to other terms of practice such as "gate of visualization" (*guānmén* 觀門) as seen in this statement from the *Fózǔ tǒngjì* 佛祖統紀 (Systematic record of Buddhas and Patriarchs, T.2035) by Zhipan (*Zhìpán* 志磐, d.u.) in which he describes the teachings of Shandao 善導: "The only way to transcend samsara rapidly is this gate of visualization" (T.2035.49:263a24–b8).

The specific term "Pure Land dharma-gate" occurs many hundreds of times in Chinese Buddhist literature. In several instances, the context makes clear that the referent is a form of Buddhist practice. Here are some examples:

In his *Wúliángshòujīng yōupótíshè yuànshēngjié pósǒupántóu púsà zàobīng zhù* 無量壽經優婆提舍願生偈婆藪槃頭菩薩造并註 (Commentary on Vasubandhu's Treatise on the Pure Land, T.1819), Tanluan (*Tánluán* 曇鸞, 476–542) wrote, "Bodily practice is to prostrate and worship; oral practice is to offer praises; mental practice is to make vows; the practice of wisdom is to do visualization; the practice of the wisdom of expedient means is to transfer the merit. Bringing all five of these practices together is to follow the dharma-gate of rebirth in the Pure Land (*wǎngshēng jìngtǔ fǎmén* 往生淨土法門) to its completion with ease" (T.1819.40:843a15–a19).

Zongxiao (*Zōngxiǎo* 宗曉, 1151–1214) included this passage in his *Lèbāng wénlèi* 樂邦文類 (Anthology of the Land of Bliss, T.1969A): "Therefore, one hears the breezes in the boughs and attains the correct contemplation; one ascends to the jeweled pavilions and the samadhi appears. This is not a provisional expedient; one spontaneously attains the Way. Thus, the Pure Land dharma-gate is the path by which one returns to the source" (T.1969A.47:186a7–a9). In this instance, a "dharma-gate" is a path that one traverses. He reinforces this point at T.1969A.47:211a28–a29 when he specifies that the Pure Land dharma-gate is something that one puts into practice (*xiūxí* 修習).

The Song dynasty literatus Wang Rixiu's (*Wáng Rìxiū* 王日休, d. 1175) collection *Lóngshū zēngguǎng jìngtǔ wén* 龍舒增廣淨土文 (Longshu's Augmented Pure Land Essays, T.1970) contains this exhortation to Pure Land practice:

> If people know about this dharma-gate, it is as if I myself know it; how could this not bring pleasure? If they do not know it, it is as if I myself did not

> know it; how could this not bring pain? [. . .] Therefore, one can counsel one person to cultivate Pure Land, and by the favorable condition [this creates] extinguish guilt and evil. [. . .] Counseling people in this good Way is called giving the alms of dharma. This Pure Land dharma-gate is considered greatest among the ways of giving the alms of dharma; by means of it one exits samsara. No other way of giving dharma-alms compares with it. (T.1970.47:261a4–a21)

For Wang, Pure Land is something to be cultivated; note how in the middle of this passage he says, "cultivate Pure Land" (*xiū jìngtǔ* 修淨土) without the addition of "dharma-gate."

One could cite many more passages such as these, but let us conclude with one more from a biography recorded in the *Sòng gāosēng zhuàn* 宋高僧傳 (Song biographies of eminent monks, T.2061) by Zanning (*Zànníng* 贊寧, 920–1001). The monk Huiri (*Huìrì* 慧日, d. 748) once undertook a strenuous retreat and fasted for seven days. On the last day, the bodhisattva Avalokiteśvara appeared to him.

> He reached down his right hand and touched my head, saying, "You desire a special dharma to benefit both yourself and others. In the west is the country of Amitābha that is the Pure Land world of Utmost Bliss. I advise you to *nianfo*, recite sutras, and transfer the merit to the aspiration [for rebirth]. Once you are reborn in that land, you will see the Buddha and me and obtain great benefit. You should know that this Pure Land dharma-gate surpasses all other practices." Having said this, he vanished. (T.2061.50:890b15–b20)

This places the Pure Land dharma-gate squarely within the category of practices.

Jìngtǔ fǎmén 淨土法門 is not the only expression in Pure Land texts suffixed with *fǎmén* 法門 in reference to a practice. The synonym "dharma-gate of *nianfo*" (*niànfó fǎmén* 念佛法門) also occurs many hundreds of times. To give one example, in the fourth fascicle of his *Zōngjìng lù* 宗鏡錄 (T.2016), Yongming Yanshou (*Yǒngmíng Yánshòu* 永明延壽, 904–975) answers a question about the *niànfó fǎmén* with specific recommendations for practice.

> Question: In previous analyses, you clearly distinguished principle from phenomena. Outside of the Buddha, there is no mind; outside of the mind, there is no Buddha. Why give additional teachings establishing the dharma-gate of *nianfo* (*niànfó fǎmén* 念佛法門)?
>
> Answer: This is solely for those who do not believe that their own mind is the Buddha and gallop about seeking something external. If they are of

> middling or inferior capacities, we provisionally lead them to contemplate the Buddha's form-body. By affixing their coarse thoughts to this condition, what is internal becomes evident by means of the external, and they gradually awaken to their own minds. (T.2016.48:506a10–a14)

Thus, we see the terms "Pure Land" and "*nianfo*" frequently paired with the suffix "dharma-gate," indicating that Pure Land is above all a tradition of practice. However, religious people do not adopt practices in a conceptual vacuum. A practice requires justification, and in searching for this, we return to the term *zōng* 宗. As noted in the previous section, we do not find the term *jìngtǔ zōng* 淨土宗 as a stand-alone marker for an institution in premodern Chinese Buddhist sources. Instead, we find the word *zōng* 宗 in several compounds that mean "primary meaning" or "cardinal tenet." We cannot leave the matter there, however. Although we now know that there is no institution understood as the Pure Land "clan," it does not follow that no group of people ever identified with or as something called "Pure Land." After all, essential doctrines and cardinal meanings are not disembodied ideas; they are essential or cardinal *to someone* about *something.*

What Makes the Pure Land Dharma-Gate: The Idea of Non-elite Attainment

Let us begin by looking at a pair of stories from Zhipan's *Fózǔ tǒngjì* 佛祖統紀 (Systematic record of Buddhas and Patriarchs, T.2035). Both recount cases of very bad people who achieved rebirth in the Pure Land by doing nothing more than calling Amitābha's name from their deathbeds.

> **Biographies of Those within the Evil Ranks Who Attained Rebirth (*wǎngshēng èbèi zhuàn* 往生惡輩傳)**
>
> There was a man from Chang'an named Jīng 京 who was a butcher. Because the monk Shandao advised the practice of *nianfo,* people throughout the city stopped eating meat. Incensed, Jing entered the temple with a knife in his hand intending to kill or inflict great harm. [Shan]dao taught [him] the marks of the Pure Land manifest in the west and he repented, vowing to climb a high tree to practice *nianfo,* stopping only when the tree fell. Those present saw a transformation-buddha lead a celestial child (*tiāntóngzǐ* 天童子) from the crown of his head ("celestial child" means the conscious spirit [*shíshēn* 識神]).[1]
>
> In Chang'an there was a man named Zhāng Zhōngkuí 張鍾馗 who slaughtered chickens for a living. As he was dying, he saw a red-robed man driving a group of cackling chickens. Four of them came up to peck out his

> eyes; the blood flowed and the pain was unbearable. There was a monk [present] who worked for the propagation of Buddhism. Upon seeing the scene he set up an image and advised [Zhang] to *nianfo.* Immediately he was aware of a fragrance filling the room and the chickens scattered and went away. Sitting upright, [Zhang] passed away. (T.2035.49:288c9–c20)

In a very stark way, these stories epitomize what I consider the essential point of the Pure Land dharma-gate. More than anything else, the teaching that non-elite Buddhists could attain the religious goals of non-retrogression (*bùtuìzhuǎn* 不退轉) and ultimately buddhahood by means of a relatively simple practice created Pure Land Buddhism as a movement embraced by ordinary people. This teaching received a very mixed response from the wider Buddhist community and required generations of apologists to defend and rationalize it. I will take this teaching, comprising both the practices and their theoretical rationalizations, as the Pure Land dharma-gate, or what I shall call the "Pure Land tradition" in the chapters to come. This tradition of practice begins with Shandao (*Shàndǎo* 善導, 613–681), building upon foundations laid by his predecessors. Let us look at the developments that led to his breakthrough and the way in which others defended and handed it down afterward.

Early Understandings of the Pure Land

According to Mochizuki Shinkō's 望月信亨 history of Chinese Pure Land doctrine, the tradition's earliest authors sought primarily to understand the nature of Sukhāvatī and the means by which beings gained access to it. To do this, the texts correlated different conceptions of the buddha-land with the three bodies of a buddha (*sānshēn* 三身; Skt. *trikāya*). That is to say, a buddha's land manifested three realities corresponding to his three bodies:

(1) For the buddha as "dharma body" (*fǎshēn* 法身; Skt. *dharma-kāya*) there was a theoretical "land of suchness" (Skt. *dharmatā*), though some authors stated that since the buddha's dharma body pervades everywhere, such a theoretical land did not really exist in a localizable way. At any rate, only the buddha could occupy it, so it was of no consequence for religious practice.

(2) The "reward land" or "enjoyment land" (*bàotǔ* 報土 or *shòuyòng tǔ* 受用土) corresponded to the buddha's "complete enjoyment body" (*bàoshēn* 報身 or *shòuyòng shēn* 受用身; Skt. *saṃbhoga-kāya*). This could be subdivided into a "land for the [buddha's] own enjoyment" (*zì shòuyòng tǔ* 自受用土), which the buddha alone perceived, and the "land for the

enjoyment of others" (*tā shòuyòng tǔ* 他受用土), a place of rebirth for those who earned it through their achievements. These would include only bodhisattvas who had achieved a particular level within the "grounds" or "levels" of advanced practice (*dì* 地; Skt. *bhūmi*).

(3) Just as a buddha manifested a "transformation body" or "response body" (*huàshēn* 化身 or *yìngshēn* 應身; Skt. *nirmāṇa-kāya*) for the sake of ordinary beings that accommodated their capacities, so there was a "transformation land" (*huàtǔ* 化土) accessible to beings at lower levels of accomplishment, though not to any being just for the wishing (summarized from Mochizuki 1942, chap. 1–15; see also Pas 1995, p. 150–157).

Broadly speaking, early authors held three different views regarding the level of accomplishment necessary for rebirth in these manifestations of the Pure Land. (1) The first held that the land of Sukhāvatī was a transformation land into which ordinary beings could be born. (2) Another declared that it was a reward land accessible only to advanced bodhisattvas. (3) A third stated that practitioners perceived or were born into the kind of land that corresponded to the relative purity of their minds. It could thus appear to them as either a reward land or a transformation land. In other words, the further one progressed in mind-purification, the more subtle and refined a Pure Land one perceived. An advanced bodhisattva could contemplate the Pure Land in a high degree of opulence, but could also see how it appeared to those at lower levels of attainment. The reverse was not true; those at lower levels could only see what their stage on the path enabled them to see and no higher (Mochizuki 1942, p. 184–185).

According to Mochizuki, it was Shandao who first proposed that devotees of Amitābha could gain rebirth in a manifestation of the Pure Land higher than that which their progress should have earned. The conceptual framework needed to make the idea of underserved, non-elite attainment of rebirth in Sukhāvatī plausible took shape under previous thinkers such as Tanluan and Daochuo. Their ideas tended in two directions, although one author could hold both in tandem; they were not mutually incompatible. The first was to explain how a relatively simple practice could bring about a disproportionately great result. The second was to attribute the achievement to the Buddha Amitābha and his fundamental vows (*běnyuàn* 本願). The first focused on the power, however slight it might seem, of the practitioner; the second focused on the power of the Buddha.

Tanluan and Daochuo

Tanluan.

Tanluan (*Tánluán* 曇鸞, 476–542), in his *Wangsheng lun zhu* 往生論註 (*Wúliángshòujīng yōupótíshè yuànshēngjié zhù* 無量壽經優婆提舍願生偈註, T.1819) addresses the question mainly from the practitioner's side with some attention to the Buddha's role. In this text, an inquirer asks how someone of the lowest grade (*xià xià pǐn* 下下品) who has committed the "Five Heinous Deeds" and the "ten evils" could attain rebirth in the Pure Land, the state of non-retrogression, and escape from the Triple World simply because a "good friend" (*shàn zhīshì* 善知識; Skt. *kalyāṇa-mitra*) appeared by the deathbed and convinced him or her to repeat the name of Amitāyus ten times. According to the law of karma as expounded in many sutras, a person with such guilt should proceed to eons of suffering in a hell; how can a practice so undemanding annul karma so heavy? (T.1819.40:834b13–b22; trans. Inagaki 1998, p. 198–199). Tanluan responds with three principles of Buddhist teaching that indicate where the practice's power resides (the so-called three places, or *sānzài* 三在): the state of mind (*zàixīn* 在心), the object (*zàiyuán* 在緣), and the degree of concentration (*zài juédìng* 在決定) (T.1819.40:834b25; Inagaki 1998, p. 198–199).

First, the state of mind that leads to wrongdoing is grounded in delusion, while the mind that repeats the Buddha's name has grasped the truth; the latter thus easily overcomes the former, just as a lamp instantly illuminates a room even though it has been dark for a thousand years. Second, objects of grasping normally arise through deluded thoughts, but the name of Amitābha is reality itself. The name thus drives out delusion because it provides the mind with a suitable object, just as the sound of a magical drum instantly expels a poisoned arrow and neutralizes its poison. Finally, imminent death concentrates the mind fully on the ten repetitions of the Buddha's name without anticipating any result; this is stronger than previous deeds of wrongdoing, during which intentions and anticipations jostled together. Being more concentrated, it prevails over past evil karma (T.1819.40:834b25–c12; Inagaki 1998, p. 199–201).

These reasons for the efficacy of ten *nian* at the time of death explain only why the brief and light practice of an unworthy practitioner can produce great results. While it is not unimportant that the recitations focus on Amitābha, the Buddha does not play an active role here; he merely provides an appropriate object for the practice. While the term "power of the original vow" (*běn yuànlì* 本願力) does appear three times in the *Wangsheng lun zhu,* it occurs only when Tanluan quotes other sources, and he seems to regard this power only as the means whereby the Buddha established his land as an object upon which one may concentrate.

While it thus may appear that Tanluan is postulating the notion of non-elite practice and attainment, Chen Chienhuang[2] 陳劍鍠 explains that something more subtle is happening. Rather than explaining how an unworthy practitioner can attain the goal, Tanluan is actually saying that the practitioner *becomes* worthy through these practices. In his reading, Tanluan is drawing upon his prior forty years of study in the Perfection of Wisdom literature to demonstrate that in the particular situation of deathbed practice and nowhere else, even the ten name-recitations of an evil person become indistinguishable from the elite practice of mental concentration and yields the same results (Chen 2009, p. 42–49). Tanluan's real concern here is to show that the deathbed practice of ten continuous *nianfo* becomes the equivalent of the virtuoso practice of an elite practitioner.

Daochuo.

Daochuo (*Dàochuò* 道綽, 562–645) considered himself Tanluan's successor even though twenty years had elapsed between the latter's death and his birth, and indeed one may find all of the ideas outlined above, often verbatim, in his *Ānlè jí* 安樂集 (Anthology of the Land of Bliss, T.1958). Identifying him as a transitional figure between Tanluan and Shandao, Chen Chienhuang regards him as the thinker who established Pure Land as an independent school (Chen alternates between *mén* 門 and *zōng* 宗; see Chen 2009, p. 92–102). While in this chapter, I will argue that Shandao deserves the credit for this, Chen's points in support of his thesis are worth noting.

According to Chen, Tanluan provided the basic distinctions of "difficult practice" versus "easy practice" and "self-power" versus "other-power." However, Tanluan followed the lead of Nāgārjuna and considered the two as options that were always available to practitioners. In other words, at any given time there were beings such as advanced bodhisattvas who could engage in difficult practices while others needed an easier path. In contrast, Daochuo employed a chronology that divided history into five 500-year periods after Śākyamuni's passing, which he found in the *Dàjí yuèzàng jīng* 大集月藏經 (Skt: *Candragarbha-sūtra*), and conflated with the three-part schematization into the periods of the Correct Dharma, Counterfeit Dharma, and Decadent Dharma (*zhèngfǎ* 正法, *xiàngfǎ* 像法, and *mòfǎ* 末法). He combined these timetables with the previously unrelated idea that the current world was corrupted by the Five Turbidities (*wǔzhuó* 五濁). He argued that belief and practice must fit the times and the capacities of beings, and declared that *nianfo* (or the *niànfó sānmèi* 念佛三昧) was the only practice that had any chance of success under the conditions of the present age. The "way of the sages" (*shèngdào* 聖道), which he equated with both the "path of difficult practice" (*nánxíng dào* 難行道) and "self-power" (*zìlì* 自力) would not work. Only the "way of rebirth in the Pure Land" (*wǎngshēng jìngtǔ* 往生淨土), which corresponded to the "path of easy practice" (*yìxíng dào* 易行道) and "other-power" (*tālì* 他力) answered the conditions of the Decadent Dharma (T.1958.47:13c6ff.).

Even if all the above is true and represents an advance beyond Tanluan's position, it seems to me that it still does not produce a conceptual framework within which the stories of butchers and chicken-slaughterers attaining rebirth make sense. I hesitate on this point because Daochuo does not clearly recommend any practice, nor does he provide a consistent set of criteria by which one may make a selection. David Chappell noted Daochuo's "ambiguity" on this point (1976, p. 272–276). I would go further and agree with Daochuo's early critic Jiacai (*Jiācái* 迦才, d.u.) that Daochuo's presentation in the *Anthology of the Land of Bliss* is incoherent:

> Recently there was Chan Master [Dao]chuo who composed the *Anthology of the Land of Bliss* in one fascicle. While broadly quoting from the sutras with brief explanations, its text is muddled and its chapters and sections are confused, and it leaves its readers undecided. (T.1963.47:83b14–b16)

For our purposes, we need only note one element of Daochuo's presentation. Like Tanluan, he remained focused on the practitioner, seeking to explain why the relatively simple practices that lead to rebirth in the Pure Land work rather than on the power of Amitābha and his vows. Very early in the *Anthology,* Daochuo asserts that the Pure Land is a reward land occupied by a reward body buddha, adding that previous masters who asserted a transformation buddha in a transformation land were greatly mistaken (T.1958.47:5c12–c15). When he moved on to demonstrate that both advanced bodhisattvas and ordinary beings can attain rebirth in the Pure Land, he did so in terms of their practices and the different ways the Pure Land manifests to beings of different levels of accomplishment.

Advanced bodhisattvas engage in the formless practice; they do not need the rich features of Sukhāvatī to entice them. He defines "ordinary beings" as those who are still attached to form and thus need concrete features to coax them to practice. Like his predecessors, Daochuo taught that the Pure Land manifests to those reborn there in accordance with their capacities. He says:

> Since ordinary people have shallow wisdom, they mostly seek birth through a practice attached to form and yet they decisively attain birth [in Sukhāvatī]. Since the practice attached to form has weak power, it simply brings about the birth in the land of form, where one only sees the [reward] and transformation Buddhas. (T.1958.47:6c3–c5; trans. Inagaki 2014, p. 26)

In addition, Daochuo explained the efficacy of an ordinary being's practice with reference to "good roots" (*shàn'gēn* 善根) laid down in past lives (T.1958.47:4c15–5a15). After quoting various sutras, he assured his audience that the mere fact that they were in a position to hear this teaching demonstrates that they have already aroused *bodhicitta* and made offerings to buddhas in past lives (T.1958.47:5a15–a17). Thus, much as Tanluan ascribed the efficacy of the practice to the non-duality of the Buddha's name and his reality, Daochuo asserted that it works because the practitioners had already done virtuoso practices in past lives.

Finally, while in Daochuo's reading the "path of rebirth" is easier and more suited to the times than the "path of sages," it is still far from an easy practice. Only in a very few places does Daochuo refer even ambiguously to the practice of *nianfo* as oral invocation of the Buddha's name. Most of his presentation advises the reader to practice the "*nianfo* samadhi," focusing on the Buddha's name as a way to achieve a particular meditative state. The entirety of the twelfth and last chapter of the *Anthology* quotes extensively from a scripture that recommends the full panoply of Buddhist practices with no mention of *nianfo* at all. In sum, Daochuo recommended practices leading to rebirth in the Pure Land as the only ones that will work in the age of the Decadent Dharma, but the practice is not easy, and he still explains its apparently undeserved effectiveness through the devotee's "good roots" from past lives rather than via Amitābha's "other-power." It fell to his disciple Shandao to take that final step.

Shandao's Contribution

With Shandao (*Shàndǎo* 善導, 613–681), we come to the figure many authors consider the real founder of the Chinese Pure Land tradition (see Pas 1995, p. 318–319; Chén Yángjiǒng 2008, p. 270). The reason is easy to see: While Tanluan and Daochuo provided some of the necessary conceptual pieces and served as exemplars, it was Shandao who stated clearly and fully that ordinary beings can attain rebirth in the Pure Land through the power of Amitābha's vows. Limitations of space preclude an exhaustive study of Shandao's contribution, so I will only discuss four key aspects of his thought that cleared the way for the establishment of a distinct Pure Land tradition: (1) his assertion that ordinary beings could perceive the Pure Land as a "reward land"; (2) his reinterpretation of the ten *nian* required for rebirth as ten oral invocations; (3) his teaching that all beings in the nine levels of rebirth in the Pure Land are ordinary beings and not *āryans*; and (4) that rebirth in the Pure Land comes about primarily through the power of Amitābha's original vows.

(1) As noted above, authors prior to Shandao had held that beings gained rebirth in Sukhāvatī only by achieving a high level of purification and perceived the land only as their level of achievement permitted. What the Buddha Amitābha accomplished with his vows was simply to establish the Pure Land as a destination. Shandao dissented from all of these views and held that the Pure Land was a reward land because it derived its form from Amitābha's past vows and the power of his merit. Even ordinary beings reborn there perceived it as a reward land, not as a transformation land (Pas 1995, p. 154–155). As he says in the first fascicle of his commentary on the *Contemplation Sutra:*

> Question: You have said that the land and the Buddha are both of the reward type. Their reward-dharmas are high and wondrous; [even] arhats (*xiǎoshèng* 小聖) attain it with difficulty. How would worldlings obstructed by defilements enter? Answer: In terms of the obstructions of defilement, it would indeed be difficult to enjoy such a place. By entrusting themselves to the Buddha's vows to fortify their conditions, beings of all the five vehicles gain entry equally. (T.1753.37:251a6–a9)

In this way, Shandao affirmed that ordinary beings attain entry into Sukhāvatī, which manifests as a reward land despite their heavy defilements, something earlier authors would not have accepted.

(2) Shandao defined the ambiguous term "ten *nian*" (*shí niàn* 十念) as "ten sounds" (*shí shēng* 十聲); neither Tanluan nor Daochuo made such a clear connection between *nian* and oral invocation (Chen Chienhuang 2009, p. 146, 167). In contrast, in the fourth fascicle of his *Guān wúliàngshòu fó jīng shū* 觀無量壽佛經疏 (Commentary on the *Contemplation Sutra*),

Shandao notes the difference between *nian* as mental cultivation and as oral invocation. His point of departure is the sixteenth contemplation, which deals with the last of the nine levels of rebirth, the lowest birth of the lowest grade (*xiàpǐn xiàshēng* 下品下生). Here the sutra says:

> When he is about to die, he may meet a good teacher, who consoles him in various ways, teaching him the wonderful Dharma and urging him to be mindful of the Buddha; but he is too tormented by pain to do so. The good teacher then advises him, 'If you cannot concentrate on the Buddha then you should say instead, "Homage to Amitāyus Buddha."' In this way he continuously says, "Homage to Amitāyus Buddha" ten times. (*shí niàn* 十念; trans. Inagaki and Stewart 2003, p. 98; T.365.12:346a15–a19)

Commenting on this passage, Shandao writes,

> The fifth [part of the text] makes clear that the guilty person, oppressed by the approach of death, has no way to contemplate the Buddha's name. Number six elucidates how the good friend, knowing that through suffering [the dying person] has lost the contemplation, switches his teaching to oral repetition (*kǒuchēng* 口稱) of the Buddha's name. Number seven clarifies the number of uninterrupted oral repetitions. (T.1753.37:277b14–b17)

Even though the sutra passage uses the term "ten *nian*" to describe the practice of the desperate sinner, it very clearly indicates oral repetition of the Buddha's name, and Shandao's commentary reinforces that point by explaining this action as "orally holding Amitāyus's name" (*kǒuchēng Mítuó mínghào* 口稱彌陀名號). Neither Tanluan nor Daochuo had read the passage in this way (Chen Chienhuang 2009, p. 167).

Shandao also applied this interpretation to other sutra passages in which the term *nian* did not so clearly mean oral repetition. For example, in his *Wǎngshēng lǐzàn jì* 往生禮讚偈 (Verses of obeisance and praise of rebirth, T.1980), he so interpreted the following phrase from the *Amitābha Sutra:*

> The *Amitābha Sutra* says that if sentient beings hear of Amitābha Buddha, they should immediately hold to that name for a day, for two days, or for up to seven days single-mindedly calling the Buddha without agitation. At the end of life, Amitābha Buddha and his holy retinue will appear before them. These people will not have their minds overturned at the last minute, and will instantly attain rebirth in that [Pure] Land. [. . .] If there are sentient beings who call Amitābha Buddha for seven days or even for one day for as little as ten oral invocations or even one oral calling or one contemplation (*nǎizhì yī shēng yī niàn* 乃至一聲一念), they must attain rebirth. (T.1980.47:447c27–448a9; the sutra citation is from T.366.12:347b10–b15)

In this way, Shandao came to interpret instances of ten *nian* systematically as ten oral repetitions or "sounds" even when the context of the sutra passage did not clearly support such an interpretation.

(3) Shandao taught that all beings in the nine grades of rebirth were ordinary beings; none was an *āryan.* He began the discussion in his *Guanjing shu* by declaring that he will discuss the teachings of past masters (*zhūshī* 諸師) with whom he disagrees (see T.1753.37:247c22ff.). They had explained that those who attain rebirth in the three births of the top grade are great Mahayanists, those who are reborn into the three births of the middle grade are Hinayanists, while those of the three lowest births are "worldlings just beginning on the Mahayana path" (*dàshèng shǐxúe fánfū* 大乘始學凡夫). In dissent, Shandao stated that no one among the nine grades of rebirth is a bodhisattva; all are worldlings. For our purposes, his discussion of the lowest birth of the lowest grade bears the most significance.

> As for the lowest [birth] of the lowest [grade], sentient beings at this level perform unwholesome acts: the Five Heinous Deeds, the ten evils, and everything that is not good. Because of their evil karma, such persons are bound for the hells for long eons without letup. At the end of their lives, they encounter a good friend (*shàn zhīshì* 善知識) who teaches them about Amitābha Buddha and counsels them to seek rebirth [in the Pure Land]. Such people then invoke the Buddha, and riding upon their recollection [of the Buddha], they instantly attain rebirth. Had they not encountered the good [friend], they surely would have sunk down. Because of conditions, they encountered the good [friend], and the seven jewels come to receive them. [. . .] The three [kinds of] people in the lowest grade refers to them as evil worldlings (*è fánfū* 惡凡夫) because of their evil deeds. At the end of their lives, they lean upon the good [friend] and ride on the power of the Buddha's vows to go to rebirth. [. . .] How can one say they are beginners in the Mahayana? (T.1753.37:249a24–249b5)

(4) Finally, Shandao definitively attributed not just the establishment of the Pure Land but also the rebirth even of depraved beings in it to the power of Amitābha's original vows. To understand the significance of this, we must make a distinction: The effect of the bodhisattva Dharmākara's vows may be taken as either (a) establishing the Pure Land and arraying its particular features, or (b) causing beings to attain rebirth within it. Tanluan, in his *Wangsheng lun zhu,* affirms only the former, not the latter, as seen in the following quotation:

> In the [*Larger Sukhāvatī-vyūha sūtra*] preached at Rājagṛha, I find in the section on the three grades of aspirants that although their practices differ according to their superior or inferior qualities, they all, without fail,

> awaken the aspiration for the highest Bodhi. This aspiration is the resolve to become a buddha. The aspiration to become a buddha is the resolve to save all sentient beings. The resolve to save sentient beings is the resolve to embrace sentient beings and lead them to attain birth in a buddha-land. It follows that those who wish to be born in the Pure Land of Peace and Bliss should awaken the aspiration for the highest Bodhi. If there is anyone who does not awaken the aspiration for the highest Bodhi but, having heard of the endless pleasures to be enjoyed in that land, desires to be born there simply because of such pleasures, he will not attain birth. [. . .] "The pleasures for their own sustenance" means that the Pure Land of Peace and Bliss has been produced and maintained by [Amitābha] Tathāgata's Primal Vow-Power (*běnyuàn lì* 本願力), and so there is no end to the pleasures to be enjoyed. (T.1819.40:842a15–842a25; trans. Inagaki 1998, p. 271)

In other words, it is up to every person who seeks rebirth in the Pure Land to arouse *bodhicitta,* the aspiration to become a buddha in order to save other beings. Amitābha's vows create and maintain a place wherein that goal may be accomplished most easily. Only near the end of the *Wangsheng lun zhu* does Tanluan connect the Buddha's vows explicitly to the attainment of rebirth with reference to the eighteenth vow of the *Larger Sutra.* However, the vow itself specifies that attainment of rebirth requires one to perform at least ten *nian* and excludes those who commit the Five Heinous Deeds or slander the dharma. As we have seen above, *nian* did not necessarily mean oral invocation of the Buddha's name until Shandao advanced this interpretation, and Shandao claimed that even the sinners excluded by the sutra attain rebirth.[3] Within Tanluan's framework, one could not make sense of Zhipan's stories of butchers and chicken-slaughterers attaining rebirth.

Shandao, in contrast, directly attributed the attainment of rebirth to the power of Amitābha's vows in all cases. His commentary on the *Contemplation Sutra* makes this assertion near the beginning: "As the *Larger Sutra* says, all ordinary beings, both virtuous and depraved, who attain rebirth [in the Pure Land], without exception avail themselves of the karmic power of Amitābha's great vows as a predominating condition" (T.1753.37:246b10–b11). Later, when speaking of the rebirth of those at the middle birth of the lowest grade, who for him are "shameless evildoers," he says, "At first, without the encounter with the 'good friend,' the fires of hell come to welcome them. After meeting the 'good friend,' transformation buddhas come in welcome. This is entirely due to the power of Amitābha's vows" (T.1753.37:249a22–a24). In passages such as these, Shandao makes clear that Amitābha's vows not only produced the

Pure Land, but also are the direct and empowering cause (*zēngshàng yuàn* 增上緣) for beings of all kinds to attain rebirth there.

This is only a brief sketch of Shandao's thought and there is much more that one could say. However, even with only these four elements in place, we have a soteriological framework within which Zhipan's rebirth stories become plausible. Shandao affirmed that (1) the Pure Land appears as a "reward land" to all beings no matter their level of attainment; (2) that the undemanding practice of reciting the Buddha's name ten times, which even someone consumed with pain and fear while dying could conceivably do, suffices for rebirth; (3) that the teachings are aimed entirely at ordinary beings and do not apply to great *āryans*; and (4) that the power of the Buddha's vows, not any human accomplishment, provide the motorics of rebirth. Put more simply, Shandao affirmed that by the power of the Buddha's vows, even the worst evildoer could say the name of the Buddha and gain immediate access to a glittering Pure Land immediately after death. While predecessors such as Tanluan and Daochuo no doubt helped guide the tradition toward the adoption of these four elements, only with Shandao did they become both explicit and essential.

These elements also made the tradition controversial. The proposition that undeserving, ordinary beings could achieve rebirth in a reward land and the stage of non-retrogression struck many as a violation of bedrock Buddhist principles, and as subsequent authors defended these propositions in apologetic texts, the tradition consolidated itself behind this notion.

Defending the Pure Land Vision

We will conclude the major portion of this chapter by briefly surveying the ways in which a number of later Pure Land authors provided support for Shandao's vision in a series of apologetic texts.

Huaigan

We may begin with Shandao's disciple Huaigan (*Huáigǎn* 懷感, d. 699), whose *Shì jìngtǔ qúnyí lùn* 釋淨土群疑論 (Treatise explaining a number of doubts about Pure Land, T.1960) added a great deal of philosophical depth to Shandao's basic framework. For example, in the first fascicle Huaigan devotes a series of questions and answers to explaining non-elite rebirth. In the thirteenth question, an inquirer says:

> Regarding the Pure Land into which ordinary sentient beings attain rebirth: ordinary beings have not yet attained the pure mind free of defilements, and in accordance with their minds, the land that appears to them will [also] have defilements. A land with defilements is called an impure land (*huìguó* 穢國). Why do you still call it a Pure Land? (T.1960.47:33c25–c27)

In response, Huaigan distinguishes purity and defilement of substance (*tǐ* 體) and characteristic (*xiàng* 相) that combine in four possible ways, the third of which is "defilement of substance with purity of characteristic" (*tǐhuì xiàngjìng* 體穢相淨). Here, the mind of the person reborn in the Pure Land is defiled in substance. Such a being should see only a defiled land, but the Buddha's power causes the land to appear pure, overriding the person's own mental karma and causing him or her to see it as described in the Pure Land sutras (T.1960.47:34a7–a10). Huaigan, following Shandao, attributes this to the Buddha's power and not to any accomplishment on the devotee's part.

In question twenty, the inquirer objects that according to Mahayana sutras, only those who have extensively studied the "ungraspable dharma" (*wú suǒdé fǎ* 無所得法) attain birth in the Pure Land, thus denying its availability to unenlightened beings. He claims that when Huaigan counsels the practices of the sixteen visualizations and invoking the Buddha's name, both of which focus on visual and aural forms, he gives rise to a mind attached to the graspable (*yǒu suǒdé xīn* 有所得心, T.1960.47:36b2–b11). Once again the inquirer presumes that rebirth in a buddha-land occurs only after a certain level of practice, purification, and realization; it must be earned.

Huaigan begins his response by acknowledging that there are very advanced practitioners who have thoroughly realized the emptiness of all phenomena; these attain rebirth in the Pure Land among the highest grades (*shàngpǐn* 上品). There are also foolish people who have no ability to study Mahayana sutras, grasp the cardinal principle, or perform contemplations free of grasping. However, they might be able to maintain the precepts or show filial piety, practice the ten virtues, or focus their minds by invoking the name. Even such practices as these, which entail thoughts of what one might grasp (*yǒu suǒdé* 有所得) can bring the inconceivably superior merit of rebirth in the Pure Land. Huaigan's main point is that if one relies on the sutras, one will find that there is not just one practice that leads to rebirth in Sukhāvatī; this is the very reason that the *Contemplation Sutra* even speaks of nine levels of rebirth (T.1960.47:36b12–b22).

The lesson Huaigan wishes to impart here is that the Pure Land has many ways of manifesting and there are many "ways of practice" (*xíng-mén* 行門) that lead to rebirth (see T.1960.47:36b22). This path takes in "the worldling and the *āryan,* covers both the small and the great [vehicles], can be done with or without characteristics, within both focused and scattered states of mind by those of sharp or dull capacities, within long or short time frames with much practice or only a little" (T.1960.47: 36c11–c13). This point bears emphasis; while Shandao provided the soteriological framework that allowed for non-elite attainment, he did not denigrate elite practices. After all, he himself had attained an intense vision of the Buddha through visualization, and he contended in his *Guanjing shu* that the main teaching of the *Contemplation Sutra* was samadhi gained through buddha-contemplation (*guānfó sānmèi* 觀佛三昧; T.1753.37:247a18). Huaigan likewise acknowledged the entire hierarchy of practices, from the complex and arduous to the simple and easy, while affirming that all lead to rebirth in the Pure Land. As we shall see in chapter 5, this is why the Chinese Pure Land tradition never developed the problem of antinomianism. Nevertheless, the attainment of rebirth in the Pure Land by those perceived as undeserving remained a source of controversy. Thus, Huaigan, like Shandao, maintained that rebirth takes place primarily through the power of Amitābha's vow (e.g., at T.1960.47: 31b18–b20).

Pseudo-Zhiyi and the **Jìngtǔ shí yí lùn** 淨土十疑論 *(Discourse on ten doubts about Pure Land, T.1961)*

The *Discourse on Ten Doubts about Pure Land* has long been attributed to Zhiyi (*Zhìyǐ* 智顗, 538–597), but it was probably written by another hand near the beginning of the eighth century, not long after Huaigan's time (Pruden 1973, p. 127–130). Indeed, some Japanese scholars see the hand of Huaigan in the text, along with significant borrowings from Tanluan and Daochuo. This makes good sense, since if the text were written by Zhiyi it would predate all the figures discussed so far and would not be useful for advancing their understandings. In some ways, this text may seem to represent a step backward since it emphasizes the practice of the *nianfo* samadhi in a manner more consonant with Daochuo's thought than with Shandao's. However, I hope to show that it also concerns itself with the question of non-elite attainment and the role that Amitābha's vows play in the achievement of rebirth in the Pure Land.

First, four of the ten topics discussed in this brief text (numbers 5, 6, 8, and 9) deal with various aspects of the rebirth of ordinary persons.

The fifth asks how ordinary beings, burdened by bad karma and prone to defilements, can attain rebirth in a Pure Land that lies outside the Triple World. The text answers by explaining that the term "other-power" means that if one believes that the power of Amitābha's compassionate vow encompasses all sentient beings who practice *nianfo,* then one will be empowered to produce *bodhicitta,* cultivate the *nianfo* samadhi and many other practices, and dedicate the merit to the attainment of rebirth in the Pure Land. Availing oneself of the Buddha's vow-power, one then attains rebirth because of the resonance between the practitioner's capacities (*jī* 機) and the Buddha's response (*gǎn* 感, T.1961.47:79a6–a10; Tan 1979, p. 87–88). At the end of this section, the author affirms that defiled beings may indeed enter the undefiled Pure Land just as a lowly person can tour the entire world in a single day by riding in the train of a *cakravartin* king (T.1961.47:79a22–a29; Tan 1979, p. 89–90).

The answer to the fifth doubt mixes affirmation that the Buddha's vow-power brings defiled beings to rebirth with pre-Shandao views that beings perceive the coarse or subtle features of the Pure Land in accordance with their own mental purity. The sixth doubt is less ambiguous. The inquirer asks how defiled beings, whose minds will continue to give rise to false views and impure thoughts, could attain rebirth and the stage of non-retrogression. The text answers that it is the power of the Buddha's vow that upholds those reborn in the Pure Land and enables them to achieve that stage. In addition, the life span they enjoy and the wholesome features that array the land all provide the time and the means to remove defilements (T.1961.47:79b3–b16; Tan 1979, p. 90–91). The response to this qualm places its entire emphasis on the Buddha's compassionate vow as the motive power behind rebirth and attainment of non-retrogression.

The eighth and ninth doubts ask about the rebirth of beings with evil karma as well as women and those with defective sense organs. The responses present material taken almost verbatim from Daochuo's *Anle ji* and Tanluan's *Wangsheng lun zhu* and thus represent no advance in Pure Land soteriology. In sum, the *Discourse on Ten Doubts about Pure Land* primarily presents a point of view that pre-dates Shandao, one that explains non-elite attainment of rebirth with reference to factors such as good roots laid down in the past or the concentration of mind at death that make seemingly trivial practices surprisingly efficacious. However, the *Discourse* does acknowledge the power of the Buddha's vows as well, affirming that this power upholds and empowers devotees' practices and brings them to rebirth. Finally, the amount of space devoted to the question of non-elite attainment in this apologetic text demonstrates the importance of this topic as the Pure Land tradition gained increased salience in the wider Buddhist world.

Tianru Weize 天如惟則 *and the* Jìngtǔ huòwèn 淨土或問 *(Questions about Pure Land, T.1972)*

Skipping ahead to the Yuan dynasty (1271–1368), we conclude our survey of the treatment of non-elite attainment with Tianru Weize (*Tiānrú Wéizé* 天如惟則, 1286?–1354) and his work *Questions about Pure Land.* Yunqi Zhuhong (*Yúnqī Zhūhóng* 雲棲袾宏, 1535–1615) cited this work along with pseudo-Zhiyi's *Ten Doubts* as a definitive defense of Pure Land teaching and practice in the preface to his *Dá jìngtǔ sìshíbā wèn* 答淨土四十八問 (Answers to forty-eight questions about Pure Land; CBETA X.1158.61:504c13–c14). In many ways, Tianru's text set the pattern for future Pure Land apologetics: the adversary is represented as a Chan monk who objects to Pure Land as dualistic and as antithetical to Buddhism's spirit of self-reliance.

Tianru's *Questions* consists of twenty-six questions and answers. Several of these deal with qualms about non-elite attainment, and Tianru's answers focus on the practitioner's seemingly ineffective practices as had been done prior to Shandao. However, in the seventeenth and eighteenth questions he addresses the matter of the truly evil person who attains rebirth with no prior practice or good karma from the past. In question seventeen, after quoting the passage from the *Contemplation Sutra* that describes those of the lowest grade who achieve rebirth along with Shandao's comments, Tianru offers his view that such persons' success depends upon three factors. First, when death is imminent a person's power of concentration becomes fierce and can accomplish much in a very short time. Second, such a person may have stores of good karma from past lives that become activated at the point of death. Third, even if the previous two factors are lacking, the dying person may repent their lifetime of evil in utter sincerity (T.1972.47:299a7–299b8). Here, Tianru stresses the role of the dying penitent's practices, explaining why they work, and his responses echo those of Tanluan and Daochuo.

However, the inquirer presses his doubt further in question eighteen. He asks, "In this wicked world of the Five Turbidities (*wǔzhuó èshì* 五濁惡世) everyone bears guilt. Perhaps they have not committed the Five Heinous Deeds, but of the remaining sins, there is none that they leave undone. If they do not repent of these but wait until the very end to *nianfo,* do they still achieve rebirth?" (T.1972.47:299b9–b11).[4] Tianru responds that anyone who recites the Buddha's name gains rebirth because of the great power of Amitābha's vows. It is like placing a great rock on a boat. By itself, the rock would sink immediately, but the boat supports it. Conversely, a grain of sand, while much smaller than the great stone, sinks in the water instantly. The boat represents the power of the original vows, the stone and grain of sand represent heavy and light karmic guilt. With the addition of Amitābha's vow-power, even those carrying heavy karmic burdens achieve rebirth while without it, even those with slight karmic guilt sink back into samsara (T.1972.47:299b11–b28). While Tianru's answer to the previous question rationalized the unexpected power of the penitent's practices, this answer puts the spotlight directly on the power of the Buddha to overcome all karmic guilt and lead the person to the Pure Land and the stage of non-retrogression. In the answer to this question, Tianru cites Zhipan's stories about the butcher and chicken-slaughterer and asks, "If this is not [due to] the Buddha's power, then please give another way to understand it" (T.1972.47: 299b21–b22).

We will end our survey of Pure Land apologetic literature here, as texts that appear after Tianru's do not add anything new to the understanding. Let me conclude this section with a few observations.

First, we have seen that Shandao was the first to state clearly and unambiguously that the power of Amitābha's original vows not only brought even the most evil sinners into the Pure Land, but also allowed them to perceive it as a buddha's reward land.

Second, neither Shandao nor the subsequent texts cited here conclude from this that human effort is of no account, nor do they fall into the snare of antinomianism. In question twenty of the *Questions,* the inquirer asks if he can just wait until he is dying to do the ten recitations and gain rebirth. Tianru calls this foolishness and presents reasons for serious religious practice (T.1972.47:299c13–300c7). Shandao enthusiastically practiced and recommended the *nianfo* samadhi, and all subsequent writers counseled their readers to practice traditional methods of Buddhist cultivation assiduously. Chapters 4 and 5 will deal with this issue more extensively.

Third, while I have highlighted the question of non-elite attainment here, Pure Land apologetic literature dealt with a wide array of other issues and objections to their chosen practice. We will revisit these issues in subsequent chapters.

The main point is that after Shandao, the belief that the power of the Buddha's vows sufficed to bring all beings into the Pure Land, even without stores of past good karma or intense and sincere deathbed practice, became a defining feature of the Chinese Pure Land tradition. Once in place, it required constant defense from detractors over the centuries, and as a steady stream of apologetic literature came from the hands of Pure Land patriarchs and other authorities, it became a fixed feature of this tradition.

Conclusions

The evidence produced in the foregoing discussion leads to the following characterization of the Chinese Pure Land tradition. It was not an institution or a set of master-disciple lineages. Rather, it was a "dharma-gate," here understood as a tradition of practice. This tradition's most distinctive feature was that it offered a chance for non-elite or even morally evil people to attain a goal that was tantamount to the attainment of buddhahood itself: rebirth in the Pure Land of the Buddha Amitābha, circumvention of the normal working out of their accumulated karma, escape from samsara, and the stage of non-retrogression. While proponents stressed that nothing about the doctrinal underpinnings of this practice contravened Buddhist orthodoxy, they also took pains to provide a theory that would underwrite their practice of *nianfo* and justify the hope they offered to ordinary people. Significant historical figures who either organized non-elite practitioners to support one another's practice of *nianfo* or wrote significant doctrinal justifications for belief in its efficacy came to be regarded as patriarchs, the term here understood to mean a revered teacher. Far from disparaging elite practices and advanced levels of realization, they sought instead to gain acceptance for a range of effective practices suited to a range of practitioners and their capacities. Let those who can realize the ultimately signless nature of the Pure Land of Suchness, but let no one derogate the efficacy of practices such as oral invocation of the Buddha's name as a means whereby the lowly may also escape from suffering.

I have also sought to demonstrate that this tradition of practice is a part of Buddhism but a bounded part. One may compare it to something like the tradition of Marian prayer within the Catholic Church. Practitioners do not seek to break with the Church and will see to it that their practice violates no canon of orthodoxy. At the same time, they will maintain its distinctiveness and hold it out as an option for those in the Church who feel drawn to it. They will provide an appropriate doctrinal justification for the practice to defend it from detractors, and they may at times form associations such as Marian Sodalities for mutual support in the practice. They generally will not disparage other traditions of practice nor call for exclusive commitment to this tradition alone. It would be wrong to regard it as a "school" or a "sect," because it does not aspire to institutional autonomy nor does it require it. It is a tradition of practice.

It is for this reason that throughout this chapter I have been referring to the object of our inquiry as the Chinese Pure Land "tradition." This is the word that, I think, best suits the character of the phenomenon. A tradition does not need institutions or lineages to endure; it simply needs people to engage it and pass it along to subsequent generations. I will not claim that this is how we should understand the Pure Land phenomenon as it is found in other places; very clearly, the Japanese schools display a very different social character, and Tibetan traditions regarding Sukhāvatī have their own unique features. Nevertheless, since this book is about Chinese Pure Land Buddhism, the understanding arrived at in this chapter will guide the analyses to follow.

Chapter 3

The Development of the Concept of the Pure Land

The western Pure Land of Amitābha goes by many names. In Sanskrit, it is called Sukhāvatī, a name based on the word *sukha,* meaning "ease," "bliss," and "pleasure," among other things. *Sukha* is directly opposed to *duḥkha,* a word used to describe all the pain, anxiety, and frustration that characterize the present Sahā world (*suōpó shìjiè* 娑婆世界, the "world to be endured"). The name Sukhāvatī thus means "Land of Bliss." Early Chinese sutra translators rendered "Sukhāvatī" phonetically into Chinese with terms such as *Xūmótí* 須摩提, *Xūmótí* 須摩題, *Xūhēmótí* 須呵摩提, and so on (Fujita 1970, p. 432). They also translated the name in many ways: authors sometimes referred to it as the "Western buddha-land" (*xīfāng fótǔ* 西方佛土) or "Buddha-country" (*fóguótǔ* 佛國土), reflecting the Indian Buddhist notion of a buddha-field as we will see below. Early translations of Pure Land scriptures also used the descriptive name "Land of Amitābha Buddha" (*āmítuófó guó* 阿彌陀佛國) or "Immeasurably Pure Buddha Land" (*wúliàng qīngjìng fó guó* 無量清淨佛國; see Xiao 2009, p. 267). Other translations emphasized the blissful nature of the land, as in "[Land of] Utmost Bliss" (*jílè* 極樂), "[Land of] Peace and Bliss" (*ānlè* 安樂), or "[Land of] Peace and Nurturance" (*ānyǎng* 安養). These three terms became very common (Fujita 1970, p. 433).

The name from which the Pure Land tradition derives its name, *jìngtǔ* 淨土, "Pure Land" or "Purified Land," is not a translation from any Indic language. When the term "Pure Land" appears in other scriptures, such as the *Lotus Sutra,* there is no corresponding term in the Sanskrit text. The word appears to be of purely Chinese origin (Fujita 1970, p. 507–508). It would not be a suitable translation in any case, since Sukhāvatī means the "Land of Bliss," not "Pure Land." Some scholars such as Xiao Yue 肖越

theorize that in sutra translations, the term was a verb-object compound meaning "to purify a land," and that early writers such as Tanluan mistook the term for an adjective-noun compound (Xiao 2009, p. 266).

Needless to say, belief in the Pure Land raises many questions, both for practitioners and scholars. Both may wonder how this Pure Land came into being. Where is it exactly? What is it like? Who dwells there with the Buddha?

Indian Roots

As noted above, the term "Pure Land" does not appear in Indian Buddhist literature; it is a later Chinese creation (Fujita 1996, p. 20). Nevertheless, insofar as Indian Buddhists conceived of buddhas as localized in space, they obviously had to be *somewhere,* and so some thinkers considered the question of where a buddha might dwell. In the Pāli textual tradition the historical buddha Śākyamuni dwells in the same world as all other beings and experiences it largely as they do. The only difference seems to be that the way he perceives it is emotionally dispassionate and philosophically correct. For example, as he was dying he saw that he was simply suffering in a world that tends to produce suffering, so he felt no resentment and acknowledged that such things ensue as part of the ordinary workings of cause and effect. He did *not* claim that the present impure world masked an inchoate purity, nor did he claim to dwell in another realm characterized by purity.

Nevertheless, even the Pāli texts hint at the idea that a buddha requires an environment that reflects his own religious achievements and purity. For example, as Fujita Kōtatsu points out, one of Śākyamuni's disciples objected to his dying in Kusinārā, a "miserable little town of wattle-and-daub" unworthy to host a cosmic event such as a buddha's final nirvana (Fujita 1970, p. 283–284; trans. Walshe 1987, p. 279). Śākyamuni answered that the town was indeed suitable, because in the past, it was a magnificent royal city called Kusāvatī, and in a past life, he had been its king named Mahā-sudassana. He described its former glory thus:

> Moreover, it was twelve *yojanas* long from east to west, and seven *yojanas* wide from north to south. Kusāvatī was rich, prosperous, and well populated, crowded with people and well stocked with food. [. . .] And the city of Kusāvatī was never free of ten sounds by day or night: the sound of elephants, horses, carriages, kettle-drums, side-drums, lutes, singing, cymbals and gongs, with cries of "Eat, drink, and be merry" as tenth. [. . .] The

> royal city of Kusāvatī was surrounded by seven encircling walls. One was of gold, one silver, one beryl, one crystal, one ruby, one emerald, and one of all sorts of gems. (trans. Walshe 1987, p. 279–280; see also the story in the Chinese version of the *Madhyamāgama* [*Zhōng āhán jīng* 中阿含經, T.26], in the section entitled *Sūtra of King Mahā-sudarśana* [*Dà shànjiàn wáng jīng* 大善見王經, T.26.1:515b3ff]. There is an English translation of this text in Bingenheimer 2013, p. 462–477.)

The text continues with a description of this city, and generations of scholars have noted its similarity to later descriptions of the Pure Land of Amitābha (Fujita 1970, p. 284). Even though this text acknowledges that Śākyamuni does not presently abide in such a magnificent environment, it still asks the reader to see the Buddha imaginatively as a great "wheel-turning king" dwelling in a rich and symmetrical city adorned with all the pleasures of the senses.

This conception of a buddha's dwelling changed with the rise of Mahayana Buddhism. Mahayana authors vastly expanded the cosmology of Buddhism, making room for multiple world-systems floating in a vast universe. In addition, buddhas no longer went into an indescribable state outside the world of ordinary beings at the end of their lives, but could remain in the world rendering compassionate aid and guidance for suffering beings for such unimaginably long periods of time that they were effectively immortal. Finally, the idea took hold that, while some buddhas such as Śākyamuni might work within the present impure world, others presided over their own "buddha-lands" or "buddha-fields" (Skt. *buddha-kṣetra*), magnificent lands whose splendor and purity matched the presiding buddha's purity and virtue. Many accounts of these buddhas and their lands appeared in Indian Mahayana texts, many of which were subsequently translated in China and became part of the textual deposit of Pure Land Buddhism there.

Of these, the three most important for later developments were the so-called "Three Pure Land Sutras" (*jìngtǔ sān bù* 淨土三部). These are, in their most widely accepted translations:

1. The *Larger Sukhāvatī-vyūha sūtra* (*Fó shuō wúliàngshòu jīng* 佛說無量壽經), sometimes known in Chinese by the shorter name *Dà jīng* 大經 (Large Sutra, T.360). Tradition holds that the obscure monk Kāng Sēngkǎi 康僧鎧 (or Saṃghavarman) translated the text in 262 CE, but today scholars think it underwent several subsequent revisions (Gómez 1996, p. 126).

2. The *Smaller Sukhāvatī-vyūha sūtra* (*Fó shuō Āmítuó jīng* 佛說阿彌陀經), popularly known as the *Xiǎo jīng* 小經 (Small Sutra, T.366). The great Central Asian monk-translator Kumārajīva translated it in 402 CE (Gómez 1996, p. 125). Because of its brevity, it is one of the texts recited daily by Chinese monks and nuns in their morning devotions.
3. The *Sūtra on the Contemplation of Amitāyus* (*Fó shuō guān wúliàngshòu fó jīng* 佛說觀無量壽佛經) or *Guān jīng* 觀經 (Contemplation Sutra, T.365) for short. While this text purports to have been translated from a Sanskrit original by the Central Asian monk Kālayaśas between 424 and 442 CE, no such original has come to light and it might be a Central Asian or Chinese text (Pas 1995, p. 35–36).

While the first two of these texts are closely related and share a common worldview, the third is very different in purpose and outlook.

In addition to these three sutras, several other Indian texts gained wide acceptance and helped shape the outlook of Chinese Pure Land Buddhism. Among these are:

The *Pratyutpanna-samādhi-sūtra* (*Bānzhōu sānmèi jīng* 般舟三昧經, T.418). This is a very early text, having been translated in 179 CE by the Indo-Scythian monk Lokakṣema. This is likely one of the earliest Indian texts to discuss visualization of Amitābha, and it provided a resource for many Chinese Pure Land thinkers. The full title of this sutra is the *Pratyutpanna-Buddha-saṃmukhāvasthita-samādhi-sūtra,* which means roughly, "the scripture on the meditation that brings one face to face with the buddhas of the present" (trans. Harrison 1998, p. 8).

The *Vimalakīrti Sutra* (*Wéimójí suǒshuō jīng* 維摩詰所說經, T.475) is mainly a scripture of the "perfection of wisdom" category, but its first chapter is entitled "On Buddha Lands" and contains a discourse on the nature of the Pure Land that was widely quoted in later Chinese debates.

The *Dà zhìdù lùn* 大智度論 (Great discourse on the Perfection of Wisdom, T.1509), translated in 405 CE by Kumārajīva, is a version of a Perfection of Wisdom sutra with commentary by Nāgārjuna. A massive and wide-ranging work, section (*juǎn* 卷) number 92 is entitled "Chapter on Purifying a Buddha-land" (*jìng fó guótǔ pǐn* 淨佛國土品); it answers many questions about the nature of the Pure Land and the means for attaining rebirth there.

The *Shí zhù pípóshā lùn* 十住毘婆沙論 (Skt. *Daśabhūmika-vibhāṣā;* Treatise on the ten levels, T.1521*)*, also attributed to Nāgārjuna, deals with the stages of bodhisattva practice. Its ninth chapter, called "Chapter on Easy Practice" (*yìxíng pǐn* 易行品), contains an early exposition of the Buddha Amitābha and his Pure Land. Chinese Pure Land literature frequently quoted its assertion that reliance on Amitābha's power constitutes an "easy path" of practice.

The *Verses of Aspiration: An Upadeśa on the Amitāyus Sūtra* (*Wúliángshòujīng yōupótíshè yuànshēng jié* 無量壽經優婆提舍願生偈, T.1524) is a work by the Indian monk Vasubandhu that comments on the dedicatory verses of the *Larger Sutra.* It describes five specific practices for attaining rebirth in the Pure Land, which may originally have constituted five parts of a single visualization ritual (see Payne 2015). Translated into Chinese in 529 by Bodhiruci, Tanluan's commentary on it (T.1819) became highly influential (see Inagaki 1998).

While a few other Indian texts are quoted from time to time, these are the texts that added most substantively to the concept of the Pure Land. What do they tell us?

The three main Pure Land scriptures give us the main story of the genesis and nature of the Buddha Amitābha and his western paradise. The most detailed version of the story appears in the *Larger Sutra,* which recounts the following story (T.360.12:267a14–270b15; trans. Inagaki and Stewart 2003, p. 9–26; Gómez 1996, p. 162–176).

There was once a great king who went to hear the preaching of a buddha called Lokeśvararāja (*Shìzìzài wáng* 世自在王). He was converted and took monastic ordination under the name Dharmākara (*Fǎzàng* 法藏). As a Mahayana Buddhist, he made vows to seek perfect awakening and liberation to help all other sentient beings. In particular, he vowed to create the most perfect buddha-land as an ideal place of practice and to devise the means to draw beings from the ten directions there in order to speed them toward liberation:

> Once I have become a Buddha, I will make my field the best of all.
> The assembly of my followers in that field will be unique and marvelous,
> And its Seat of Awakening all-surpassing.
> My land will be like nirvana, it will be incomparable.
> I will feel compassion for living beings, and I will ferry across and liberate all of them.
> Those who come from the ten directions to be reborn in my field will be glad in their hearts and pure.

> Once they arrive in my land, they will have happiness and peace.
> (Gómez 1996, p. 164; T.360.12:267b10–b13)

In response, the Buddha Lokeśvararāja showed him billions of buddha-fields, describing the gods and humans living in them and distinguishing the coarser fields from the subtler.[1] After spending five eons (*kalpa*) contemplating practices for arraying a perfect buddha-land, Dharmākara set forth forty-eight vows, many of which state that, if such-and-such a feature of his buddha-land does not become reality, he will not accept perfect awakening. Other early Chinese translations of this text have different numbers of vows ranging from twenty-four to forty-eight, indicating that different versions of the original served as the bases for translation. However, the essential features remain the same. In addition, several of the vows do not deal with the features of his future buddha-land, but the effect that hearing his name will have on beings dwelling elsewhere. I will not list all forty-eight here, but call attention to a few that provide an essential understanding of the Pure Land.

In the first vow, Dharmākara declares that his buddha-land will not have the three "evil paths" of hell, hungry ghosts, and animals. This leaves only the paths of gods and humans, and the fourth vow states that even these two types of beings will be indistinguishable one from the other. These vows tell us that the Pure Land is not a typical world-system encompassing all possible rebirths. In addition, this buddha-land will be accessible to all beings who aspire to be reborn there even for "ten moments of thought" (vow 18), cultivate all virtues (vow 19), and, upon hearing his future buddha-name Amitābha, dedicate the merit of their practices to gaining rebirth (vow 20). He will personally appear to such beings at the moment of death (vow 19). Once born in his buddha-land, they will have many of the abilities and bodily features of a fully awakened buddha, such as the divine eye, the divine ear, and the ability to read others' minds (vows 6, 7, 8), and the 32 bodily marks of a buddha (vow 21). The requirements that beings first perfect all virtues and attain such abilities and features before gaining rebirth might lead one to think that they are effectively buddhas upon arrival, but other vows make clear that the purpose of rebirth in this buddha-land is the acquisition of buddhahood. Beings born there are promised limitless time to practice (vow 15), they will never perish and revert to a lower rebirth (vow 2), and they will assuredly achieve buddhahood (vow 11). The land itself is to be so clear and pure that it perfectly reflects all other world-systems (vow 31). All the accoutrements of the land will be so finely wrought as to be unperceivable (vow 27), and the land itself, with all its trees and buildings, will be adorned with all seven kinds of brilliant jewel (vow 32).

After enumerating all of Dharmākara's vows and reporting the inconceivable time and effort he expended in fulfilling them, the *Larger Sutra* reveals that he succeeded and became the Buddha Amitābha. Since all his vows stated that he would not accept perfect buddhahood unless the conditions of his vows were fulfilled, then he must have realized all of them and created a buddha-field exactly as described (Gómez 1996, p. 175–176; T.360.12:270a4–a6). The sutra then describes the features of this "Land of Peace and Bliss" extensively. While much of the imagery focuses on the magnificence and comfort of the land (as shown by its multicolored jeweled trees and constantly temperate climate), equal attention is given to features of the land that help its inhabitants to achieve buddhahood. The wind in the trees produces the sound of the teachings; in fact, all the sounds in the air will bring to mind Buddhist teachings (Gómez 1996, p. 180, 182; T.360.12:271a–b).

But with whom does the Buddha share the Pure Land? Here the picture becomes less clear, because in some passages the scriptures seem to say that only the most highly accomplished bodhisattvas achieve rebirth there, while other passages open the door wide for all to enter, from the greatest to the worst. For example, the vows contained in the *Larger Sutra* describe those who will achieve rebirth in Sukhāvatī as manifesting the 32 bodily marks of a buddha (vow 21), traveling to all worlds to gather offerings for the Buddha (vow 22), preaching perfect wisdom (vow 25), having limitless inspired speech (vow 29), and so on. In a later section, the *Larger Sutra* says that, based on the practice of giving and compassion, those born in the Pure Land will manifest magnificence immeasurably greater than that of the highest gods (Gómez 1996, p. 184–185; T.360.12: 272a1–a5). Passages such as these emphasize the efforts that practitioners must have made cultivating their virtue and laying down "roots of merit" in order to gain rebirth in the Pure Land, and the high status and splendor they will enjoy there as a result.

However, other passages in both the *Larger Sutra* and the *Contemplation Sutra* indicate that beings of lower levels of achievement, or even possessing no accomplishments or good qualities at all, achieve rebirth with far less exertion. Both scriptures correlate various levels of prior practice and attainment with different levels of rebirth within the Pure Land. The *Larger Sutra* states that any being who hears Amitābha's name and vows to be reborn in Sukhāvatī gains rebirth immediately after death, and is thereby guaranteed to gain buddhahood without backsliding (technically, to achieve the state of non-retrogression, or *bùtuìzhuǎn* 不退轉) (Gómez 1996, p. 186–187, T.12:272b12–b13). Only those who have committed the Five Heinous Deeds or slandered the dharma are barred from rebirth. It then describes three kinds of Buddhists. The highest are monks or nuns who practice all possible good deeds and think single-mindedly of the Buddha Amitābha. The middle group consists of laypersons that engage in devotional and ritual practices and desire to be reborn in the presence of Amitābha. The lowest group is comprised of people who, as it were, wish they could practice virtue and are gladdened by Buddhist preaching, but can only cherish a desire to gain rebirth. The Buddha meets each of these at the time of death, though manifesting in a different way for each, and their status in the Pure Land varies according to their level (trans. Inagaki and Stewart 2003, p. 35–36; T.360.12:272b16–c10).

The *Contemplation Sutra* also sorts devotees into different levels of accomplishment and rebirth. However, it presents nine categories covering a broader moral range of believers from the best to the worst imaginable. The sutra organizes candidates for rebirth into three grades (*pǐn* 品), each divided into three births (*shēng* 生). Those who attain rebirth at the highest birth of the highest grade represent the ideal Buddhist practitioner: They possess firm faith, demonstrate strong resolve in making and keeping vows, recite advanced scriptures, and so on. Upon their death, the Buddha Amitābha comes to meet them personally accompanied by the two great bodhisattvas Avalokiteśvara and Mahāshtāmaprāpta and a great retinue. They are reborn in the Buddha's immediate presence, receive direct teaching while seated on an adamantine throne, and achieve buddhahood almost instantly (trans. Inagaki and Stewart 2003, p. 92–93; T.365.12:344c10–345a4).

At the other extreme are those born at the lowest birth of the lowest grade, who represent the most heinous offenders in the Buddhist moral imagination. While the *Larger Sutra* disqualified those who committed the Five Heinous Deeds, the *Contemplation Sutra* declares their inclusion. As they experience the terrors of hell on their deathbeds, a "good friend" (*shànzhīshì* 善知識) may come to them and tell them about the Pure Land and the vows of Amitābha. If they are too tormented by pain and fear to perform mental contemplation, then they may recite "Hail to the Buddha Amitābha" ten times and escape hell for rebirth in the Pure Land. However, no great retinue comes to escort them, only an empty lotus seat, and they are reborn on the outskirts of the Pure Land enclosed in a lotus bud. After twelve *kalpas,* the bud opens, and they emerge to receive instruction from bodhisattvas rather than the Buddha. Over a great span of time they gradually perfect their practice and attain buddhahood (trans. Inagaki and Stewart 2003, p. 98–99; T.365.12:346a12–a24). As noted in the last chapter, this sutra laid the foundation for the acceptance of the idea of non-elite attainment that came to define the Pure Land tradition in China.

As should be evident, these various texts on the conditions leading to rebirth present a seemingly intractable ambiguity. On the one hand, it would seem that rebirth requires a prior store of past merit gained by moral exertion and spiritual attainment. One might get the impression that only bodhisattvas of the highest caliber populate the Pure Land. On the other hand, the texts make great claims for the much simpler practice of invoking Amitābha's name. Many of the Buddha's own vows as recorded in the *Larger Sutra* describe the gifts that come to a devotee who only hears the Buddha's name (see vows 34–37, 41, 43, 44, and 48), and the *Contemplation Sutra* asserts that a mere ten repetitions of the name will extinguish the karma of even the most evil actions.

A linguistic coincidence permanently enshrined this ambiguity in Chinese teaching. To understand this, we must note that one of the most prominent practices for gaining rebirth in the Pure Land was visualizing the Buddha Amitābha. Most of the text of the *Contemplation Sutra* deals with this practice, and Julian Pas calls attention to other Buddhist scriptures whose principal teaching concerned the art of contemplating one or another buddha or bodhisattva (1985, p. 42–43). Even the *Larger Sutra*'s emphasis on hearing the Buddha's name and rejoicing in it appears to describe an internal practice (Pas 1985, p. 25) that the later Chinese tradition called "holding the name" (*chí míng* 持名). Literary Chinese had a word that could mean both "to think about" and "to recite"; this word is *niàn* 念 (Kroll 2015, p. 324a). Thus, while Chinese Pure Land vocabulary did include ways of naming practices that distinguished between contemplation (e.g., *guān* 觀 or *chí míng*) and external recitation (e.g., *chēng míng* 稱名, "to praise the name," or *kǒuchēng* 口稱, "to praise orally"), the term that came to predominate was *niànfó* 念佛, which could mean either of these.

All of the practices described so far entail thinking of the Pure Land as a place "over there," a pure realm far to the west that contrasted with this impure Sahā realm. There was another way of regarding the Pure Land, however, and that was to see it as coextensive with the present world. In this view, this Sahā realm is inherently pure; the perception that it is impure and not conducive to practice and attainment arises only because the impure minds of unawakened beings project impurity on to it. As the *Contemplation Sutra* famously put it, "This mind produces the buddha; this mind is the buddha" (*shì xīn zuò fó, shì xīn shì fó* 是心作佛，是心是佛), indicating that the purification of the mind by visualization makes one a buddha (trans. Inagaki and Stewart 2003, p. 8; T.365.12:343a21). The most frequently cited texts in support of this version of the Pure Land were the *Vimalakīrti Sutra* (*Wéimójí suǒshuō jīng* 維摩詰所說經, T.475) and the *Platform Sutra of the Sixth Patriarch* (*Liù zǔ dàshī fǎbǎo tán jīng* 六祖大師法寶壇經, T.2008; hereafter *Platform Sutra*). Since the latter is a Chinese composition, we will look at it later.

Of these two, the *Vimalakīrti Sutra* develops this theme more extensively. In the first chapter, called "On Buddha Lands" (*Fóguó pǐn* 佛國品), a young seeker asks the Buddha Śākyamuni how one purifies one's future buddha-land. The Buddha replies that this comes about through the purification of the mind by means of good deeds and practice. When a bodhisattva learns a point of doctrine or perfects a virtue, then that virtue accrues to his future buddha-land as well as to him personally, and beings who share that virtue will be drawn to his Pure Land. This part of the exposition ends with the oft-quoted summary, "Therefore . . . if the bodhisattva wishes to acquire a pure land, he must purify his mind. When the mind is pure, the buddha-land will be pure" (trans. Watson 1997, p. 29; T.475.14:538c4–c5).

This causes the Buddha's disciple Śāriputra to wonder if his master is indeed fully awakened. After all, the Buddha dwells in the present world, which is clearly not a pure land but a world of suffering and ignorance. The Buddha reads Śāriputra's thoughts and addresses this concern by teaching that the present world's impurity must not be ascribed to the buddha whose buddha-field it is, but to the impure minds of ordinary beings. To demonstrate the point, the Buddha touches the earth with his toe, and empowers all in attendance to see this very world as he sees it with his purified mind. The land suddenly manifests jeweled radiance, and the Buddha explains to Śāriputra, "My Buddha land has always been pure like this. However, because I wish to save those persons who are lowly and inferior, I make it seem an impure land full of defilements, that is all. . . . If a person's mind is pure, then he will see the wonderful blessings that adorn this land" (trans. Watson 1997, p. 30–31; T.475.14:538c26–c29). The Buddha then withdraws his foot, and everything appears as before.

The *Nirvana Sutra* (*Nièpán jīng* 涅槃經, T.374) answers the same question in an entirely different way. Here the Buddha Śākyamuni explains that he has his own pure land, which lies to the west beyond buddha-lands numbering as many as the sands of thirty-two Ganges Rivers. This land is called "Unsurpassable" (*Wúshèng* 無勝) because it is the equal of both the western Land of Peace and Bliss (*Ānlè shìjiè* 安樂世界) and the eastern Land of the Full Moon (*Mǎnyuè shìjiè* 滿月世界). From his base in that pure land, Śākyamuni manifests in this world of Jambudvīpa in order to turn the wheel of dharma and save all its sentient beings (T.374.12:508c25–509a4). This sutra thus affirms that the Sahā world *is* indeed defiled, and that the pure buddha-land of Śākyamuni lies elsewhere, contradicting the "mind-only" position.

Thus, the Chinese Pure Land tradition inherited from India two distinct ways of conceptualizing the Pure Land. The first position came to be known as either "western-direction Pure Land" (*xīfāng jìngtǔ* 西方淨土) or "other-direction Pure Land" (*tāfāng jìngtǔ* 他方淨土). This entailed the belief that Sukhāvatī literally existed far to the west of this Sahā world, and that one could attain rebirth there after death by religious practices such as visualization of the Buddha or the simpler method of reciting the Buddha's name with faith. The second position came to be known as "mind-only Pure Land" (*wéixīn jìngtǔ* 唯心淨土) and was favored by the Chan (Zen) School. This position held that the world is inherently pure and that impurity only appears because a defiled mind mistakenly projects its own impurity on to the landscape. In this conception, one gains the Pure Land by exerting oneself, purifying one's mind, and achieving enlightenment. These competing ideas provided the basis for a long series of polemical writings right up to the twentieth century.

On the topic of polemics, we may conclude this survey of the Indian sources by noting that, even before reaching China, early Pure Land ideas provoked opposition among more traditional Buddhists who felt that practitioners ought to be self-reliant and achieve awakening through their own efforts. Some of the literature that entered the Chinese Pure Land tradition had to explain how asking for the Buddha Amitābha's help did not violate basic Buddhist principles.

For example, a long section of the *Great Discourse on the Perfection of Wisdom* (Skt. *Mahāprajñāpāramitā-śāstra;* Ch. *Dà zhìdù lùn* 大智度論, T.1509) describes the buddha-land in the same sensuous terms as the sutras just examined. It also explains that the quality of devotees' offerings to the Buddha in the present will help to "adorn" their future buddha-lands. When offering the seven types of precious gem, one states, "May the karma of this offering cause my land to be adorned with the seven gems"

(T.1509.25:710b16–b17). One does the same when offering music, incense, food, and even wives and concubines (T.1509.25:710c2–c5, 710c17–c18, 710c26–c27, 711a6).

A questioner asks why a buddha should want any of this, since some of it is forbidden to monks by the monastic code (*vinaya*), while others simply seem superfluous (e.g., why does a buddha require entertainment?; T.1509.25:710c2–c5). In addition, the Buddha always taught that the five desires are like fire, like a pit, like a disease, like a prison, etc., so why would one wish sentient beings to enjoy them in their future buddha-lands? (T.1509.25:711a8–a10). Furthermore, why would a compassionate buddha exclude the "three evil paths" (of animals, hungry ghosts, and hell-beings) from his buddha-land? Finally, why should the song of the birds preach the dharma when a buddha is at hand to preach in person (T.1509.25:711c9–c11)?

The author answers that the five desires may indeed be poisonous to individual ordinary beings, but they are purified when offered to all sentient beings. In the present world, the five desires are the cause of suffering, strife, and violence, but at the level of gods and above, they are not. In a place where the objects of the five desires are in plentiful supply and no one has to compete for them there is no occasion for committing the ten non-virtuous deeds, so there is no need to forbid them (T.1509.25:711a13–b3). Thus, such things as music, incense, and jewels make one's future buddha-land more pleasant. As to the absence of the three evil paths, the commentator reminds the questioner that buddhas operate in all realms, including "mixed realms" (*zá guótǔ* 雜國土) where the pure and the impure abide together (T.1509.25:711c11–c22).

The last point raises issues that will recur in Chinese Pure Land literature. After quibbling about birds preaching, the text goes on to wonder why, of all the buddhas who preach diligently all through the cosmos, Amitābha gets pride of place, and why beings gain rebirth in his land simply by reciting his name when all the other buddhas preach repentance and arduous spiritual practice (T.1509.25:712a17–a18). With regard to the trees and birds, the text replies that if a buddha appears as a buddha in all places, his appearance will be too commonplace and will not engender belief. However, when the dharma is preached by the breezes and birds, this attracts attention, and the factor of surprise arouses faith (T.1509.25:712a20–a28). Finally, the reason that Amitābha occupies a central place is that he is a "dharma-nature body" (*fǎxìng shēn* 法性身). He emits innumerable buddhas from every hair-pore, and while unawakened beings might think that some are superior and others inferior, in fact they are not different. If one believes this, then one has deep roots of faith, and one will certainly become a buddha (T.1509.25:712b6–22).

Chinese Developments

We cannot know for certain when Pure Land Buddhism appeared in China, for we cannot identify the first time a Chinese Buddhist vowed to be reborn in Amitābha's Land of Bliss after death and took up the practices necessary to assure success. We know that it took shape slowly as the various elements of the Indian tradition we have outlined above developed after Buddhism's introduction into China, and required time for translation, absorption, and adaptation until a Pure Land movement appeared in the fifth and sixth centuries as described in the previous chapter. Mochizuki Shinkō points to the translation of the *Pratyutpanna-samādhi-sūtra* in 179 CE as the beginning point, and I agree that this is the first textual evidence of proto–Pure Land thought (1942, p. 5). Possibly the earliest account of Pure Land practice is that of the monk Que Gongze (*Què Gōngzé* 闕公則) recorded in the *Fǎyuàn zhūlín* (法苑珠林, T.2122). According to this text, he died during the reign of Emperor Wu of the Western Jin dynasty (r. 265–290), and while scriptures were being recited during a memorial service for him he appeared to the assembly and announced that he had "been born in the western land of Ease and Bliss." He had returned with a retinue of bodhisattvas to hear the scriptures (T.2122.53:61b15–c1; the text dates from 668 CE; see Ono 1932–1936, p. 10:5b).

The monk Huiyuan of Mount Lu (*Lúshān Huìyuǎn* 盧山慧遠, 334–416), the first "patriarch" (*zǔ* 祖) of the Pure Land tradition in China, ranks among the earliest recorded Chinese figures to promote the practice of *nianfo* in order to secure rebirth in Sukhāvatī. We find the evidence of his Pure Land activity in two brief texts. The first, from the *Biographies of Eminent Monks* (*Gāosēng zhuàn* 高僧傳, T.2059), describes how he convened an assembly of 123 laymen in the year 402 CE at the request of a lay follower to fast and meditate before an image of Amitābha and vow to attain rebirth in the Pure Land. The same lay follower composed the texts for the ritual (T.2059.50:358c18–359a20; English in Zürcher 1959, p. 240–253). The second story concerns one of Huiyuan's monastic disciples, Sengji (*Sēngjì* 僧濟). When this monk fell critically ill while visiting his master, Huiyuan facilitated a vigil to enable Sengji to gain rebirth in the Pure Land (T.2059.50:362b12–b27). There is a third text containing an exchange of correspondence between Huiyuan and the famous Kuchean monk-translator Kumārajīva based on a reading of the instructions for visualizing buddhas in the *Pratyutpanna-samādhi-sūtra*. Aside from the fact that it mentions the Buddha Amitābha, it is not a strictly Pure Land topic, but one focused on a general form of meditation (T.1856.45:34b4–135a4; see chapter 8).

We will devote an entire chapter to Huiyuan later on. For this chapter's purposes, we need only look at the way members of Huiyuan's "White Lotus Society" (*Báiliánshè* 白蓮社) thought of the goal toward which their joint practice was aimed. For this, we will look closely at the society's charter, composed by Liu Yimin (*Liú Yímín* 劉遺民) at Huiyuan's behest. Does the text specifically refer to Sukhāvatī as the goal or describe it in recognizable terms? It seems not. First, the paragraph introducing the text and the text itself as reproduced in the *Biographies of Eminent Monks* (T.2059.50:358c22–359a20) contain only four references to the goal: the "western direction" (*xīfāng* 西方, 50:358c22), the "western region" or "western border" (*xījìng* 西境, 50:359a5), the "most distant region" (*juéyù* 絕域, 50:359a12), and the "spirit realm" (*shénjiè* 神界, 50:359a13). When Erik Zürcher translated this text, he emended each of these terms, adding "Sukhāvatī" in parentheses after the first and fourth references, and "of the Western Paradise" after "most distant region" (1959, p. 244–245). None of these additions is justified by the text, and their inclusion gives a false indication of the extent to which Huiyuan's followers understood the nature of the Pure Land.

Upon reading Liu's conception of what it will be like to enjoy the goal, one becomes even more suspicious that Huiyuan and his followers had no clear understanding of the nature of the Pure Land. Using Zürcher's translations but omitting his emendations, Liu says that rebirth in "the western region" will look like this:

> Their knowledge will be renewed by Enlightenment, and their bodies will be changed by transformation. They will sit on lotus flowers in the midst of streams and sing their words (of praise) in the shadow of the *ko*-tree [*kē* 柯] of jade; they will move in their cloud-woven garments to the eight borders of the earth and float around on fragrant wind till the end of their lives. Their bodies will grow oblivious of rest and yet become more sedate; their minds will rise above pleasure and thereby become naturally joyful. [. . .] They will join the host of supernatural beings and continue in their traces, and, directing themselves to the great repose, they will regard this as their final term. (Zürcher 1959, p. 245; T.2059.50:359a15–359a20)

This does not match any canonical description of the Land of Bliss, and indeed seems to express something more like an aspiration to Daoist immortality! This may not be surprising in a time when Kumārajīva's translation of the *Amitābha Sutra* was not yet in circulation and among men who saw themselves as "secluded scholars" (*yǐnshì* 隱士). The facts that they carried out their practice in front of an image of Amitābha and located their goal vaguely in the west provide the only connection to later Pure Land developments. At this point in Chinese Buddhist history, it seems the idea of the Pure Land was still quite vague and idiosyncratic.

Turning now to later developments in the conception of the Pure Land, we may note one early controversy and three later trends. The early controversy had to do with a question relating the Pure Land to the theory of the Three Bodies of the Buddha (Skt. *trikāya;* Ch. *sānshēn* 三身). The later three trends had to do with the nature of the Pure Land as a place literally existing to the west of the present world, a construction of the mind, or a goal to be achieved in this world.

As noted briefly in the previous chapter, early authors held that the nature of the Pure Land corresponded to each of the three kinds of buddha-body that manifested with it. Behind this discussion was the theory of two kinds of karmic consequence that I will translate "proper recompense" (*zhèngbào* 正報) and "dependent recompense" (*yībào* 依報). The first term indicates the karma of past actions that brings results in one's personal body and mind: size, health, gender, intelligence, and so on. The second refers to the karma that leads one to a certain environment: family, land, economic conditions, availability of Buddhist teaching, etc. Logically, then, a buddha's purified karma should lead not only to a pure body and mind, but a pure buddha-field as well; the *Vimalakīrti Sutra* affirmed as much. How did this align with the teaching of the Three Bodies of a Buddha?

(1) All buddhas manifested dharma-lands to match their dharma-bodies. However, only buddhas could perceive them, and so they were not relevant to present practitioners.

(2) Since the past merit accrued by a buddha brought him a magnificent reward body (Skt. *saṃbhoga-kāya;* Ch. *bàoshēn* 報身 or *shòuyòng shēn* 受用身), then the buddha-land ought to be a reward land (*bàotǔ* 報土 or *shòuyòng tǔ* 受用土). Later Chinese sutra commentaries distinguished two varieties of reward land. The first, the "land for the [buddha's] own enjoyment" (*zì shòuyòng tǔ* 自受用土), manifested the full merits of a buddha only for that buddha and not for others. The second, called the "land for the enjoyment of others" (*tā shòuyòng tǔ* 他受用土), was available for the benefit of others. The Tiantai commentator Zhanran (*Zhànrán* 湛然) used this device to explain how Vulture Peak functioned as a reward land both for the Buddha Śākyamuni (as the first type) and his

audience (as the second type) in the *Lotus Sutra* in his *Fǎhuá wénjù jì* 法華文句記 (Notes on [Zhiyi's] Commentary on the Text of the Lotus Sutra; see T.1719.34:340c10–c14).

(3) If the presiding buddha manifested as a transformation body (Skt. *nirmāṇa-kāya;* Ch. *yìngshēn* 應身 or *huàshēn* 化身), then his buddha-field should correspondingly be a transformation land (*biànhuà tǔ* 變化土 or simply *huàtǔ* 化土). As a buddha accommodated his appearance and manner of teaching to his audience, so a transformation land could appear in a way that corresponded to the state of the devotee's consciousness and karma.

Early masters took sides on various aspects of these classifications, but not over the question of which of the three kinds of land a buddha manifested; insofar as a buddha had three bodies, he manifested all three lands. Rather, as noted above, the question was soteriological: Into which of these three lands would a practitioner gain rebirth? When it came to the question of what kinds of buddha-field actually were to be found in the universe, the tradition proved very conservative. As we shall see near the end of this chapter, the tradition came to accept that a buddha-field manifested wherever a buddha was, and any kind of environment that the sutras said a buddha inhabited was real enough. Thus, rather than argue about what kind of Pure Land was real and what kind was not, several authors made efforts to catalogue and classify all the buddha-lands attested in scriptures.

Before we move on to examine these classificatory schemes, let us note one area in which a broad consensus emerged early: that the Pure Land of Amitābha is not part of the Triple World consisting of the Desire, Form, and Formless Realms. This was important both in understanding the nature of the Pure Land and for soteriological reasons. For the Pure Land to represent a definitive escape from samsara, it had to be an extraordinary realm outside of the Triple World. In his *Wangsheng lun zhu,* Tanluan, quoting Vasubandhu, asserts that the Pure Land "surpasses" (*shèngguò* 勝過) the Triple World through its purity and absence of inverted views (Inagaki 1998, p. 138–139; T.1819.40:827c29–828b1). Daochuo devoted a section of his *Anle ji* to this question in which he cites the *Great Discourse on the Perfection of Wisdom:*

> Furthermore, we rely upon the *Perfection of Wisdom Discourse,* which says, "The reward of a Pure Land is without desire, and so it is not of the Desire Realm. One dwells upon its ground, and so it is not of the Form Realm. It has

> shape and form, and so it is not of the Formless Realm." (T.1958.47:7b2–7b4; translation mine, see Inagaki's translation [2014, p. 31])

Later in the text, this becomes a reason to advise against seeking rebirth in the Tuṣita Heaven; although it is the abode of the future buddha Maitreya, it is still within the Triple World and therefore part of samsara. One will not find the requisites for successful practice there. Its pleasures are purely sensual and lack the edifying properties of Sukhāvatī. Those who gain rebirth in Sukhāvatī attain the state of non-retrogression, and are forever free of samsara (T.1958.47:9c1–9c5; see Inagaki 2014, p. 49).

As noted in the last chapter, arguments based on these three kinds of buddha-land generally revolved around soteriological issues. They were arguments about who could access which manifestation of the Pure Land, not about the Pure Land per se. Other conflicts arose later over three competing visions of the nature of the Pure Land. The first two, which coexisted and at times competed throughout most of the history of Chinese Pure Land Buddhism, are known as "mind-only Pure Land" (*wéixīn jìngtǔ* 惟心淨土) and "western-direction Pure Land" (*xīfāng jìngtǔ* 西方淨土) or "other-direction Pure Land" (*tāfāng jìngtǔ* 他方淨土). These were introduced in the previous section. The third way of presenting the Pure Land appeared early in the twentieth century and reflects the growing social concerns of Buddhism; it is called "the Pure Land in the human realm" (*rénjiān jìngtǔ* 人間淨土).

"Western-Direction Pure Land" and "Mind-Only Pure Land"

Competition between the doctrines of "mind-only Pure Land" and "western-direction Pure Land" became inevitable after Shandao provided the rationale for non-elite attainment. The former position reflects the earlier masters' assertions that the Pure Land that one perceived accorded with the level of mental purity one had achieved, while the latter position comported well with Shandao's claim that everyone who achieves rebirth sees the Pure Land as Amitābha's power caused it to manifest. However, I wish to look at this matter from the perspective of religious need as well. We may interpret these two positions as reflecting the conflict between Pure Land eschatology's need to remain consistent with Buddhist philosophy and the need to envision the Pure Land as a suitable object of devotion. As the needs of philosophers and devotees differ, the conceptions of the Pure Land required by each were difficult to harmonize. The devotee wishing to engage in visualization of the Buddha Amitābha and his Pure Land required rich imagery and the hope that even the unawakened could achieve rebirth. The philosopher needed to know that the doctrine of the Pure Land did not violate widely accepted Buddhist concepts such as non-duality, emptiness, and the mentally constructed nature of all reality, buddha-lands included.

Consequently, texts and teachers that aimed to arouse faith and inspire devotional practice tended to dwell on the magnificence of the Pure Land and its availability even to the vilest sinner. As an example, we may look at Tanluan (*Tánluán* 曇鸞, 476–542) and his *Wangsheng lun zhu*. The greater part of this text is taken up with contemplations of the seventeen "glorious merits" (*miàosè gōngdé* 妙色功德) of the Pure Land. These merits include its purity, its vastness, its basis in the Buddha's compassion, its luminous appearance, its adornment with precious jewels, its blazing illumination, and so on (Inagaki 1998, p. 136ff.; T.1819.40:827c29ff.). The last of the seventeen merits is that "whatever aspirations sentient beings may have will all be fulfilled." The section concludes with the lines, "For this reason, I aspire to be born in [Amitābha] Buddha's land" (Inagaki 1998, p. 168–170; T.1819.40:831b4–b13). The phrase "for this reason" makes clear that the text's purpose in describing all the glorious merits of the Pure Land is to arouse faith and motivate practice.

Other such exemplary texts could be cited, but it should be clear that the devotional and aspirational conception of the Pure Land requires at least two things. First, the Pure Land should be separate and distant from the present defiled world. Second, descriptions of it must include a wealth of magnificent features to arouse the desire to go to it. Those religious leaders who attracted and ministered to congregations of devotees resisted attempts to minimize, denigrate, or psychologize these aspects of the Pure Land, insisting that it was a real place separated from the present world and vastly preferable to it. As recently as the late nineteenth century, the 13th patriarch (*zǔ* 祖) of Pure Land, Yinguang (*Yìnguāng* 印光, 1861–1940), instructed his followers to accept this sort of detailed, literal interpretation of the Pure Land:

> Have deep faith in the Buddha's words, penetrate [them] without doubt or delusion; this alone can be called true faith. [. . .] [I] teach that if [one takes] the various and inconceivable supreme splendors of the Pure Land as fables, metaphors, or psychological states, then this is not true perception. If one maintains this kind of heretical knowledge and ludicrous view, then one loses the actual benefit of rebirth in the Pure Land. (Yìnguāng 1991, p. 4)

The insistence that the Pure Land is literally away to the west is the reason that this view acquired the name "western-direction Pure Land" or "other-direction Pure Land."

Other thinkers believed that the "western-direction" position violated several fundamentals of Buddhist thought. By distinguishing this world from the Pure Land, purity from impurity, unawakened beings from buddhas, and so on, it denied the basic Mahayana belief in the nonduality of all things and all views. Asserting that the Pure Land exists external to the mind and can manifest as pure even to an impure consciousness was incompatible with the view that beings live in a mind-constructed world; the phrase, "the Triple World is mind-only" (*sānjiè wéixīn* 三界唯心) is a shibboleth repeated again and again in Chinese Buddhist literature.

The *Vimalakīrti Sutra* and the *Contemplation Sutra* provided the primary scriptural supports for the "mind-only Pure Land" position. We saw in the previous section how the former presented the story of the Buddha temporarily manifesting the purity of the present world as perceived by a pure buddha-mind, and the latter's declaration that the land is pure in proportion to the purity of the mind. In addition, the *Platform Sutra,* while not an Indian text, was also widely quoted in later Chinese debates. In chapter three, a government official asks the Chan patriarch Huineng (*Huìnéng* 慧/惠能, 638–713) why he sees people chanting the name of Amitābha in order to gain rebirth in the western Pure Land. Huineng replies that it is because people take the Buddha's symbolic speech literally, believing, for instance, that he meant to say that the Pure Land is 8,000 or 10,000 *lǐ* 里 away, when in fact these terms refer to the "ten evils and eight heterodoxies" (trans. McRae 2000, p. 51; T.2008.48:352a15–a17). Deluded people recite the Buddha's name in hopes of rebirth in a land far to the west, while superior people who have realized their self-natures as ultimately empty know to seek the Pure Land by purifying their minds (trans. McRae 2000, p. 52; T.2008.48:352a20). He goes on to derogate the naive realism of the "western-direction" position:

> The deluded person recites the Buddha's [name] and seeks for rebirth in that other [location], while the enlightened person purifies his mind. Thus, the Buddha said, "as the mind is purified, so is the Buddha land purified." (T.2008.48:352a19–a21; trans. McRae 2000, p. 52)

The debate between those who held the "western-direction" position and those (mostly associated with the Chan School) who held to the "mind-only" position lasted well into the twentieth century.

Some thinkers felt such a dichotomy was too stark and sought out ways to reconcile the two positions. One strategy was to declare that the presentation of Sukhāvatī as a paradise literally off to the west was an expedient device (*fāngbiàn* 方便; Skt. *upāya*) that the Buddha deployed to entice devotees of lesser capacities to seek rebirth there. For example, Yunqi Zhuhong (*Yúnqī Zhūhóng* 雲棲袾宏, 1535–1615) divided different aspects of the Pure Land into the provisional (*quán* 權) and the real (*shí* 實). The boundaries are not firm, however: what may be provisional for one being might be definitive for another depending upon their levels of attainment. In truth, the Buddha has no land at all, since, as a scripture says, his spirit (*shén* 神) pervades everywhere and has no need of a land. Nevertheless, he manifests a land as an expedient to lure in weak beings. Sages know better, so it does no harm to use the term "land" (CBETA X.424.22:634b9–b21).

Zhuhong, in his commentary on the *Amitābha Sutra,* also relied on the distinction between principle (*lǐ* 理), a term meaning reality-as-it-is and as-it-operates, and phenomena (*shì* 事), or the world as construed by individual minds into concrete appearances. By applying these concepts to the Pure Land itself, Zhuhong argued that, like any other reality, it could be perceived correctly by an awakened mind or incorrectly by an unawakened mind. Amitābha himself has arranged its phenomenal aspects to attract unawakened beings to it, but once there, they hear the preaching of the Buddha and gain awakening, thereupon realizing the mind-only nature of the land. At the highest level, the practitioner realizes that principle and phenomena interpenetrate; one does not abandon the concrete appearances of the Pure Land (or anything else) to seek for principle elsewhere:

> As to "non-obstruction": The field of senses and the mind [encompass both] principle and phenomena; both fundamentally and thoroughly interpenetrate. The field of the senses is phenomena; this is called "following the characteristics" (*suíxiàng* 隨相). The mind is consciousness-only (*wéishí* 唯識). Principle is the return to its nature (*guīxìng* 歸性). All thoroughly interpenetrate. (CBETA X.424.22:617b8–b9)

According to Zhuhong, then, because of this interpenetration one may hold both the "western-direction" and "mind-only" positions concurrently without contradiction. The first "follows the characteristics" while the second "returns to nature."

Another strategy involved setting up a typology that arranged all the various kinds of buddha-lands encountered in scripture into categories capable of accommodating all needs. Both Zhuhong and Yuan Hongdao

(*Yuán Hóngdào* 袁宏道, 1568–1610) employed this strategy. Zhuhong and Yuan surveyed a wide range of Buddhist literature and identified several different kinds of buddha-land. Here is Yuan's presentation from his *Xīfāng hélùn* 西方合論 (Comprehensive Treatise on the West, T.1976), published in 1599:

1. Pure Land of Vairocana (*pílúzhēnà jìngtǔ* 毘盧遮那淨土): The primordial buddha Vairocana pervades all of reality as its ground and substance, so this is the formless pure land. It is the entire *dharmadhātu* in which all things co-inhere: purity and defilement, buddhas and beings, all perfectly interfuse.
2. Mind-only Pure Land (*wéixīn jìngtǔ* 惟心淨土): This is the pure land described in the *Vimalakīrti Sutra* and the *Contemplation Sutra,* which manifests when the practitioner succeeds in purifying his or her mind.
3. Constant-truth Pure Land (*héng zhēn jìngtǔ* 恒真淨土): Referring to the *Lotus Sutra,* this indicates the pure land manifested during the assembly on Vulture Peak, which included both bodhisattvas and worldlings.
4. Conjured-manifestation Pure Land (*biànxiàn jìngtǔ* 變現淨土): Occasionally, as when the Buddha altered the environment on Vulture Peak in the *Lotus Sutra* or touched the earth with his toe in the *Vimalakīrti Sutra,* an impure land is caused to manifest its purity. This pure land manifests only for a short time, and is not one to which beings can aspire for rebirth.
5. Sent Reward [-body] Pure Land (*jì bào jìngtǔ* 寄報淨土): This is the peak of the Form Realm, where the highest bodhisattvas manifest their reward bodies. However, it is still within samsara, and so does not provide an escape from the world as would rebirth in Sukhāvatī.
6. Divided Body Pure Land (*fēnshēn jìngtǔ* 分身淨土): Here Yuan cites two scriptures, including the passage from the *Nirvana Sutra* noted above, that describe Śākyamuni as dwelling simultaneously in this Sahā land and in a pure buddha-land.
7. Other-dependent Pure Lands (*yītā jìngtǔ* 依他淨土): Yuan quotes the *Fanwang jing* 梵網經, which portrays Vairocana as emanating billions of buddhas and buddha-lands from his own substance, making them dependent on the first category given above.
8. Pure Lands of All Directions (*zhū fāng jìngtǔ* 諸方淨土): This category covers the pure lands of all the buddhas in the cosmos, but

Yuan asserts that, for a variety of reasons, none is as good as the Pure Land of Amitābha.

9. Four Types of Pure Land in One Mind (*yī xīn sì zhǒng jìngtǔ* 一心四種淨土): This is a composite category that actually encompasses four distinct types of pure land, possibly in an attempt to keep the overall number of categories to ten. These comprise:

    1. Lands in which Worldlings and Sages Dwell Together (*fánshèng tóngjū tǔ* 凡聖同居土)
    2. Lands of Expedient Means with Remainder (*fāngbiàn yǒuyú tǔ* 方便有餘土)
    3. True Recompense Unobstructed Lands (*shíbào wú zhàng'ài tǔ* 實報無障礙土)
    4. Land of Eternally Quiescent Light (*chángjì guāng tǔ* 常寂光土)

    While the fourfold framework derives from Tiantai thought, Yuan divided each of these four categories into many subcategories in an effort to ensure that every previous categorization of pure lands in Buddhist texts and every scriptural description of a place where buddhas dwelt would be covered.

10. The Inconceivable Pure Land that Receives Sentient Beings of the Ten Directions (*shèshòu shífāng yīqiè yǒuqíng bùkěsīyì jìngtǔ* 攝受十方一切有情不可思議淨土): While the first type of pure land, that of Vairocana, described the cosmos as the inconceivable body of this primal Buddha, this last category refers specifically to Sukhāvatī where Amitābha dwells. While it is similarly all-pervasive and transcends all conventional knowledge, it is superior to the first in that it also takes on a particular phenomenal appearance, thus allowing for the presence of unawakened beings who cling to concrete perceptions. Thus, it is a suitable dwelling for all beings. (T.1976.47:389c27–392a27)

Zhuhong presents a schema of four categories as found in number nine in Yuan Hongdao's list, from the "Lands in which Worldlings and Sages Dwell Together" to the "Land of Eternally Quiescent Light" (CBETA X.424.22:634a14–a23). The main difference between Zhuhong's and Yuan's schemas is that for Zhuhong, the "Land of Eternally Quiescent Light" is the land of Vairocana, whereas Yuan made the "Pure Land of Vairocana" the first in his list of ten and did not identify the "Land of Eternally Quiescent Light" with any particular buddha. He merely said that it was the "*dharmadhātu* of suchness illuminated by marvelous awakening and supreme wisdom." He further said that "its name is called a land, and that it is also called the land of dharma-nature" (T.1976.47:391b19–b20).

While very complex, Yuan's typology served to resolve the conflicts and contradictions inherent in thinking about the Pure Land (or buddha-lands in general) in a number of ways. It took into account as wide a range of Buddhist scriptures and Chinese exegetical works as possible, in particular those that were popular and influential such as the *Lotus Sutra,* the *Huayan Sutra,* the *Nirvana Sutra,* and the *Vimalakīrti Sutra.* It reconciled the devotional need for a richly imagined pure land with the need for philosophical rigor by showing the sheer variety of pure lands and the way their manifestations accommodated every being's capacity, from the impure Sahā land where the Buddha preached to lands that transcended all images and limitations of time and space. Lastly, it served the needs of Pure Land followers by demonstrating the superiority of Amitābha's Land of Bliss.

The Pure Land in the Human Realm

Until the end of the nineteenth century, these two ways of portraying the Pure Land sufficed for both common and elite devotees, but with the onset of the twentieth century, a new set of challenges called for another way of envisioning the goal. The revolutionary spirit running through China at this time caused many to reject all previous conceptions of the Pure Land as otherworldly (*chūshì* 出世), escapist, and unconnected to the needs of living people. "Mind-only Pure Land" manifested only to the elite practitioner who could claim awakening, while the "western-direction Pure Land" was a postmortem destination that distracted practitioners from the problems of life here and now. Threatened by cultural irrelevance and the possible confiscation of temple lands for practical use, Buddhist leaders re-thought the Pure Land.

The monk-reformer Taixu (*Tàixū* 太虛, 1890–1947) declared that Buddhism is a religion to benefit human life rather than serve spirits, and should do so in this world and not in the afterlife. Thus, he coined the terms "Buddhism for Human Life" (*rénshēng fójiào* 人生佛教) and "Buddhism in the Human Realm" (*rénjiān fójiào* 人間佛教, also translated as "Humanistic Buddhism") to express these new priorities. This led him to reimagine the prospect of life in an ideal Buddhist environment as something to be achieved here and now, not after death. Thus, he came up with the idea of "The Pure Land in the Human Realm" (*rénjiān jìngtǔ* 人間淨土). Heretofore scholars have focused on the progressive and forward-looking aspects of his thought. Here, I wish to present a fuller view of his ideas on the nature of the Pure Land to show him as a transitional figure who espoused both the traditional and the modern.

In Taixu's major statement on the subject, the 1926 essay "On the Establishment of the Pure Land in the Human Realm" (*Jiànshè rénjiān jìngtǔ lùn* 建設人間淨土論), we see that he does not repudiate traditional conceptions of rebirth in the Pure Land of Amitābha. He begins his diagnosis of the problems of human society by acknowledging that human beings have two basic needs: first, security of life and property, and second, immortality. The first is best fulfilled by rebirth in the mythical northern continent of Uttarakuru, and Taixu provides a very long scriptural description of its blessings and emphasizes the necessity of practicing the traditional Ten Virtues (*shíshàn* 十善) as a means to get there (1956, p. 24:357–371). In an effort to harmonize Buddhist mythic geography with modern science, he speculates that Uttarakuru may be a planet within our solar system (p. 24:356–357). However, even rebirth in Uttarakuru does not fulfill the desire for immortality, and so he presents another long quotation from the *Larger Sutra* that describes the qualities of the western Pure Land (p. 24:372–382).

Only after these considerations does Taixu turn to modern social problems and ways in which to achieve a Pure Land in the Human Realm. He notes that people have employed various means to address these problems, but since most of these means were rooted in ignorance, they produced unsatisfactory results. To be workable, the Pure Land in the Human Realm must include the presence of the Buddha, Dharma, and Sangha. However, as these are not always present, he recommends basing this Pure Land on a "rationalized" (*lǐxìng* 理性) Buddha, Dharma, and Sangha. This meant redefining these concepts. The Buddha will manifest as human intelligence and imagination; the Dharma in wise interactions between humans and their environment; and as people form families, mass societies, nations, and the entire human realm, a Sangha will appear (Taixu 1956, p. 24:396–397). In this way, one can conceptualize the Pure Land in the Human Realm in an abstract way. These ideas will lead people to work toward social reform in order to improve people's lives. Taixu also desires that world governments take part in this project by fostering an international union of Buddhists who would respond to the needs of the masses both by mobilizing for relief efforts, and also by carrying out esoteric rituals and prayer services for the welfare of the nations. The effort, in other words, will require both exoteric and esoteric methods (*xiǎnmì shuāngróng* 顯密雙融; Taixu 1956, p. 24:398–399).

After this, Taixu goes on to describe the concrete establishment of the Pure Land in the Human Realm as an ideal Buddhist community in a specific location, preferably Mt. Putuo (1956, p. 24:399; Goodell 2017, p. 174). Using land provided tax-free by the government, he envisioned a place wherein the monastic community, organized according to eight specific "schools" (*zōng* 宗) of Buddhism, would preside over a community of laypeople. This site would include agricultural fields allocated to families in proportion to their level of initiation into Buddhism (Three Refuges, Five Lay Precepts, Ten Virtues), and would include schools, police stations, and everything needed to form a viable community based on Buddhist teachings. This center would send out missionaries to the world and draw in delegates seeking to learn from it (Taixu 1956, p. 24:399–404).

As one reads this essay, one finds scant evidence that Taixu advocated social welfare and reform work as a way of establishing a Pure Land in the Human Realm, but that he retained a great deal of traditional Buddhist teaching. He notes that social reform only benefits people in this present life, and that the need for personal salvation and immortality may only be answered by recourse to traditional Pure Land practices, such as those leading to rebirth either in the Pure Land of Amitābha or the Tuṣita Heaven of Maitreya (Taixu 1956, p. 24:405). While he did coin the term "Pure Land in the Human Realm," he defines the "Human Realm" very broadly as any place in the Buddhist cosmos where humans dwell, including not only the present world with all its problems, but also Uttarakuru, the western Pure Land, and the domain of a *cakravartin* king.[2] Direct calls for social action occupy very little of the essay, while quotations from Buddhist scriptures that describe the Pure Land of Amitābha and traditional paradises take up a great deal of room. Nevertheless, Taixu did set forth the concepts and terminology upon which later thinkers and activists could build. (For more information and context about Taixu's contribution to modern Pure Land thought, see Goodell 2012, 2017, and Ritzinger 2017.)

Taixu's disciples took his teachings in different directions. Some actively denigrated Pure Land practices, such as Yinshun (*Yìnshùn* 印順, 1906–2005) did in his book *Pure Land and Chan* (*Jìngtǔ yǔ chán* 淨土與禪), in which he compared the Pure Land to a Marxist paradise (Yinshun 1992, p. 12) and cast Pure Land as a debased practice (English summary in Jones 1999, p. 126–131). Other followers such as Sheng Yen (*Shèngyán* 聖嚴, 1931–2009) and Cheng Yen (*Zhèngyán* 證嚴, b. 1937) further refined the concept of the "Pure Land in the Human Realm." By this, they meant that Buddhists, far from desiring escape from a world of incurable suffering by seeking rebirth in a distant paradise, are to engage in social reform and charitable work in order to transform *this* world into a Pure Land. In this model, the Pure Land will appear when the environment is cleansed and healed, the rights of women and children are safeguarded, and economic and social justice prevail (Sheng Yen 1997; see also Jones 2003).

Sheng Yen has written theoretical works on Pure Land, but here I will focus on a book published after his death, *Master Sheng Yen Teaches the Pure Land Dharma-Gate* (*Shèngyán fǎshī jiào jìngtǔ fǎmén* 聖嚴法師教淨土法門). This book, consisting of dharma-talks given to lay participants at a *nianfo* retreat, presents his pastoral recommendations for incorporating Pure Land practice into daily life. Reading these transcripts, one notices that he follows Taixu in adopting an eclectic approach that excludes nothing. Far from using the idea of the Pure Land in the Human Realm to supersede the traditional ideas and practices of the past, he finds ways to fit all these elements together: *nianfo* to gain rebirth in Sukhāvatī through the power of Amitābha's vows, efforts in self-cultivation in order to make as much personal progress as possible, affirmation that the Pure Land is a manifestation of the mind, and attention to benevolent work in the present world in order to create a Pure Land here and now.

Sheng Yen asserts that there is no inherent conflict between traditional "western-direction Pure Land" thought and the "Pure Land in the Human Realm" (2010, p. 88). This is because the practice of Humanistic Buddhism does not conflict with the aspiration for rebirth in Amitābha's land; in fact, it prepares one for rebirth there (Sheng Yen 2010, p. 89). In asserting this, Sheng Yen implicitly repudiates prior critics who held that the wish to attain rebirth in the Pure Land arises from a loss of all hope for this world. In contrast, he states that all Mahayana Buddhists ought to generate *bodhicitta,* the desire to save all other beings. When one has this attitude, then one accords with the aspirations set forth by all buddhas as exemplified by Amitābha's forty-eight vows. Normatively, one should vow *both* to bring about the "Pure Land in the Human Realm" by assisting living beings in the present world *and* seek rebirth in Sukhāvatī after death. In this way, one gains a higher rebirth in the Pure Land, becomes a buddha sooner, and can go about aiding other beings (Sheng Yen 2010, p. 90–93). Later, Sheng Yen states that the Pure Land is not inherently otherworldly and escapist; to the contrary, escapism signifies an unbalanced understanding of Pure Land (2010, p. 111).

Besides denying any conflict between a traditional "western-direction" idea of the Pure Land and social action in the present world, Sheng Yen also sought to harmonize the more traditional dichotomy between "western-direction" and "mind-only" Pure Land. In the course of counseling retreatants to engage in all the traditional Buddhist methods of self-cultivation, Sheng Yen mentions that, in keeping with the principle of mind-only (*wéixīn* 唯心), every Pure Land is only as pure as the mind experiencing it. To a buddha, even the present defiled world presents itself as utterly pure (Sheng Yen 2010, p. 162). The Pure Land is a kind of "one-room schoolhouse" in which students from various grades inhabit the same space but only receive such instruction as their prior experience has prepared them. This does not falsify the "western-direction" concept; if that is what a given being is ready to receive, then it will be given and will be as real as any other experience to an unenlightened mind. Nevertheless, such beings *will* be in the Pure Land and *will* attain buddhahood. Sheng Yen goes so far as to speculate that there may be as many Pure Lands as there are minds (2010, p. 163).

To summarize, Sheng Yen goes beyond Taixu's rather eclectic conception of the Pure Land in the Human Realm to present a more concise and coherent scheme. Taixu moved indiscriminately among such ideas as rebirth in Uttarakuru, rebirth in the Inner Court of the Tuṣita Heaven and subsequent presence when Maitreya attains buddhahood in this world, the purchase of land and the construction of an ideal Buddhist community with government support, social action to benefit human beings here and now, and rebirth in the Pure Land of Amitābha or of other buddhas. Sheng Yen, by contrast, omitted many of these ideas (e.g., rebirth in Uttarakuru and government-sponsored Buddhist utopias do not figure in his writings), and took the three elements of Pure Land previously assumed to be mutually inconsistent and brought them together. "Western-direction," "mind-only," and "the Pure Land in the Human Realm" do not contradict one another, and all can have their place even within the life and practice of an individual devotee. He also brings back to the fore the pre-Shandao notion that beings born in the Pure Land see it only as their level of mind-purification allows while eschewing the traditional typology of lands that correspond to the three bodies of a buddha in favor of a radically individualized vision.

Not all Chinese Pure Land followers have adopted the notion of the Pure Land in the Human Realm, however. As noted above, Taixu's contemporary Yinguang warned against believing that the Pure Land was anything but an existing goal located countless buddha-lands to the west, and a more traditionalist strain has existed alongside the modernizing movement. Venerable Daan (*Dàān fǎshī* 大安法師, b. 1959), one of the foremost advocates of the Pure Land tradition in modern China, serves as an example. His book *A Course in Pure Land* (*Jìngtǔ zōng jiàochéng* 淨土宗教程) contains a chapter on the Pure Land that explains "Pure Land ontology" (*xīfāng jìngtǔ běntǐlùn* 西方淨土本體論) in strictly traditional terms. The land of Sukhāvatī exists solely by means of Amitābha's forty-eight vows (Dàān 2006, p. 341). Whereas Taixu tried to harmonize traditional ideas about the Pure Land with modern science by suggesting that the Pure Land might be a planet, Daan more subtly notes that Albert Einstein theorized that time and space are mental constructs. This gives him the scope to say that traditional teachings that place the Pure Land to the west and give it a temporal beginning in the bodhisattva Dharmākara's forty-eight vows provide "coordinates in time and space" (*shíkōng zuòbiāo* 時空座標) that represent the Buddha's expedient means. In the Buddha's reality, the Pure Land is outside of time and space (Dàān 2006, p. 342–345). A search of the electronic version of Daan's text reveals that the term "Pure Land in the Human Realm" occurs only three times and is never elaborated. Scholars of modern Chinese Buddhism therefore must not think that "Humanistic Buddhism" and its corollary "the Pure Land in the Human Realm" have a monopoly on the field.

Conclusions

As a concept, the Pure Land has had a rich and dynamic history. It has crossed from Indian religious culture into China, which grappled with the necessity to make it serve a variety of needs in a variety of contexts. It has answered the question of where a Buddha dwells; it has served as an object of contemplation for advanced meditators; it has served as a practical goal for ordinary people who lacked confidence in their ability to escape suffering through arduous practices; and it has served to motivate a new generation of social activists. Its very flexibility made it responsive to many types of religious needs, and thus it endures to the present day.

Chapter 4

Self-Power and Other-Power in Chinese Pure Land Buddhism

In East Asian Pure Land Buddhism, few terms are more fundamental than "self-power" (*zìlì* 自力) and "other-power" (*tālì* 他力). The way that the practitioner's religious exertions and Amitābha's support on the path relate to each other defines this tradition, and understanding the nature of this relationship is one of its most central and enduring preoccupations. Scholars of the tradition are generally aware of the way in which Japanese Buddhists construed this relationship, at least from the times of Hōnen (法然, 1133–1212) and especially Shinran (親鸞, 1173–1263): Self-power (J.: *jiriki*) does nothing to advance the devotee, who would thus be foolish to trust in it. The person who sincerely desires rebirth in the Pure Land must rely solely on the other-power (J.: *tariki*) of Amitābha.

However, Chinese Buddhists never took this view. Rebirth in the Pure Land results when the two powers work together, an idea that the modern Taiwan Pure Land master Zhiyu (*Zhìyù* 智諭, 1924–2000) captured with the phrase "the two powers of self and other" (*zì-tā èr lì* 自他二力). He writes:

> If one wishes to be reborn in the west, then one must abandon greed, anger, delusion, pride, doubt, and evil views. If these are not abandoned, then one is entangled in karma and will not attain rebirth. Abandoning these is self-power; the Buddha [Amitābha] coming to conduct one [to rebirth] is other-power. Therefore, attainment of rebirth is the dharma-gate of the two powers. (Shì Zhìyù 1992, p. 58)

In another dharma-talk, Zhiyu went so far as to say that this way of combining self-power and other-power was the distinctive mark of the Pure Land path (1988, p. 29).

Since rebirth in the Pure Land results from the devotee and the Buddha working together in some fashion, the task of this chapter will be to describe the nature of this cooperation. We will first look at other Buddhist ideas about how buddhas and believers combine their powers to provide context, then look at the meaning of the terms "self-power" and "other-power" to see what is distinctive about the Chinese Pure Land conception of them. Finally, we will determine as precisely as possible just what the devotee's efforts contribute to the process, what the Buddha does to supplement these efforts, how other-power works in making the path to rebirth "easy," and how other-power contributes to the devotee's overall progress toward the ultimate goal of buddhahood.

Self-Power and Other-Power in a Wider Context

The terms "self-power" and "other-power" are distinctive to the Pure Land tradition, but they denote concepts that inform other Buddhist schools and practices, and they have synonyms and connections within concept clusters found both within and without the Pure Land tradition. In this section, I will touch on four such connectors: (1) transference of merit; (2) empowerment; (3) synonymous terms within the Pure Land tradition; and (4) related concepts within Pure Land, specifically the closely connected ideas of "easy path" and "difficult path" (or "path of sages"). The first two will situate the terms "self-power" and "other-power" within a wider Buddhist landscape where the confluence of a practitioner's efforts with a buddha's supporting power was taken for granted. The latter two will show that we need to look beyond these two terms to fill out the Pure Land tradition's particular understanding of this confluence.

Transference of Merit

Transference of merit was one of the earliest concepts by which the nascent Mahayana movement distinguished itself from earlier teachings. Even pre–Mahayana Buddhism entertained the notion that a practitioner's acts of charity or self-cultivation could bring benefit to others, as demonstrated by votive inscriptions that made such wishes explicit (see Schopen 1997, chap. 2). Mahayana texts such as the *Lotus* and *Huayan Sutras* promised the devotee that buddhas and great bodhisattvas constantly transferred their merit to believers in a way that augmented the fruits of their practices. Jingying Huiyuan (*Jìngyǐng Huìyuǎn* 淨影慧遠, 523–592) wrote about this in his *Dàshèng yì zhāng* (大乘義章, T.1851).

Drawing on the *Huayan Sutra,* Huiyuan defined merit transference (*huí-xiàng* 迴向) as orienting wholesome practices (*shànfǎ* 善法) in a certain direction (*qùxiàng* 趣向; T.1851.44:748b22–b23). He then defined ten forms of merit transference, including those that free living beings from the characteristics that defined them as worldlings by absorbing them into the practice of the six perfections. This leads them out of all their defilements and unskillful ways of thinking (T.1851.44:748b28–c4). However, Huiyuan presented this as rather diffuse in its effect. For example, the fourth of his ten categories stipulates that the merit-power of bodhisattvas' practices radiated in all directions to assist all beings. The effects of this included making all buddha-lands more magnificent and better able to gather in all living beings (T.1851.44:748c17–c19).

Early Buddhism also put forward the idea that the worthiness of the object of one's practice elevated the merit one accrued proportionately. Pāli Buddhism taught that a gift to an animal paid returns one hundredfold, and that rewards increased as the object of offering moved further up the hierarchy. At the highest extreme, a gift to a *tathāgatha* repaid with immeasurable merit (Adamek 2005, p. 140). In early Mahayana, the *Lotus Sutra* frequently claimed that seemingly minor acts of devotion directed at the sutra itself such as reciting even a single *gāthā* would redound to the devotee at a level vastly disproportionate to the offering. Thus, we find that almost all Buddhists believed in the two ideas that (1) one being may consciously turn the merit accrued through religious cultivation over to another being, and (2) the greater the disparity of religious status between these two beings, the greater the benefit that accrued to the lesser who gives to the greater.

Proponents of Pure Land thus had no need to convince other Buddhists of these possibilities; they already believed. However, belief in merit-transference did not necessarily entail a direct relationship between one individual and one buddha or bodhisattva, though a practitioner could solicit one in particular. Wendi Adamek provides an example of this in her reading of Jingying Huiyuan: "so (for example), when one solicits the bodhisattva Samantabhadra, the entirety of the merit of Samantabhadra is available" (2005, p. 146; see T.1851.44:749a16–a17). In the practice of empowerment, however, we do find the establishment of such particular relationships becoming the norm.

Empowerment

While the idea of merit-transference is virtually pan-Buddhist, one may also find an analogue to other-power called *jiāchí* 加持 in both Pure Land texts and those of other specific Buddhist traditions. I will translate this term "empowerment" and provide three examples of its use.

(1) The first is its use as a Chinese translation of the Sanskrit word *adhiṣṭhāna* in Chinese Esoteric initiation texts. This is the practice whereby the initiate calls upon the support and empowerment of a buddha or bodhisattva ritually assigned (see Orzech 1998, p. 147 for *adhiṣṭhāna* as "grace"). This buddha or bodhisattva then protects and empowers the initiate's meditation, and becomes his or her object of visualization. In this capacity, he partners with the practitioner and adds his power and support.

(2) Similarly, precept-conferring ceremonies sometimes include petitions to buddhas and bodhisattvas to act as witnesses and supporters of the recipient's vows. For example, a Song dynasty ritual for expressing filial gratitude to parents called *Rúlái guǎngxiào shí zhǒng bào'ēn dàochǎng yí* 如來廣孝十種報恩道場儀 (CBETA ZW68) contains a section called "Declaration to the Buddhas and Petition to the *Āryans* (*báifó qǐngshèng* 白佛請聖). In it, the aspirant confesses the heaviness of his or her past karma and invites the buddhas and bodhisattvas of the ten directions to come and offer support and protection (*jiāchí fùhù* 加持覆護; see CBETA ZW08n0068_p0077a02-a20; see also Jones 1997, p. 133–134). During my fieldwork in Taiwan in the early 1990s, I heard anecdotal evidence for the power of this support for preceptees. A woman who had received the Five Lay Precepts, which includes a prohibition on intoxicants, told me that once she was sick and was prescribed medicine that contained alcohol. Her doctor and family encouraged her strongly to take it, since the purpose was not to get drunk but to get well. She reluctantly agreed, but told me that once it entered her mouth, she reflexively spit it out and was unable to swallow it. She credited this to the empowerment of her precepts that she received by asking for the "other-power" of the Buddha.

(3) Third, the term *jiāchí* appears in Pure Land literature as well. In the Pure Land section of his anthology *Fǎhǎi guānlán* 法海觀瀾, Ouyi Zhixu (*Ǒuyì Zhìxù* 藕益智旭, 1599–1655) cited a scripture called the *Dà fāngděng dà jí jīng xián hù fēn* (大方等大集經賢護分, *Bhadrapāla-sūtra*, T.416) in regard to the attainment of the *nianfo* samadhi (*niànfó sānmèi* 念佛三昧). In the third fascicle of this scripture, the Buddha Śākyamuni tells Bhadrapāla that there are three causes for the attainment of this

samadhi. The first is having the proper conditions for this samadhi, the second is the empowerment of the buddha to be visualized, and the third is the maturation of the practitioner's good roots (Ǒuyì Zhìxù 1989, p. 3:2161; T.416.13:877a12–a14). While the term *jiāchí* was never widely adopted as an equivalent for "other-power" in the Pure Land tradition, other terms did function in this way, as we will see next.

Synonyms within Pure Land Texts

Within Pure Land literature, one finds the ideas of self-power and other-power under other names. For example, the *Wànshàn tóngguī jí* 萬善同歸集 (T.2017) by Yongming Yanshou (*Yǒngmíng Yánshòu* 永明延壽, 904–975) uses the terms "internal power" (*nèilì* 內力) alongside "self-power" and "external power" (*wàilì* 外力) in place of "other-power" (T.2017.48:961c28). Yuan Hongdao 袁宏道 quotes Yanshou in his *Xīfāng hélùn* 西方合論 (Comprehensive treatise on the west, T.1976), but substitutes *tālì* 他力 for Yanshou's *wàilì* 外力 (T.1976.47:403c221–c222). In other texts, synonyms for "other-power" are generally variants of the phrase *fó yuàn lì* 佛願力, or "the power of the Buddha's vow." For example, the *Jìngtǔ shí yí lùn* 淨土十疑論 (Discourse on ten doubts about Pure Land, T.1961) attributed to Tiantai Zhiyi uses such a term to define other-power: "Other-power is when one has faith in the power of the Buddha Amitābha's great compassionate vows as covering all beings that practice *nianfo*" (T.1961.47:79a6–a7).

Related Concepts

Conceptually, the terms "self-power" and "other-power" are often bundled with the terms "path of difficult practice" (*nánxíng dào* 難行道) and "path of easy practice" (*yìxíng dào* 易行道), respectively. The *locus classicus* for this terminology is the "Chapter on Easy Practice" (*yìxíng pǐn* 易行品) in the *Shí zhù pípóshā lùn* 十住毘婆沙論 (Treatise on the ten levels, T.1521). This chapter states that the path of difficult practice entails great risks. The attainment of highest enlightenment requires the completion of an extremely long and arduous path, and practitioners may fall away from the path between lives and lose what they have gained (T.1521.26:40c29–41a2). For frail worldlings, the text recommends the "path of easy practice," which it describes in this manner: "If a bodhisattva wishes to attain to the stage of non-retrogression in this body and accomplish supreme highest enlightenment, he should contemplate (*niàn* 念) all the buddhas of the ten directions and invoke their names" (T.1521.26:41b16–b17). While the text does not prescribe the recitation of

Amitābha's name in particular and aims at the attainment of the stage of non-retrogression rather than rebirth in Sukhāvatī, its recommendations applied easily to later Chinese Pure Land practice.

Daochuo uses a similar pair of terms in his *Ānlè jí* 安樂集 (Anthology on [the Land of] Peace and Bliss, T.1958). In the course of arguing the exclusive suitability of Pure Land practice for beings of the present age, he opposes the "path of sages" (*shèngdào* 聖道) to the search for "rebirth in the Pure Land" (*wǎngshēng jìngtǔ* 往生淨土; T.1958.47:13c6; trans. Inagaki 2014, p. 78). He identifies the first path as difficult and not fitting for the diminished capacities of beings of his time. In contrast, the path of *nianfo* removes all hindrances and smooths the way toward buddhahood. In other places, Daochuo uses the terms "path of easy practice" and "path of difficult practice," indicating that he considered these interchangeable with "rebirth in the Pure Land" and "path of sages" respectively.

In sum, the Chinese Pure Land tradition accords with the general Mahayana belief that buddhas and bodhisattvas are available to infuse their power into an individual's practice. While it often uses the familiar terms "self-power" and "other-power" to denote the believer's and the buddha's contributions to the process, its texts use other terms as well, such as *jiāchí* 加持, *fó yuàn lì* 佛願力 and its variants, and *nèilì* 內力/*wàilì* 外力 as synonyms. It also correlates the ideas of self-power and other-power with the paths of difficult and easy practice. In keeping with our main topic, however, it is important to note that only in this last instance, when presenting easy practice versus difficult practice, does any text require one to choose between the two. In all other cases, the terms appear complementary rather than oppositional. That is, they all speak of self-power and other-power (or their analogues) working together to maximize progress.

Images of Self-Power and Other-Power in Early Chinese Pure Land Texts

Texts that speak directly of self-power and other-power usually illustrate their relationship with similes rather than through theoretical arguments. This tendency goes back to the earliest days of the Pure Land tradition in China. For example, let us look at a set of seven similes put forward in Tanluan's *Lüèlùn ānlè jìngtǔ yì* 略論安樂淨土義 (Brief discussion on the meaning of the Pure Land of Peace and Bliss, T.1957) that were echoed later in Daochuo's *Ānlè jí* 安樂集. In answer to an objection that such a simple practice as *nianfo* cannot possibly eliminate eons of accumulated karma, they present the following:

1. It is like a pile of firewood accumulated by a hundred men for a hundred years that can be burned in half a day by a bean-sized spark.
2. It is like a lame man boarding a boat and travelling a thousand *li* in one day.
3. It is like a poor man who finds a great treasure. When he presents it to the king, he is rewarded with emoluments and titles for which other men might work for a lifetime without success.
4. It is like a lowly man on a donkey who cannot fly on his own, but can sail effortlessly through the skies by riding in the train of a *cakravartin* (universal king).
5. It is like a rope of great girth. Even though a thousand strong men cannot pull it apart, a young child wielding a sharp sword can cut it with ease.
6. It is as if a *Zhèn* 鴆 (a mythical poisonous bird) were to enter the water and kill all the fish and shellfish. Later, contact with a rhinoceros horn revives them all.
7. Finally, it is like the *Huánghú* 黃鵠 (another mythical bird) which called to Zǐ'ān 子安 and restored his life. (Tanluan's text is at T.1957.47:2b13–c3; Daochuo's text is at T.1958.47:10b22–c16; English translation of Daochuo's text at Inagaki 2014, p. 56–57)

Tanluan and Daochuo both conclude this list of similes with the following (citing Tanluan's somewhat clearer phrasing):

> Every one of the myriad dharmas has self-power and other-power, self-encompassment and encompassment by others. A thousand come into being; ten thousand cease, immeasurable and boundless. Will those with obstructed consciousnesses doubt the unobstructed dharma? Among the five inconceivables, the buddha-dharma is the most inconceivable of all! Also, for one who doubts the attainment of rebirth [in the Pure Land] because [they believe that] a hundred years' worth of evil deeds is heavy while ten *nianfo* is light and tries to enter into right meditation, it will not seem so. (Tanluan's text is at T.1957.47:2b28–c3; Daochuo's text is at T.1958.47:10b11–c16; English at Inagaki 2014, p. 57; because that translation is not accurate, this is mine)

From this coda, we see that, in response to the objection, they used these similes to illustrate the relationship of self-power to other-power. However, the similes are not all alike in their referents. The first, third, fifth, and sixth similes address the objection on its own terms: How can a seemingly trivial and easy practice produce such great results? The second, fourth, and seventh answer a slightly different question: How does a greater power intervene in order to assist lesser powers achieve their aims? That is to say, the simile of the spark that burns the great pile of kindling demonstrates that even a small cause can produce tremendous effects under the right circumstances. This kind of illustration will continue to appear in later texts in order to explain how the practice of *nianfo* produces immediate beneficial effects even before the practitioner's death, such as purifying the mind or eliminating vast amounts of past karmic guilt. The simile of the lame man boarding the boat illustrates the way in which a helpless being can take advantage of a greater power. This represents a second line of argument that will also continue to appear in order to illustrate the working of Amitābha's other-power. Texts of the later tradition will use both of these understandings.

Yunqi Zhuhong, Yuan Hongdao, Jixing Chewu, and Daan: Other-Power and the "Easy Path"

In this section, I want to turn my attention to late Ming, mid-Qing, and modern materials, in particular the works of Yunqi Zhuhong (*Yúnqī Zhūhóng* 雲棲袾宏, 1535–1615) and Yuan Hongdao (*Yuán Hóngdào* 袁宏道, 1568–1610). These are the two Pure Land thinkers of the period most noted by scholars for their lasting influence (see Guō Péng 郭朋 1982, p. 162–166). I will look into their works, with some references as well to the writings of the mid-Qing figure Jixing Chewu (*Jìxǐng Chèwù* 際醒徹悟, 1741–1810) and the modern Pure Land proponent Daan (*Dàān* 大安, b. 1959) to find answers to the following questions regarding self-power and other-power:

1. How do self-power and other-power work to speed the practitioner's progress?
2. How "easy" is the "easy path" of other-power?
3. To what specific goal does other-power lead the practitioner?

If we can answer these three questions, we will have a good picture of the ideal forms of Pure Land life and practice as they had developed by the late imperial period.

The Workings of Self-Power and Other-Power

The quotation from Zhiyu's modern essay given above maintains that progress in the Pure Land path requires that the practitioner and the Buddha Amitābha both contribute their powers. Such a reading, however, can mislead the reader if he or she assumes that these are two discrete beings contributing different amounts and types of effort to a common task. When one looks at the works of Zhuhong, Yuan Hongdao, and Jixing Chewu one immediately sees that they deny any such clear distinction and talk instead about a process that cannot be circumscribed by such concepts. For instance, here is a quotation from the section "Superior Expedient Means" (*shèng fāngbiàn* 勝方便) from Yuan's *Comprehensive Treatise on the West* (*Xīfāng hélùn* 西方合論):

> This expedient is not self-power, nor is it other-power. In the midst of the ocean of conditioned self-nature, there is plenty of the kind of spontaneous, unobstructed merit by which all things manifest. For this reason, a single utterance of the holy name [of Amitābha] contains no word that would bring suffering back. The merit brought to completion by ten utterances will [cause the] sudden transcendence of [the karma of] many *kalpas*. It is like the power of angry howls in ten thousand apertures during a cyclone; because of the apertures, it manifests. It is like the brightening of a cave in a deep valley. The power comes from the morning sunlight, but it manifests in the valley. It is like a string of ant-holes threading through the slopes of a mountain range. The power of water does it, not the strength of the ants. Again, it is like a single reed mat (i.e., sail) that moves a boat of ten thousand *hú* (斛, a measure of capacity; thus a large cargo barge). It is the power of the wind, not the strength of the reeds. In summary, everything is of the *dharmadhātu*'s ocean of nature, and does what it does without doing or intending. Not of itself, not from outside; everything together becomes sufficient. That is why one can have a superior expedient means such as this, a shortcut through the shortcuts. To abandon [the Pure Land path] would indeed be foolish and ignorant. (T.1976.47:393b28–393c9)

Like Tanluan and Daochuo, Yuan argues through similes, though his images convey somewhat different thoughts. In general, he presents two ideas here. First, he declares that there is no ultimate distinction between the practitioner and the Buddha Amitābha, and so no point in distinguishing the self-effort of the one from the outside assistance of the other. All share a single dharma-nature, and so all participate as one in the process of deliverance. Second, and despite this, one may still account for the working out of this unified process of deliverance in terms of the cooperation of a single large power and several individual smaller powers. One mighty wind produces its howling noise in dozens of small apertures. The trickling of large amounts of water through a mountain assists thousands of ants in their tunnel making. Sails made of reed mats help many boats catch the power of the wind to get them to their destinations. All these are rightly to be opposed to unstated counter-images: apertures whistling by themselves, ants carving through a mountain using only their minuscule power, or cargo barges moving by the power of the reeds that make up their sails.

Zhuhong's writings are much more extensive and nuanced than Yuan's, and so it is more difficult to distil his teachings into a few points. We may begin by noting Zhuhong's belief that the practitioner's efforts connect with the Buddha's power by *gǎnyìng* 感應, a term that Robert Sharf translated as "sympathetic resonance" (2002b, p. 82–88). This term has circulated in Chinese thought since the Warring States period. For example, the term appears in the "Rectification of Names" (*Zhèng Míng* 正名) chapter of the *Xúnzǐ* 荀子, where it means a congruence of sense stimuli with a person's inner nature (see *Xúnzǐ* 1999, p. 2:706–707). The influential Song dynasty Neo-Confucian philosopher Zhang Zai (*Zhāng Zǎi* 張載, 1020–1077) used the concept in his theory of *qì* 氣. Sympathetic resonance provided an explanation for action at a distance and through obstacles, as when a magnet attracted iron or when plucking one string of an instrument sets another string of identical pitch vibrating spontaneously (Chéng 1986, p. 85–86; Kim 2015, p. 18–20, 63–67). For Zhuhong, the term denoted a connection that the believer's practice made with Amitābha, as in this passage from his *Dá jìngtǔ sìshíbā wèn* 答淨土四十八問 (Answers to forty-eight questions about Pure Land; CBETA X.1158) in which he responds to the question: Why does only Amitābha come to meet the practitioner upon death rather than all the buddhas?

> Answer: The buddhas can know everything, but they do not go forth in an unruly crowd. Since one assiduously concentrates on one buddha, [that buddha] is automatically in accordance through sympathetic resonance. A practitioner of Pure Land causes all the buddhas to manifest equally, but there must be a main [buddha] and attendant [buddhas]. Amitābha manifests alone, with clouds of transformation-buddhas following. The principle of cause and effect is like this; it is not that the attainment is one-sided and shallow. (CBETA X.1158.61:510a7–a9)

Thus, the devotee's mental focus on Amitābha produces a resonance that evokes a response from him, and it is *this* buddha who arrives to conduct him or her to rebirth.

Other Pure Land thinkers have followed Zhuhong's reasoning. For instance, the twelfth "patriarch" (*zǔ* 祖) of Chinese Pure Land, Jixing Chewu (*Jìxǐng Chèwù* 際醒徹悟, 1741–1810), utilized the concept but in a slightly different way. In his *Recorded Sayings* he established that the practitioner and Amitābha, while non-dual, remain distinct from one another. The practitioner performs *nianfo* by holding the Buddha's name in his or her mind, and this is sufficient to evoke the whole reality of the Buddha. At a basic level, self-power and other-power work together in a relatively uncomplicated way: The practitioner generates the proper state of mind, and the Buddha responds. The picture becomes more complex and the interlocking nature of the practitioner and the Buddha comes out when Chewu goes on to show how Amitābha also holds the practitioner in mind. It is within their simultaneous mutual regard that the mechanism of sympathetic resonance takes effect. Chewu says:

> Now the reason that Amitābha can be Amitābha is that he deeply realized his self-nature as mind-only. However, this Amitābha and his Pure Land—are they not [also the practitioner's own] self-natured Amitābha and a mind-only Pure Land? This mind-nature is exactly the same in both sentient beings and buddhas; it does not belong more to buddhas and less to beings. If this mind is Amitābha's, then sentient beings are sentient beings within the mind of Amitābha. If this mind is sentient beings', then Amitābha is Amitābha within the minds of sentient beings. If sentient beings within the mind of Amitābha recollect (*niàn* 念) the Amitābha within the mind of sentient beings, then how could the Amitābha within the mind of sentient beings fail to respond to the sentient beings within the mind of Amitābha? (CBETA X.1182.62:337a2–a8; see also Jones 2000, p. 63–64)

As in all other cases, the practitioner and the Buddha work together to manifest this simultaneous mutual effect.

The modern Pure Land master Daan (*Dàān* 大安, b. 1959) has put forward yet another way of understanding the matter. First, like Zhiyu, he utilizes the phrase "two powers of self and other" (*zì-tā èr lì* 自他二力), but only in describing the path laid out by the first patriarch Lushan Huiyuan. He contrasts this with the sole reliance on other-power that he ascribed to Shandao, but rather than declare one orthodox and the other not, he says that these thinkers, both honored as patriarchs by the tradition, help to provide Chinese Pure Land with a balanced approach (Dàān 2006, p. 125, 140). Later, he describes how both ordinary practitioners and the Buddha Amitābha blend their efforts together to create the Pure Land. He describes the process in this way:

At first, he merely reiterates what generations of masters had already said: that the land of Sukhāvatī with all its marvelous adornments is an expedient teaching meant to draw in unenlightened beings. From the viewpoint of Amitābha, it is a *dharmakāya* land devoid of characteristics. That Amitābha sets up a Pure Land in time and space for sentient beings mired in illusions of time and space is an instance of "using a wedge to remove a wedge" (*yǐ xiē chū xiē* 以楔出楔; Dàān 2006, p. 344). However, when explaining why the Pure Land lacks a Mt. Sumeru as a central support, Daan introduces a surprising new element. The Pure Land needs no Mt. Sumeru because it is held up by the two powers of the sages and worldlings (*shèng fán èr lì* 聖凡二力). The Buddha Amitābha supports it through his spiritual powers and the power of his vows, and worldlings who have attained rebirth support it through the power of their merit and virtue. In addition, the Buddha creates it by manifesting his wisdom, while we who practice Pure Land respond to it (*gǎn* 感) as a transformation in our consciousnesses. Since practitioners have varying states of mind, the Pure Land manifests in various ways. The minds of Amitābha and of Pure Land practitioners both interactively cause the Pure Land to manifest, and the light of buddhas and worldlings mutually interpenetrate and complement each other. When one begins practicing *nianfo,* a lotus bud appears in the Pure Land with one's name on it. If one is diligent, it thrives; if one slackens, it withers. This means practitioners participate in the arraying of the Pure Land (Dàān 2006, p. 347–349).

Thus, we have seen that from its earliest history in China, Pure Land thought has held that the practitioner has a role to play in effecting his or her own rebirth in Sukhāvatī. In addition, between the quotation from the modern master Zhiyu given at the beginning of this chapter, Yuan Hongdao, Yunqi Zhuhong, Jixing Chewu, and Daan, we have seen five different ways of explicating the collaborative dynamic between the devotee's exercise of self-power and the contribution of the Buddha Amitābha's other-power in attaining rebirth in the Pure Land. It is a sailor raising a reed sail to catch the wind (Yuan); it is the Buddha responding to the devotee's focus upon him (Zhuhong); it is a confluence of consciousnesses as the practitioner and the Buddha hold one another in mutual contemplation (Chewu); it is a simple division of labor in which the practitioner lives the Buddhist life while calling upon Amitābha (Zhiyu); it is the practitioner supplying the state of mind to which the Buddha responds by arraying the land (Daan); it is all this and more.

How "Easy" Is the "Easy Path"?

Judging from the series of images that Yuan Hongdao provided to illustrate the Pure Land path given above, this is indeed quite an easy path compared with other forms of practice. However, Zhuhong's recommendations for practice may lead us to wonder just how easy this "easy path" really is, and in comparison to what?

We may begin by looking once again at the "Chapter on Easy Practice" of the *Shí zhù pípóshā lùn* 十住毘婆沙論 (Treatise on the ten levels, T.1521). An oft-quoted line from this chapter puts it thus: "There are innumerable gates to the buddha-dharma. Just as there are difficult and easy paths in this world, going over land being wearying while taking a boat over water is pleasant, just so are the bodhisattva paths" (T.1521.26:41b3–b4). This passage, repeated many times in Chinese Pure Land texts, gives the impression that attaining rebirth and enlightenment is a pleasant rafting trip down a placid river. To what extent do the actual practices recommended by Pure Land authorities reflect this sense of ease and pleasure?

When assessing the ease of the path, according to Zhuhong, we must look at two things: the number and complexity of methods he prescribes and the amount of effort he believes the practitioner must expend for them to be effective. Zhuhong's answer is clear: The method is *nianfo*. However, there are several different ways of performing *nianfo*, and in Zhuhong's writings, it often seems that his conception of the practice little resembles the peaceful images of ants and barges that Yuan employs. Rather, *nianfo* seems very arduous indeed. For example, during a "Water-Land Ceremony" (*shuǐlù fǎhuì* 水陸法會), Zhuhong named the traditional four kinds of *nianfo:* holding the name, or oral recitation (*chímíng* 持名), contemplation of an image (*guān xiàng* 觀像), visualization (*guān xiǎng* 觀想), and contemplation of the true character (*shí xiàng* 實相). These categories go back at least to the Tang dynasty (618–907) in Pure Land thought, and we will review them in chapter 7. Here we simply note that he regarded the middle two as too difficult for most people, and stated that simple oral invocation produces the contemplation of the true character, effectively giving even the least skilled practitioners the highest benefit of *nianfo* (Zhuhong [1973], p. 8:4711–4712).

This seems easy enough, but in other passages, Zhuhong prescribes a level of diligence that seems heroic, and he demands that these be combined with a strictly disciplined lifestyle that conforms to Buddhist piety and morality. Thus, we must carefully examine his writings to see in exactly what way he relates *nianfo* as an easy practice to other practices, and under what circumstances he prescribes diligence in the Buddhist life.

In his *48 Questions,* Zhuhong makes clear that he is recommending only *nianfo* as oral invocation; practices connected with gaining rebirth in Sukhāvatī in earlier texts are no longer appropriate in this age of the Decadent Dharma (*mòfǎ* 末法). In response to a question about the variety of practices found in other texts, Zhuhong says:

> Invocation of the name is easy to do; achieving a visualization is difficult. In the *Pratyutpanna* one first visualizes the wheel-marks on the [Buddha's] feet and then moves up against the grain of one's conditioning. Is this not in the same category as [the visualizations of] the *Contemplation Sutra?* The realm of the buddhas is transcendent and the mind of worldlings is coarse, and it is hard to approach the Three Contemplations in One Mind. Idleness is natural and strenuous effort goes against the grain; who would want to give up sitting for the constantly-walking practice when the six-word invocation of the name is something even a small child can manage? This sutra inclines toward the salvation of the end times; how could this be without due cause? (CBETA X.1158.61:511c21–a3)[1]

Thus, Zhuhong makes clear that he recommends only oral invocation to his contemporaries. However, even given this, the level of practice he advises seems onerous. In a sermon, he tells those who have married off their children and now have grandchildren to make great efforts in *nianfo,* reciting several thousand or even tens of thousands of times per day. He goes on to give lower numbers to semi-busy and then to very busy people (Zhuhong [1973], p. 8:4708). In addition, he never wavers from his insistence that the practice should lead to a particular mental state called the "single, unperturbed mind" (*yī xīn bú luàn* 一心不亂). Thus, while it is clear that Zhuhong conceives the main practice of *nianfo* as much easier than conventional Buddhist practices or even the Pure Land practices of prior ages, he still demands a great deal of sustained "self-power."

Yuan Hongdao likewise emphasized reliance primarily on oral invocation, but he accounts for the power of this simple practice not by the believer's own power to bring about the results, but by claiming that the practice to some extent works *ex opere operato.* For example, in the second fascicle of the *Comprehensive Treatise* he says, "A single utterance of 'Amitābha' enables one to enter into and accomplish all of the previously mentioned great dharma-gates, without any mark of 'one who accomplishes' and 'that which is accomplished.' Otherwise, it would constitute purity with something left over. The *nianfo* samadhi is not like that" (T.1976.47:395a28–b1). Later, in the sixth fascicle, he describes how the simple practice of *nianfo* constitutes practice of all the six perfections. Furthermore, since the practice of each perfection is connected to the Buddha (*xì fó* 繫佛) by invoking his name, and because it is so tied to one's own mind, it converts each perfection from a distinct worldly practice to a perfection of nature: Almsgiving becomes "almsgiving of nature" (*xìng shī* 性施), precepts becomes "precepts of nature" (*xìngjiè* 性戒), and so on. He concludes, "Because of this, the gate of *nianfo* is able to serve as all practices. Why? *Nianfo* is the dharma-gate of one mind, because outside the mind there are no practices. It also does not dispense with the practices, because to dispense with the practices is to dispense with the mind" (T.1976.47:405b14–b27). Since he believed that traditional Buddhist cultivation gains efficacy when infused by the Buddha's power through *nianfo,* Yuan exhorted his readers to adopt the full panoply of serious Buddhist ethical and religious practices. This is the subject of the entire ninth fascicle. In eight of this fascicle's ten sections, he emphasizes the need for faith, contemplation, recollection/recitation, confession, vows, precepts, avoidance of impure places such as brothels and wine houses, and the need for pure companions.

All this might lead one to think that the Pure Land path is very difficult. On the other hand, in several places both authors appear to make the practice appear exceptionally easy. *Nianfo* is only simple oral invocation of the Buddha's name as few as ten times, and works by the name's own virtue to purify the mind and cleanse *kalpas* of evil karma (see, for example, CBETA X.1158.61:507b20–507c1). Thus, the picture is inconsistent. How can the Pure Land path be so arduous and so easy at the same time? The answer to this question has several parts.

First, the point of comparison is always the practices by which the buddhas and bodhisattvas themselves attained liberation and enlightenment. The *Larger Sutra,* for example, states that the bodhisattva Dharmākara undertook many astonishingly rigorous practices over the span of many eons on his way to becoming the Buddha Amitābha.

Second, the practice requires long dedication because it produces its effect only while the practitioner engages in it; when dropped, the benefits immediately cease. Zhuhong is quite explicit on this point. One of the questions he addresses in his *48 Questions* concerns a hypothetical devotee who once practiced *nianfo* diligently but fell away because of distractions. Could such a one still achieve rebirth? Zhuhong answers that should this person resume the practice on his deathbed, it is possible, but once death occurs and he enters the intermediate state, it is too late (CBETA X.1158.61:506b19–506c1). Yuan describes how Amitābha appears when beings keep him in mind, and disappears when they cease to think of him (T.1976.47:391c4). Zhiyu says, "If your faith is not steady and you are plagued by egoism, how will you be able to receive the Buddha to conduct you [to the Pure Land]?" One must practice every moment of one's life in order to be ready to maintain this faith on one's deathbed; otherwise, the pain and worry of dying could easily drive it out (Shì Zhìyù 1988, p. 29).

Third, it appears that *nianfo* was not intended to be the devotee's *sole* practice, but only an underpinning and guarantor of success. In a sermon, Zhuhong says, "Ignorantly talking about Chan principle is not as good as keeping the precepts and practicing *nianfo*." He continues with a series of parallel illustrations, always dismissing some practice he considers heretical and asserting that it is not as good as engaging in one or another standard Buddhist practice *and* practicing *nianfo* (Zhuhong [1973], p. 8:4708). This matters because in debating with Chan partisans who saw Buddhist practice as a solitary heroic quest to be accomplished for oneself, Zhuhong and Yuan both insisted that this entailed too much risk; if one did not accomplish full and perfect enlightenment by the end of one's life, one might well lose all the benefits of practice and suffer a grievous setback. *Nianfo* leading to rebirth in the Pure Land guaranteed that one could conserve the fruits of one's practice and continue on the upward path. *Nianfo* therefore did not supplant all other practices, but was a necessary fixative to prevent loss and backsliding.

Fourth, both authors sought to take into account the different capacities of practitioners under the umbrella of the Buddha's skillful means, and this is why their presentations on the relative ease of the path seem so inconsistent at times. Recall that Zhuhong did not demand the same level of intensity of all people, but in a sermon taught that practice could be adjusted according to one's stage in life and familial and societal obligations; those that were more busy could recite less and vice versa (Zhuhong [1973], p. 8:4708). He also pointed to the famous nine grades of rebirth taught in the *Contemplation Sutra*. Because of their karmic burdens, people had different moral proclivities. Some did indeed carry on strict and austere practices and could advance a great distance toward liberation in this life; others were at the opposite end of the moral spectrum and became so depraved that only birth in a hell awaited them at death. Most Buddhists are somewhere in the middle, but the buddhadharma covers all of them. All could practice *nianfo* at their own level of ability and could attain rebirth (Zhuhong [1973], p. 8:4708–4709). Elsewhere, Zhuhong explained that the quality of one's practice of *nianfo* might also make a difference in this life:

> In sum, make the mind correct and extinguish evil. If one can *nianfo* like this, one is called a good person. Collect the mind and put an end to scatteredness. If one can *nianfo* like this, one is called a worthy. Enlighten the mind and cut off delusion. If one can *nianfo* like this, one is called a sage. (Zhuhong [1973], p. 8:4708)

This brings us to our fifth and final point. Zhuhong and Yuan Hongdao both recognized these different levels of attainment and ability among practitioners, which meant that the level of self-power that people could contribute to the process of liberation might vary widely. However, it was still incumbent upon them to contribute as much as they could. While on one reading Zhuhong's sermon referenced above might celebrate the flexibility of the teachings in accommodating the amount of free time that people in various stages of life can devote to practice, on another it insists that one must still do the most one can. Why? Because, by following the teachings on the nine grades of rebirth, it made a difference. While all in the nine grades attained rebirth, they did so at vastly divergent levels. As we saw above, the highest of the high (*shàngpǐn shàngshēng* 上品上生) arrive in the middle of the Pure Land in the presence of the Buddha and attain complete awakening after a brief sermon, while the lowest of the low (*xiàpǐn xiàshēng* 下品下生) found themselves on the periphery locked in a lotus bud for twelve *kalpas*, after which they attained buddhahood only after a very long time. As I will show in the next chapter, other Pure Land authors asserted that if one were serious about the bodhisattva vows and wished to gain buddhahood in order to save other beings, then one should do what one could to become a buddha as quickly as possible. Engaging in serious practices in order to gain a higher-level rebirth in the Pure Land helped with this.

What Does Nianfo *Accomplish?*

One of the questions that arose repeatedly in the history of Chinese Pure Land Buddhism had to do with the goal of practice. As we will see, there are two answers to this question. We will begin by examining the most obvious ostensible goal, that of gaining rebirth in the Pure Land and the attainment of the stage of non-retrogression. We will see, however, there are immediate, this-worldly benefits as well: *Nianfo* purifies the mind and erases past karma.

The first set of goals, rebirth in the Pure Land and the stage of non-retrogression, have been promoted since the inception of the tradition. While this in itself is nothing new, this inquiry into the relationship of self-power to other-power requires us to give the matter a fresh look. Since, as we have seen, a question frequently put to Pure Land advocates was how such a simple practice as oral invocation of Amitābha's name could lead to such great results, it pays to be clear as to how great the results really are. The Buddha's other-power does not lead to complete awakening and perfect enlightenment; it leads only to the Pure Land, which, as Yuan Hongdao stated, was not the final destination but only a way station or "hostel."

> The buddhas also have greatly built residences to bring peace [to beings]. One [Śākyamuni] comes and goes through the prison gate in order to prepare the way. The other [Amitābha] waits outside the prison for long periods to prepare a hostel (*lǚguǎn* 旅館). (T.1976.47:392c2–c3)

Once in the Pure Land, the devotee could remain until the achievement of buddhahood. As we saw in the last chapter, the Pure Land is outside of the Triple World and samsara, so rebirth there is the equivalent of the stage of non-retrogression.

This posed a problem for detractors: It appeared to run afoul of the law of karma. A very evil person who ought to be bound for rebirth in hell or in some other undesirable state not only avoided these by redirection into the Pure Land, but achieved a state that traditional Buddhist literature reserved only for very advanced bodhisattvas who had engaged in serious practice for many lifetimes. We have already seen the answer to this objection: The Buddha Amitābha had made and fulfilled great vows, and the power of these vows sufficed to overcome the practitioner's past karma. This was the Buddha's other-power at work.

At the same time, the practice of *nianfo* itself, in whatever form and at whatever level of complexity, had inherent power to purify the mind and redirect one's fate, though this worked only while the believer engaged in it. The effect could be lost completely the moment he or she stopped. As Jixing Chewu put it:

> Moreover, the other gates of cultivation require one to confess one's present karma; if any manifest karma is not confessed, then it constitutes an obstacle on the Way and leaves one without a path for advancement. However, the one who practices pure karma (*jìngyè* 淨業, often a synonym for Pure Land practice) goes to rebirth carrying their karma with them; there is no need to confess one's karma. This is because when the mind reaches the point of

> reciting the Buddha's name just once, one is able to extinguish the faults [accumulated over] 8,000,000,000 *kalpas*. (CBETA X.1182.62:335c14–335c17)

One might also repeat the words of Tanluan and Daochuo: *Nianfo* was like a spark thrown into a pile of kindling accumulated for a hundred years.

However, two other images became the dominant means of illustrating this idea: First, *nianfo* practice was like lighting a lamp in a room that had been dark for many years. No matter how long the darkness had been present, the light of the lamp banished it instantly. Second, it was like a *maṇi* gem, as Daochuo explained:

> [I]t is like putting a luminous *maṇi* gem into muddy water; the water instantly becomes clear. If a man, though defiled with karmic evils which would cause him to transmigrate for countless births and deaths, hears the supreme, luminous gem of the Name of [Amitābha] Tathāgata, [. . .] his karmic evils will be destroyed and his mind purified. (trans. Inagaki 2014, p. 64; T.1958.47:11c18–c22)

This is self-power. The practitioner engages in the practice, and it produces the result of mental purification and expiation of karma independently of the result of rebirth in the Pure Land and the state of non-retrogression.

These two effects, rebirth and non-retrogression brought about by Amitābha's other-power and mental purification and erasure of karma brought about by the devotee's self-power, are not unrelated. Both work through the mechanism of sympathetic resonance. The fact that the practice put one in tune with the Buddha accounted both for purification and for rebirth. Thus, the danger of suspending the practice was the same in both cases. If the darkness of ten thousand years could be dispelled by lighting a lamp, the darkness could also come back the instant the lamp went out. If the practice of *nianfo* could in like manner dispel all mental impurities and bad karma, these could also return immediately upon ending the practice. This also meant that rebirth in the Pure Land could take place only if the devotee was practicing *nianfo* at the time of death.

This clarifies a little more the relationship between self-power and other-power in the practice of *nianfo*. While the ostensible goal of the practice is to attain rebirth and non-retrogression, these results obtain only when both powers work together at the crucial last moment of life. However, the self-power aspect of *nianfo* can be utilized for immediate benefits as well. In chapter 7 we will explore the uses of *nianfo* further. For now, let us examine more closely the difficulties caused by the belief, seen several times now, that *nianfo* only works while one is occupied in it.

The Ongoing Dilemma

So far, it seems that Chinese Pure Land thinkers of various periods found a way to coordinate ideas about self-power and other-power that, while complex, worked fairly well. The solution was not perfect, however, and in this section, we will examine an enduring problem that the tradition could never quite resolve.

In order to set the stage, let us look at three possible ways of relating the two powers. One might postulate that all religious accomplishments follow from one's own efforts, and that self-power alone brings about the results. This would be the way of virtuoso practice, and I compare it to climbing a stairway. The evident problem with this formulation is that it works only for elite practitioners; the vast majority of religious people would have no hope of accomplishing the goal and the path would be irrelevant to their anxieties.

A way of alleviating this difficulty is to assure people that their own abilities and circumstances pose no obstacle because the Buddha will do all the work. This is the path of total reliance on other-power, and the schools of Pure Land Buddhism founded in Kamakura Japan became mass movements by adopting this model. This is like ascending in an elevator; one is assured of reaching the top without having to contribute any effort at all. While this resolves the problem of elitism that stems from total reliance on self-power, it too involves difficulties. Some people, when told that their own efforts are unnecessary for reaching the goal, embrace antinomianism, believing that no religious or moral striving at all is required of them. This creates institutional problems as followers of the movement bring bad publicity and unwanted official attention for the group through lax practice or evil behavior.

At first blush, it seems the Chinese way of synchronizing the two powers averts these two difficulties. It is like riding an escalator: If one truly is powerless, it will take one to the top, but one can still contribute to the process by walking. Adding one's own effort to the escalator's motion increases the speed with which one attains the top. As the next chapter will demonstrate, this solution avoided the potential problem of antinomianism by giving followers a reason to be moral and engage in religious practice. However, insofar as Chinese Pure Land thinkers insisted that *some* level of self-power was necessary, it did not quite fix the problem entailed by the first position. That is, so long as it remained incumbent on the practitioner to contribute to the effort, the possibility of failure remained. Indeed, we occasionally find stories in the literature of practitioners who failed to attain rebirth due to some lapse in their own effort. Let us look at Shandao's advice on deathbed practice and then two stories of near-failure and total failure.

In his practical manual *Guānniàn Āmítuófó xiànghǎi sānmèi gōngdé fǎmén* 觀念阿彌陀佛相海三昧功德法門 (The dharma-gate for the merit of the samadhi of contemplating Amitābha Buddha's ocean of marks, T.1959), Shandao devotes a section to instructions on deathbed practice. This section includes the following caution:

> If the practitioner's family members within the six relations come to see him or her when sick, do not admit any who have consumed wine, meat, or the five pungent plants. Those that are present should not be allowed to come to the sick person's side, as this will cause the loss of right concentration. Devils and spirits will cause confusion, and the sick person will die in delusion and fall into the three evil rebirths. (T.1959.47:24b29–24c2)

Shandao thus believed that failure at the final moment was possible if impure persons defiled the ritual space and allowed demonic beings to invade.

Yuan Hongdao confirms this fear in a story in which his nephew almost lost his chance for rebirth due to inadvertent ritual pollution. In Jonathan Chaves's translation, the story runs as follows:

> My friend Fang said: "I have heard the monks of Cloud Perch [i.e., Yunqi] Temple assert that if one recites Buddha's name, one may achieve birth in the Pure Land. Is this true?"
>
> I replied: "Yes. Without going into all the written accounts, let me just refer to cases I have experienced myself. Deng, the second son of my older brother Boxiu [i.e., Yuan Zongdao], became terminally ill at the age of twelve. He himself knew he had no hope of living. When he was on the point of dying, he spoke to me tearfully: 'I will die today. Is there any way to save me?' I answered: 'If you only recite Buddha's name, you will immediately be reborn in Buddha's land. The present world, with its Five Ages of Decay, is not worth yearning for. Just concentrate on Buddha with one mind and all will be well.'"
>
> "I then had my nephew chant Buddha's name while holding the palms of his hands together in an attitude of devotion. The entire family stood around him in a circle, praising Buddha in rich tones. After a while, my nephew smiled slightly and said: 'I see a lotus flower, the color of earth, but slightly reddish.' He then continued to chant. After some more time, he suddenly spoke of the extreme brilliance of the lotus, which he said was incomparably superior to any in this world, and was now bigger than before. Still another period of time—and suddenly, he said that Buddha had

> arrived, the radiance of his features filling the entire room! A little later he said that there was an impure person in the room, whose presence had caused the lotus and Buddha to disappear. Boxiu looked around and noticed that a maidservant, who had just arrived, was standing in front of the folding screen. This girl, as it happened, had just had her period that evening, so Boxiu called to her to leave and had the other people encircle his son and chant Buddha's name as before. The boy then grew short of breath, and Boxiu said: 'If you just recite one character of my name, that will be enough.' The boy asked me: 'Is that all right?' and I replied: 'Yes.' But when he had chanted a few syllables more, he died, still holding his palms together." (Yuán Hóngdào 1978, p. 82–83; Romanization adapted for consistency; Chinese text in Yuan 1981, p. 1:476–477)

In this instance, the simple intrusion of a ritually impure person came close to scuttling young Deng's chances of rebirth altogether.

Another way in which insufficient effort could derail one's progress toward rebirth stems from the concept of sympathetic resonance. As we have noted a couple of times already, one had to be engaged in practice at the very point of death for the power of sympathetic resonance to take one to rebirth. The point of long years of practice was to ensure that one stood a better chance of maintaining the proper frame of mind at the critical moment. The modern Taiwan master Zhiyu once told this story to a group assembled for a *nianfo* retreat in order to spur them to diligence:

> I will tell you a true story: There was an elderly layman whose practice of *nianfo* was very good. He enjoyed this world and had two wives. Since his practice of *nianfo* was good, when he was on the point of dying during a grave illness, the image of the Buddha [Amitābha] appeared before him, and he himself said, "I see the Land of Bliss!" But there was an obstruction at the last moment. His junior wife came running in crying and said, "When you're dead, how will I go on living with our young son?" He said, "Don't worry, I'll write up a will. You will definitely be taken care of." His mind having been perturbed, he cried out, "Oh, no! I don't see the West anymore, and the Buddha has disappeared! There is just a stretch of darkness and the signs of hell." (Shì Zhìyù 1992, p. 58)

As Zhiyu explains, the layman left himself open to distraction because of deficits in his prior practice. While he had practiced *nianfo* faithfully for a long time, he had not cultivated his mind so as to rid it of greed. This is why he had failed to attend to his will, and why he was unable to regain concentration after his wife interrupted the ritual to express her very reasonable distress.

In these examples, we see how the similes of Chinese Pure Land can take a sinister turn. One may have good instruction and ritual support in one's last moments, but a menstruating maid can render it all useless. One may practice *nianfo* diligently for years and develop the habits of mind that enable one to maintain *ganying* even in the rigors of death, but a distraught young wife can still ruin everything at the last minute. Thus, as coherent and sensible as many of the solutions to the problem of relating the two powers are, it seems that *any* residual reliance on self-power leaves open the possibility that one may fail in the end. The fact that Zhiyu could tell this story as late as 1992 indicates that this dilemma has not been fully resolved. It may be that this tension is inevitable, if not for theoretical reasons, at least for practical or pastoral ones. The Pure Land tradition always attempted *both* to reassure those who could not perform hard practices that they still had hope *and* to challenge those who were able and ready to engage in practice to push themselves to their utmost. One needs different kinds of theories and stories to comfort the first group and motivate the second, and so the inconsistency abides.

Conclusions

After the religious innovations of such figures as Hōnen, Shinran, and Ippen, Pure Land Buddhism in Japan came to deprecate self-power and preach complete and sole reliance on the other-power of the Buddha Amitābha. Chinese Pure Land Buddhism never taught this, but developed its own way of relating the two powers as a cooperative venture in which both the devotee and the Buddha contribute to the process of achieving rebirth. This has three aspects.

First, while they never agreed with the Kamakura reformers that self-power had no part to play in the process, they did teach that reliance on self-power alone was risky. While it sometimes worked for extremely gifted practitioners, such people were rare and most of us needed to supplement our own efforts with the power of the Buddha's original vow. This view has a long history in Chinese Pure Land. In the first fascicle of his *Wangsheng lun zhu* (T.1819) Tanluan said the fifth of the five obstacles to successful completion of the difficult practice in this age of five impurities (*wǔzhuó* 五濁) is "exclusive reliance on self-power without the support of other-power" (T.1819.40:826b5–b6; see also Chen 2008, p. 109).

Second, the Buddha's compassion led him to set forth the means by which even the meanest person who repented only on his or her deathbed and uttered ten invocations of the name could still attain rebirth. However, the tradition assumed that such people did not represent the norm, and those with the ability to engage in meditation, morality, and precepts ought to do so. By this means, they could achieve buddhahood more rapidly after gaining rebirth and then go about doing a Buddha's compassionate business. *Nianfo* and reliance on other-power provided a safety net in the very likely event that one's own power proved insufficient for complete liberation.

Finally, as Yuan Hongdao and Jixing Chewu both stated in their own terms, there really was no stark distinction between self-power and other-power because there was no strict separation of self and other. The two intertwined and merged in a process that worked to bring the believer to a place hospitable to the buddha-dharma and to the final achievement of buddhahood.

This position had both advantages and disadvantages for Chinese Pure Land Buddhism. James Dobbins and Fabio Rambelli have amply documented the problem of antinomianism that crops up when any religion, whether Buddhism or Christianity, postulates the utter futility of human striving and thus negates the value of morality (Dobbins 1989; Rambelli 2004, p. 177–179, 187). By providing a coherent account of the contribution that the believer's efforts made to the pursuit of the goal, Chinese Pure Land avoided this pitfall. On the other hand, it could not avoid the pitfall to which the Japanese teaching of total reliance on other-power served as the antidote: the anxiety that comes with any need for human effort in religious practice. As we have seen, Chinese Pure Land authorities taught that *nianfo* provided a connection to the Buddha through *ganying* 感應 only while the practitioner was engaged in it. Its effect ceased as soon as the practice ceased and the devotee's mind moved to other things, and if one got out of the habit, all the fruits of practice could disappear, leaving one to revolve in samsara. Perhaps lighting a lamp will drive away 10,000 years of darkness, but when the lamp goes out, the darkness returns instantly. Perhaps this is a dilemma with no ultimately satisfactory solution.

At this point, then, we have seen that self-effort in Buddhist practice has a positive role to play in the practitioner's progress toward buddhahood. However, the Chinese tradition did continue to affirm that the other-power of Amitābha could bring a weak practitioner to the Pure Land without the expenditure of effort. The question remained, then: Why *should* a Buddhist make efforts in the Way? This will be the subject of the next chapter.

Chapter 5

Ethics and Precepts in Chinese Pure Land Buddhism

Defining the Problem

This chapter grew out of a long-standing dissatisfaction that I have had with the study of Pure Land Buddhism. A particular historical narrative predominates in which Kamakura period Japanese Pure Land Buddhism represents the norm, the *telos,* or both for *all* Pure Land Buddhism. In hindsight, it seems that a kind of logic intrinsic to the narrative of Amitābha and his Pure Land led inexorably to the doctrines and practices of the Jōdo Shū 淨土宗, the Jōdo Shinshū 淨土真宗, and the Jishū 時宗. The teachings elaborated by Hōnen (法然, 1133–1212), Shinran (親鸞, 1173–1262), and Ippen (一遍, 1239–1289) denied the efficacy of all human action or "self-power" (*zìlì* 自力; J. *jiriki*) and attributed exclusive salvific potency to Amitābha's "other-power" (*tālì* 他力; J. *tariki*). This development became, as it were, the Omega Point of Pure Land Buddhism's historical trajectory, and all forms of Pure Land teaching prior to it came to be seen as its precursors. They simultaneously point to it and, insofar as they fail to conform to it perfectly, await their fulfillment in it.[1]

Such a construal of Pure Land history misrepresents it as a linear progression, a chain of developments that moved link by link to its logical endpoint or climax paradigm. In reality, this history is more like a tree than a chain: Branches appear at various points and then continue their growth parallel to other branches. I have been struck in my own study of the Chinese Pure Land tradition by the way that it has trodden its own path and has never produced anything like the theologies of the Kamakura reformers. As we saw in the previous chapter, it never denied the necessity or effectiveness of self-power or of all forms of moral striving and spiritual cultivation. While recognizing the need for reliance on the other-power of Amitābha, it has seen the path to rebirth more as a cooperative venture involving both, as captured in Zhiyu's formulation noted in the last chapter, "the two powers of self and other" (*zì-tā èr lì* 自他二力; Shì Zhìyù 1992, 58–60).

Even if one grants that Kamakura Pure Land Buddhism provides no service as either a heuristic or a *telos* by which to understand the Chinese Pure Land experience, a comparison of the two can still alert scholars to doctrinal and practical issues hitherto unexamined. Historical circumstances peculiar to Japanese Buddhism, such as Hōnen's problems with his disciples' antinomian behavior or the crises Shinran underwent when he was forced to return to lay status and thought his religious practices had failed, led the Japanese to think long and hard about the relationship between self-power and other-power. Their deprecation of human religious striving came about as the conclusion of their reflections.

This being the case, I began to wonder if any Chinese Pure Land thinker had ever examined the relationship between human religious activity and the saving power of Amitābha so as to encourage Buddhists to apply themselves to self-cultivation and avoid evil actions. I knew that the Chinese had certainly never judged self-effort useless, but had they ever formulated their own systematic account of this relationship as the Japanese had? Had the issue been addressed at all? The primary goal of this project was to find a Chinese text that took on this topic and treated it rigorously, but I failed to find such a discussion in historical documents prior to the Qing dynasty (1644–1912). As we shall see, at least two modern masters put all the pieces together to make recommendations for their followers. We will examine their syntheses at the end of this chapter. First, I shall look at several earlier texts to draw on scattered indications, which, added together, constitute a fairly complete and consistent soteriological scheme that affirms the sufficiency of the Buddha's other-power while still valorizing self-effort. These proof-texts from works spanning many separate times and places will show the foundation upon which the modern synthesis rests. I will assemble this synthesis by focusing on a particular arena of human religious activity: ethics and precepts—"ethics" indicating general norms of human behavior, and "precepts" meaning specific vows taken in ritual contexts.

First, however, a couple of qualms call for our attention. It may appear that, in asking whether Chinese Pure Land thinkers ever formulated a soteriology that methodically related the roles of moral effort and the Buddha's power in effecting rebirth in the Pure Land, I am assuming the existence of a self-contained Pure Land "school" or "sect" with its own religious agenda pursued independently of other "schools." I have already disposed of this notion in chapter 2 and noted that Pure Land is the common property of all Chinese Buddhists, one of a number of "dharma-gates" (*fǎmén* 法門) open to those with a need or an aptitude for it. In light of this, it is reasonable to ask: Why look for a "Pure Land account" of the need for ethics and precepts? If "Pure Land" is a tradition of practice and not a sect or denomination, then an account of morality and vows could be sought elsewhere, in the writings of *vinaya* masters, preceptors, or any Buddhist author that cared to address the topic.

To this, I would respond that, far from obviating the need for the present inquiry, this point only increases its relevance. If the Pure Land tradition really belongs to all Chinese Buddhists and not to just one "school," then the questions we will raise in the next section must perforce be of concern to *all* Chinese Buddhists. Unlike Japanese Buddhism, in which well-bounded schools may indeed look only to their own literature for answers to their own problems, Chinese Buddhism's boundaries are quite porous, and so the availability of Amitābha's other-power as a resource on the path to buddhahood raises the question "why be moral?" for *everyone,* including the *vinaya* masters and preceptors. In fact, as we shall see, very few of the thinkers whose works we shall consult thought of themselves exclusively as Pure Land sectarians. Many, such as Ouyi Zhixu (*Ǒuyì Zhìxù* 藕益智旭, 1599–1655), wrote on a wide variety of topics that included both Pure Land soteriology and precepts.

A second qualm relates to the focus on ethics and precepts in this chapter. At its most general level, the question I am raising is this: How exactly did Chinese Pure Land thought relate the practitioner's own self-power to Amitābha's other-power? "Self-power" is an extremely broad and inclusive term that can denote anything that a Buddhist does to achieve liberation from suffering: meditation, making vows, chanting sutras, joining the monastic order, study, ritual, ethical living, and so on. I choose ethics and precepts mainly because the last chapter, having dealt with the broader question of the relationship between self-power and other-power left open the question of antinomianism. It dealt with soteriology (how does one achieve rebirth and buddhahood) rather than ethics (how should one live one's present life). In other words, having seen that people who cannot engage in practices can still ride the power of Amitābha's vows to rebirth in the Pure Land, we still do not know how the tradition convinces its followers *not* to follow this path and leave everything to the Buddha. Examining the specific problems of ethics and precepts within a Pure Land framework will allow us to address that concern.

Furthermore, ethics and precepts have historically been the most problematic items on the list. If one wishes, one may choose not to meditate, study sutras, or chant mantras, and it will only affect one's own progress. Dismissing ethics, however, affects one's relationships with others and can negatively affect the image Buddhism presents to the wider community. When the founders of the Kamakura Pure Land schools in Japan took the step of negating the efficacy of ethics as a way of attaining rebirth in the Pure Land, it led immediately to the problem of antinomian behavior justified as "licensed evil" (Dobbins 1989). This makes ethics, and to a lesser extent precepts, the most potentially fraught aspect of self-power. A soteriology that, even in potential, gives people a reason to disregard ethics has the capacity to do great harm to the image and credibility of those who teach it.

Even in China, where no thinker ever seriously contemplated such a soteriology (although they were sometimes accused of doing so, especially by Chan practitioners), Pure Land thought still had the potential to lead one down the road to antinomianism. This next section will examine this potential, and the following section will show how it was neutralized.

The Disjunction of Precepts and Rebirth in the Pure Land Tradition

I have frequently noticed in Pure Land literature the simultaneous affirmation of two seemingly contradictory messages. On the one hand, all Chinese Pure Land thinkers maintain that human moral efforts, such as ethical living, taking and keeping precepts, and making vows, are integral to Buddhist life and practice. On the other hand, they are also aware that, as stated in texts such as the *Contemplation Sutra,* the power of Amitābha's vows is enough to deliver even the wickedest deathbed convert to the Pure Land. His or her rebirth in the Pure Land amounts to attainment of the stage of non-retrogression and will lead inevitably to his or her attainment of buddhahood. As we have already seen, the power to bring this rebirth about belongs to Amitābha, not the penitent, and so his or her lack of moral rectitude or good karmic roots did not necessarily matter. This means that ethics and precepts are *not* essential to Buddhist practice. This constitutes a paradox requiring resolution.

Most texts maintain both of these ideas as simple assertions, which the authors affirm without any effort at reconciliation. For example, if one looks at Siming Zhili's (*Sìmíng Zhīlǐ* 四明知禮, 960–1028) ritual for transmitting the bodhisattva precepts, one finds statements such as the following:

> [If] one wishes to receive the Buddhist precepts, [but] there is no one from whom to obtain them, [then] it is right that one should exert him/herself and strive to find them. Abandon the conditions of this world; discipline yourself in the precepts and [practice] *nianfo;* bring all to a successful conclusion and complete these endeavors, and one will most certainly gain passage and obtain rebirth into the Pure Land of Peace and Nurture. (T.1937.46:859b13–b15)

In one sentence, Zhili exhorts his preceptees *both* to exert themselves ceaselessly in Buddhist discipline *and* to practice *nianfo* in order to gain rebirth. This example also shows how authors of works such as this typically did not even see the need to harmonize these counsels to diligence with the *Contemplation Sutra*'s assurance that those who do not engage in these practices and even commit great evil may attain rebirth and eventual buddhahood. Jumping ahead to the Qing dynasty (1644–1912), we see the ambiguity more clearly in a popular work by Wukai (*Wùkāi* 悟開, d. 1830) entitled *One Hundred Questions about Nianfo* (*Niànfó bǎi wèn* 念佛百問). Question 48 asks whether those who practice *nianfo* need to maintain a vegetarian diet, and Wukai affirms that they should, noting that the arousing of *bodhicitta* should point practitioners in that direction (CBETA X.1184.62:359c13–c16). However, in number 49, the inquirer wonders what happens to the person of *nianfo* (*niànfó rén* 念佛人) who is unable to do this; can they still attain rebirth? Wukai responds,

> In general, it will constitute a fault, but a very minor one. Furthermore, it functions as a hidden fault. [Nevertheless,] if one practices *nianfo* and seeks birth in the Land of Bliss, and his or her mind is deeply committed, then at the end of life, the power of the Way will overcome the power of karma, and he or she will most certainly achieve rebirth. (CBETA X.1184.62:359c17–c19)

In two consecutive questions, then, Wukai assures the reader that vegetarianism is essential for fulfilling the compassionate intentions of *bodhicitta,* but with the right zeal in the practice of *nianfo,* one can achieve the goal without it. The scholar is thus confronted by a tradition whose various authorities presented two seemingly conflicting propositions: Ethics and precepts are absolutely essential, but one can still attain rebirth and buddhahood without them.

The paradox emerged with the popularization of the three sutras traditionally taken as foundational for the Pure Land tradition in China and the line of thought springing from Shandao. The passages that give rise to this paradox with special force are those in the *Larger Sutra* (*Fó shuō wúliángshòu jīng* 佛說無量壽經, T.360) and more acutely in the *Contemplation Sutra* (*Fóshuō guān wúliángshòu fó jīng* 佛說觀無量壽佛經, T.365) that posit levels or grades of rebirth based on the individual's level of practice, realization, and ethics. The problem arises when one considers the situation of those at the "lowest grade, lowest birth" in these schemes (*xià bèi* 下輩 in the *Larger Sutra, xià pǐn xià shēng* 下品下生 in the *Contemplation Sutra*). These passages teach that even the most evil person that Buddhism can imagine can still gain rebirth through the power of Amitābha, an idea that sunders the relationship between the practice of morality and the attainment of rebirth. As we have already seen, this teaching became the hallmark of the Pure Land tradition after Shandao reassigned the motive power of rebirth to Amitābha's vows rather than to the extraordinary efficacy of the aspirant's practices. The later "patriarchs" of Pure Land continued to affirm, right to the present day, that other-power was the *sine qua non* of rebirth in Sukhāvatī. Only within this framework could the tradition tell tales of butchers and chicken-slaughterers who gained rebirth through last-minute deathbed practice.

Historical developments kept this belief alive over the centuries and even strengthened it. In response to continued polemics between Pure Land masters and various opponents, mostly from the Chan School, later Pure Land writers continued to emphasize the futility of depending solely upon one's own efforts to achieve buddhahood. Many Chan critics insisted on the need for efforts in the Way, and Pure Land writers such as Yuan Hongdao (*Yuán Hóngdào* 袁宏道, 1568–1610), Jixing Chewu (*Jìxǐng Chèwù* 際醒徹悟, 1741–1810), and Yinguang (*Yìnguāng* 印光, 1861–1940) consistently denigrated the efficacy of human effort. They held that attainment of buddhahood depended upon a thorough realization of reality, the elimination of even the most subtle obscurations, the achievement of moral perfection, and profound attainments in meditation. Who, they pointedly asked, could hope to achieve this in one human lifetime within this Sahā world? Yinguang, for example, phrased the critique in this way:

> Even though a person may be thoroughly enlightened and may have illuminated the mind and seen into their own true nature within a Chan lineage, they still cannot easily cut off the disturbances of views and thoughts. One

> must practice continually for a long period of time and bring oneself to the point where one is completely and utterly purified; only then can one cut off samsara and find escape. It does not matter if [only] one hair's breadth remains to be cut off. One is still one hair's breadth away from complete purification, one will revolve around in the six paths as before, and escape will be difficult. The ocean of samsara is deep, and the road to wisdom long. The end of one's life comes, and one still has not made it home. (Yìnguāng 1991, p. 1:368–369)

Thus, Yinguang and others continued to emphasize the practitioner's need for the other-power of Amitābha to get them to the Pure Land and deprecated unaided human striving as futile (Yìnguāng 1991, p. 1:361).

What exactly did Amitābha's power do? Most Chinese Pure Land thinkers understood the effect of their practices as tapping into the power of *gǎnyìng* 感應, or "sympathetic resonance." Whereas the Japanese Pure Land founders denigrated efforts in cultivation and made faith (J. *shinjin* 信心) the necessary condition of gaining rebirth in the Pure Land, the Chinese saw *ganying* (or its equivalent *xiàngyìng* 相應) as the key factor, and this provided the rationale for engaging in *nianfo.* To focus the mind on Amitābha, or to repeat his name, or to engage in any form of *nianfo* put one's mind "in tune" with Amitābha's, and the more that one engaged in *nianfo,* the stronger and more enduring this resonance became. The ideal, then, was to keep one's mind focused on the Buddha as much as possible, so that it became more and more likely that the resonance of mind and Buddha would be at its peak at the critical moment of death (e.g., Wukai at CBETA X.1184.62:359c7–c12). Such a practice was not easy and required constant vigilance and effort on the devotee's part. The difference between this practice and those of other dharma-gates, such as Chan, lay in the fact that the "resonance" brought Amitābha's power into play in cooperation with the practitioner's, creating the cooperation of self-power and other-power detailed in the last chapter. This, as Yinguang explained, was why deathbed recitation could be effective even for the worst sinner: With a vision of hell looming before one, the mind focused on Amitābha with a special intensity that created a very strong resonance even without prior practice. As he put it: "However, even though [deathbed converts] do not recite very many times, they can still reap this great benefit because of their fierce determination. You cannot compare the sheer number of repetitions between them and others who recite listlessly" (Yìnguāng 1991, 1:368).

As indicated above, however, the very authors who pointed to this teaching as a source of hope also continued to live as monks or pious laymen, kept their precepts strictly and advised others to do so and pursue traditional Buddhist ideals. The Chinese scholar Liu Changdong 刘长东 points out that, in the latter half of the Tang dynasty, the records of those who attained rebirth included several renowned *vinaya* masters (Liú 2000, p. 452–459). The ninth "patriarch" of the Chinese Pure Land School, Ouyi Zhixu, was active in transmitting precepts and wrote on philosophical issues relating to Tiantai contributions to the problem of defining the concept of "precept-essence" (*jiètǐ* 戒體; see Eiki 1998, p. 77–80). Clearly, precepts, and by implication ethical living, were still necessary components of the path, even if one counted on the power of the *ganying* one hoped to establish with the Buddha Amitābha to reach the goal in the end.

Even the tradition's consistent affirmation of the special focus and power of deathbed *nianfo* did not lead anyone to counsel putting off Buddhist practice and stake everything upon it. The Yuan dynasty monk Tianru Weize (*Tiānrú Wéizé* 天如惟則, 1286?–1354) said emphatically that one should not adopt this as a strategy ahead of time. In the twentieth question of his *Jìngtǔ huòwèn* 淨土或問 (Questions about Pure Land, T.1972), an inquirer asks about the strategy of going about one's ordinary business until the time of death and then beginning the practice of *nianfo* in the expectation that Amitābha's power would bring one to the Pure Land. Tianru calls this plan greatly deluded and gives many reasons why it would not work: The suffering that accompanies dying makes concentration difficult, one may not meet the "good friend" who will lead one to recite the name, a mind accustomed to dealing only with mundane matters will continue to worry about worldly affairs, one might meet a sudden death, and so on. If one can engage in disciplined Buddhist practice, then one ought to do so and not avail oneself of measures intended for those who have no other options left (T.1972.47:299c13–300c7; an English translation may be found in Sutra Translation Committee of the United States and Canada 1991, p. 86–93). We must also note that this is far from a call to "licensed evil": The inquirer's question and Tianru's response both assume that one seeking rebirth in this manner intends to live at least a conventionally moral life.

Thus, even though one ought not to rely *solely* on the power of one's own practice, Buddhist masters still insisted that one needed such practice to elicit Amitābha's support and other-power through the connection of sympathetic resonance. However, the desperate deathbed convert seemed to negate half of the equation: precepts and morality. If the dying sinner's focused recitation of the name produced sufficient sympathetic resonance without precepts and morals and he or she achieved rebirth at the last minute by relying exclusively on the power of the Buddha's vows, then why be good? Tianru's warning that the circumstances of one's death may not be conducive to last-minute practice is valid, but it is contingent. Is there a more systematic way to answer the question, why engage in Buddhist practices? In the next section, we will begin to sketch the outlines of the answer.

Establishing a Basis for a Pure Land Ethic

As mentioned before, no work or treatise earlier than the twenty-first century has come to my attention so far that treats this subject systematically. However, a search through earlier materials and texts provides the basic building blocks with which later thinkers could construct a coherent account and offer recommendations to practitioners.

One's Level of Rebirth Matters

One of the required threads is given by Wang Rixiu (*Wáng Rìxiū* 王日休, d. 1173) in his *Lóngshū zēngguǎng jìngtǔ wén* 龍舒增廣淨土文 (Longshu's augmented Pure Land essays, T.1970). Wang points out that the nine grades of rebirth taught in the *Contemplation Sutra* can serve as much as an incentive for moral action as a disincentive. While it is true that even the lowest of the low gains rebirth and this might undermine one's motivation to practice, Wang calls attention to the fact that rebirths in the nine grades are not at all equal. We have already described the high birth and rapid progress of those born in the highest grade and contrasted it with the inferior birth and glacially slow progress of those born in the lowest grade, so we will not review it here (see the *Contemplation Sutra*, T.365.12:344c–345a).

While both the highest and the lowest practitioners attain rebirth in the Pure Land and break free from samsara, in all other respects the first type of rebirth is greatly preferable to the second. All things being equal, Wang asks whether it would not be better to aspire to a higher rebirth in the Pure Land? For example, the essay entitled "Food, Drink, and Sex," is largely devoted to discussing the evil consequences of gluttony and lasciviousness. In the essay's last sentence he says, "Although these [two vices] may be hard to avoid, one can still practice Pure Land and liberate oneself from the wheel of samsara. Nevertheless, those who wish to practice the way of the highest grade cannot but restrain these!" (T.1970.47:279c17–280a7). He repeats this idea in another essay, in which he says:

> The *Laṅkāvatāra-sūtra* says, "Today's pleasure is the seed of future suffering." A *gāthā* says:
>
> Practice meritorious karma and wisdom together
> *Nian* Amitābha as well.
> In the nine levels of the Lotus land,
> What doubt is there that the first is attained?
>
> This is because a practitioner who observes fasting and the precepts and has bright understanding is born in the highest birth of the highest grade. (T.1970.47:280b10–b13)

To state Wang's point another way, it is true that even the lowest of the low attains rebirth, and this is indeed a cause for comfort and assurance that all will be saved through Amitābha's other-power. However, one still has a chance to better one's level of rebirth in the Pure Land, and the benefits of doing so are significant: rapid attainment of enlightenment, instruction by Amitābha himself, and so on. Thus, one should make some moral efforts and restrain one's behavior.

A second example will show that this way of thinking extended beyond elite authorities and was shared at the popular level as well. It comes from Zongxiao's (*Zōngxiǎo* 宗曉, 1151–1214) *Lèbāng wénlèi* 樂邦文類 (Anthology of the Land of Bliss, T.1969) in the story of Lady Yueguo (*Jīng wáng yuèguó fūrén wǎngshēng jí* 荊王越國夫人往生集, T.1969.47.189c9–190a27), which Zongxiao culled from the writings of Huang Ce (*Huáng Cè* 黃策, 1070–1173).

Lady Yueguo, an ardent Pure Land devotee, converted her entire household to Pure Land practice with the exception of one young maidservant. One day, the lady admonished the maid, who realized her sinfulness and sloth and decided to repent. Not long afterward, the maidservant died, and the lady had a dream of her in which the maid took her to see the Pure Land. Once there, the lady was shown a pond with lotus blossoms of varying color and splendor. In Daniel Stevenson's translation, the maid interpreted these differences to the lady as follows:

> The lady of the house set off with the maid, and in time, they came to two pools of water, both of which were filled with white lotus blossoms of varying size. Some were glorious. Others were withered or drooping. However, each one was different. Her ladyship said, "Why are they like this?"
>
> To which the maid replied, "They all represent persons of the mundane world who have made the resolution to seek rebirth in the western pure land. With the arousing of the [first] flicker of thought [of the pure land],

> one's wholesome [karmic] roots will have already sent forth a sprout. Eventually it will form a single blossom. However, because people's degrees of diligence are not the same, there are differences in the quality of the blossoms. For those who are unrelenting in their efforts, [the blossom] is fresh and resplendent. For those who are sporadic, it is withered. If people continue to practice for a long time without giving up, to the point where their mindfulness becomes stabilized [in *samadhi*] and their contemplation reaches fruition, then when their physical bodies perish and their life [in the mundane world] reaches its end they will be reborn by miraculous transformation in the center [of one of these lotus blossoms]. (Stevenson 1995, p. 599)

As the lady looks on, one of the blossoms opens, and a person described as an exemplary practitioner emerges from his blossom decked in regal garments covering an adamantine body. Another opens, but this blossom is withered, and the occupant's raiment and body are far less impressive. The lady responds by asking in what estate she will be reborn, and the maid assures her that her high level of practice and virtue will gain her rebirth at the highest level (Stevenson 1995, p. 599–600). It is important to recognize that both of the figures that the lady sees emerging from their lotus calyxes have achieved rebirth in the Pure Land; thus, for both of them, salvation is assured. Nevertheless, the story shows a great concern for the level and quality of their rebirth, and the lady's own desire to know the degree of rebirth she will attain in the future demonstrates that this was not insignificant for the Chinese Pure Land practitioner. Rebirth was assured, but at what level? This question mattered.

We find a final example of this teaching from the early twentieth century in the autobiographical statement that opens Yinguang's *Treatise Resolving Doubts about Pure Land* (*Jìngtǔ Juéyí lùn* 淨土決疑論). Yinguang describes his religious attitude after joining the monastic order as a mixture of both despair and aspiration. He despaired of his poor fortune and lack of good karma, disabilities that led him to believe that it would be impossible for him to attain buddhahood through his own intelligence and effort. Thus, he says, "The Buddha was my only thought, the Pure Land my only goal" (Yìnguāng 1991, p. 1:357; 2012, p. 30). Nevertheless, he did keep the precepts to the best of his ability and engaged in study and meditation. The purpose of these, according to his testimony, was to "attain the necessary qualifications for a superior-level (*shàng pǐn* 上品) rebirth in the Pure Land" (Yìnguāng 1991, p. 1:357; 2012, p. 30). Yinguang clearly took Wang Rixiu's counsel seriously.

Thus, for Wang Rixiu, Huang Ce, and Yinguang, the point is that even when one puts one's faith in the other-power of Amitābha's vows, practice still matters because it gives one a higher level of rebirth in Sukhāvatī after death. This in itself could constitute a fairly persuasive rationale for ethical action and religious practice within a Pure Land context, but it might strike one as rather weak or selfish. After all, one who has attained rebirth in the Pure Land at whatever level has achieved freedom from further rebirth in samsara. As Yinguang observes,

> Regardless of whether or not one's good roots have ripened, or whether one's bad karma is light or heavy, one need only be willing to generate faith and make the vows and recite the Buddha's name, and at the end of one's life, Amitābha Buddha will compassionately descend to meet and guide one to rebirth in the Pure Land. This is in order that those whose good roots have ripened may immediately attain to the sudden fruition of perfect buddhahood, while those whose evil karma is heavy may enter the holy stream. (Yìnguāng 1991, p. 1:359; 2012, p. 33)

In other words, one obtains good results even without serious ethics or practice. In addition, the Pure Land is pleasant enough even at the lowest rebirth. As the layman Yu Chunxi (*Yú Chúnxī* 虞淳熙, 1553–1621) observed to his master Zhuhong, those reborn in the lowest grade according to the *Larger Sutra* pass twelve *kalpas* within lotus calyxes that are comparable to the Heaven of the Thirty-Three (*Dāolìtiān* 忉利天; see CBETA X.1158.61:512a21–512b2)! It should not really matter how long they reside there. Why tax oneself with moral striving in order to shorten one's stay or improve one's status within it? In order to answer this question, we must note the relationship between two factors: the nature of the Pure Land as an intermediate goal and the normative Mahayana Buddhist motivations for practice. We will examine each of these in turn.

The Pure Land is not the Final Goal

It is essential to remember that Pure Land Buddhism in every region and time advances two sequential goals for the path: rebirth in the Pure Land first, and then the attainment of buddhahood. Furthermore, whenever Pure Land authors speak about relying on Amitābha's other-power, it is for the attainment of the first of these goals and not the second. The Pure Land is an intermediate goal, a way station on the path to buddhahood, a place wherein one attains the stage of non-retrogression so that one is assured of the eventual achievement of the final goal. The fact that one relied upon Amitābha's vow-power to attain rebirth in the Pure Land does not imply that his other-power will take one all the way to buddhahood. This happens when one completes one's practice there with the Buddha's teaching and support. The Pure Land simply provides a place where the environment, the absence of distractions and temptations, the provision of all requisites, and the presence of perfect teachers gives one the ideal *dàochǎng* 道場 within which to achieve buddhahood by self-exertion.

Yuan Hongdao makes just this point in his *Xīfāng hélùn* 西方合論 (Comprehensive treatise on the west, T.1976). The fourth fascicle outlines the characteristics of various levels of teaching and has six sections. The first pertains to non-Buddhists who lead ethical lives, and the last five correspond roughly, though using different terms, to the Huayan five-fold *pànjiào* 判教 scheme. The first section is very interesting for the purposes of this chapter. It describes all the values of ethical conduct and the practice of virtue. According to Yuan, moral conduct helps even non-Buddhists avoid rebirth as hell-beings, hungry ghosts, or animals; they remain in the realms of humans and gods. Buddhist practitioners attain the final goal proposed by the form of Buddhism in which they have taken refuge: Some become *arhats,* some *pratyekabuddhas,* and some bodhisattvas. At the highest level of the Mahayana, Yuan teaches that one does not achieve the final goal of becoming a buddha without practicing ethical conduct. It allows one to develop a stock of "good roots" (*shàn gēn* 善根) over many lifetimes, and, as Yuan says in other places, one's very ability to practice Pure Land depends upon having these good roots. All of this necessarily involves taking the Three Refuges, then receiving and keeping the various sets of precepts (T.1976.47.398c14–399b8). Thus, Yuan emphasizes that buddhahood is the goal, not the Pure Land.

Yuan's presentation depends for its coherence on the assumptions that (1) the final goal is the attainment of buddhahood, (2) rebirth in the Pure Land is a step along the way to this goal, and (3) ethical conduct is essential for producing the "good roots" that both goals require. He clearly distinguishes the first two as separate goals and posits the third as a prerequisite for both. While this supports my major point that rebirth in the Pure Land is not the final goal, it also makes the very interesting case that, while Amitābha's other-power is necessary for gaining rebirth, one's own ethical practice, undergirded by the formal reception of precepts, is essential for generating one's ability to call upon the Buddha's power for help in the first place.

The Mahayana Vow to Save All Beings

Thinkers within the Pure Land tradition all acknowledged that if a Buddhist engaged in religious practice, then *some* level of attainment was possible in this present life, and this would be "credited" toward the attainment of buddhahood in the future. Absent Pure Land practice, it would be quixotic to plan on achieving complete and perfect buddhahood in this life or assume that one will continue to enjoy uninterrupted progress in subsequent lives. Nevertheless, one's practice in this life still has some value in gaining rebirth at a higher grade or level in the Pure Land, and this affected the length of time that it would take to achieve buddhahood once there. This difference in time could be considerable: from the instantaneous achievement of the "highest of the high" to the twelve *kalpas* that the "lowest of the low" spent locked in the lotus bud before even beginning practice. The final question we must answer is this: Why should it matter how long one dwelt in the Pure Land?

The answer has to do with the normative Mahayana motivation for practice. The generation of *bodhicitta* that put one on the Mahayana path made the salvation of all beings the motivation for seeking buddhahood. If one was serious about this motivation, then it made sense to choose the path that led to buddhahood sooner rather than later, for the sooner one reached the goal, the sooner one could get about the task of saving all other sentient beings. This makes sense of the section in Siming Zhili's ceremony for the conferral of the bodhisattva precepts in which he administers the Four Great Vows (*sì hóng shìyuàn* 四弘誓願) with the admonition that all the recipients keep these vows in order to attain rebirth in the highest grade (*shàng pǐn* 上品) of the Pure Land (T.1937.46:862a10). The first of the Four Great Vows is to save all sentient beings without limit, and indicates that the bodhisattva's goal is to attain the highest Buddha Way in order to do so. Rebirth at the highest grade brings about completion of this vow in the shortest possible time.

Yuan Hongdao also made this connection. In a brief section of the first fascicle of his *Comprehensive Treatise on the West* devoted to the "inconceivability of cause and effect," he used the progression from practice to attainment to subsequent service as his example: "For example, practicing *nianfo* is the cause, and seeing the Buddha is the effect. Seeing the Buddha is the cause, and becoming a buddha is the effect. Becoming a buddha is the cause, and saving all sentient beings is the effect" (T.1976.47:391c29–392a2). The fact that Yuan brings this up as a casual illustration in the course of making another point demonstrates that he took for granted that the purpose of Pure Land practice was buddhahood, and the purpose of buddhahood was compassionate service for the liberation of other sentient beings.

Jixing Chewu made the same point in much the same way. As a way of illustrating the simultaneity of past, present, and future, he said:

> The very moment of contemplating the Buddha (*nianfo*) is the very moment of seeing the Buddha and becoming the Buddha. The very moment of seeking rebirth is the very moment of attaining rebirth *and the very moment of liberating all beings* (*dù shēng* 渡生). The three margins of time are all a single, identical time; there is no before and after. (CBETA X.1182.62:334b18–b20)

Like Yuan, Chewu takes this progression so much for granted that he uses it without further elaboration to illustrate another point, knowing that his audience will accept it unquestioningly.

Yinguang is more explicit in connecting rebirth in the Pure Land with the aspiration to achieve buddhahood for the sake of others:

> Because of this [that is, most beings' inability to achieve buddhahood on their own], the Tathāgata leads people to rebirth in the Pure Land, where they can see the Buddha and hear the teachings, and realize the Forbearance of the Unborn. Afterwards, riding on the power of the Buddha's compassion and the wheels of their own aspiration, they can reenter the Sahā world and bring other sentient beings to liberation. (Yìnguāng 1991, p. 1:367; 2012, p. 44)

Yinguang is quite clear here that the aspiration (*yuàn* 願) impelling believers into Pure Land practice is (or should be) the desire to save other beings. In fact, the concluding section of his *Treatise Resolving Doubts about Pure Land* contains a ritual formula to be used by those embarking on the Pure Land path in which the new convert makes this aspiration explicit:

> I, [So-and-so], from this day forward, will practice pure karma[2] exclusively. I ask only that when I die, I may be reborn in the highest grade, so that upon seeing the Buddha and hearing the teachings I may at once attain to the Unborn. Afterward, without separating from the Pure Land, I will enter into all ten directions universally. With the stream or against it, using all manner of expedient means, *I will carry this teaching to all places and liberate all beings.* Not a single moment will I rest during all future times. In space without limit, I vow to reach the furthest extremity. May Śākyamuni, Amitābha, and all of the eternally abiding Three Jewels have pity on my foolishness and sincerity, and all come to receive and enfold me. (Yìnguāng 1991, p. 1:370; 2012, p. 50)

Jixing Chewu ties this motivation directly to the generation of *gǎnyìng* 感應, the "sympathetic resonance" that effects one's rebirth in the Pure Land in a way that adds philosophical depth to the simple assertions of Yuan Hongdao and Yinguang, explaining *why* these basic Mahayana motivations matter for the successful completion of the Pure Land dharma-gate:

> If I do not think of universal liberation, but seek only to benefit myself, then I am deficient as to the principle. If the mind is not pacified, how much more will I not generate the Great Mind? This being so, then externally I will not resonate (*gǎntōng* 感通) with all of the buddhas, and internally, I will not be in accord with my own fundamental nature. Above, I will not be able to attain the perfect Buddha Way, and below, I will not be able to benefit widely the multitude of beings. (CBETA X.1182.62:333b18–b20)

In other words, because the mind of the Buddha Amitābha is marked by great compassion for all beings, the Pure Land practitioner's mind also needs compassion as a fundamental motivation. Unless one's mind and the Buddha's mind are consonant in this respect, one will not create sympathetic resonance and will not elicit the Buddha's other-power and attain rebirth in the Pure Land. Furthermore, Chewu emphasizes the value of getting to buddhahood expeditiously as he explains that true compassion for others entails the desire to gain the ability to render aid as quickly as possible:

> Therefore, I need to generate the great mind of enlightenment in accordance with nature, and, having generated it, cultivate great practices. Further, from among the various dharma-gates, I should choose the one that is easiest to set my hand to, and easiest to have success with. As to the most stable, the most perfect and quick, there is nothing to compare with having profound faith in the calling out of the Buddha's name. (CBETA X.1182.62:333b23–c2)

Chewu thus puts elements of motivation and practice into a cyclical, self-reinforcing formula. One wishes to practice and attain rebirth in the Pure Land. In order to do this, one must establish sympathetic resonance with the Buddha Amitābha. Establishing resonance requires the emulation of the Buddha's compassionate mind. For compassion to be genuine it must, among other things, seek the fastest and most reliable way to attain buddhahood, for only a buddha has the requisite wisdom and skill to help others. The fastest and most reliable path to buddhahood is to practice *nianfo* and attain rebirth in the Pure Land.

This perspective on the individual's need for precepts, meditation, and study differs markedly from the Kamakura period Japanese construction of Pure Land. All these efforts on the part of practitioners retained their value as integral parts of the Buddhist life because they speed the practitioner to the final goal by combining his or her attainments with the other-power of Amitābha. The description of the deathbed conversion that brought the lowest of the low to rebirth as depicted in the *Contemplation Sutra* was never generalized to cover the condition of all humanity living in the Age of the Decadent Dharma but was taken at face value. It was an expedient means for the miscreant who faced the terrors of hell and *had no other recourse* but to call upon the Buddha and rely exclusively on other-power to gain rebirth. For the rest, the example simply did not apply, and practice remained necessary.

Wukai in his *One Hundred Questions* (1825) makes this explicit:

> [Question 50:] Within the *nianfo* school one hears teachings such as "Go to rebirth carrying your delusions" and "Upon the completion of ten *nian*," etc. In the ears of a student [of the Way], this is the height of great error.
>
> [Answer:] The Buddha does not mislead people; they mislead themselves. What is this misleading of self? Depending upon [the maxim] "Go to rebirth carrying your delusions" some go on creating karma, and on account of [the teaching] "Upon the completion of ten *nian*," they deliberately carry on as they always have. Do they know that "carrying your delusions" just means one does not have to wait until the three kinds of delusion are completely eliminated [to attain rebirth], or that "ten *nian*" is said for busy people who do not have time for a lot of repetitions? If they are not aware of these points, those who practice *nianfo* stumble and commit faults. At the end of their lives, the power of their karma overcomes the power of the Way; how can it be avoided? Therefore, in the ordinary course of your days, you must rinse yourself clean of evil habits and spur on the growth of good roots. This is what is meant by not misleading yourself. (CBETA X.1184.62:359c20–360a3)

In other words, Pure Land teachings that appear to simplify practices and eliminate the need for serious cultivation are aimed at beings with genuine limitations. Those who have the ability to carry out ethical practices and religious cultivation must do so; they cannot shirk these based on accommodations made for others without courting disaster.

This correlates well with Daniel Stevenson's findings in his study of deathbed testimonials. As he describes it, long before a devotee's death, he or she looked for signs that he or she had forged karmic links to the

Pure Land and activated a sympathetic resonance with its Buddha; such assurances generally took the forms of dreams or waking visions of Amitābha. However, since these indicators were typically not sought while on the deathbed, and thus not *in extremis,* there remained an expectation that the person's life would actually be in accord with Buddhist norms of practice and conduct:

> Both forms of experience [that is, dreams or waking visions] were considered valid proof that the "connection with the pure land" was or would soon be secured—provided, of course, that the character and behavior of the individual who claimed the experience fit the profile of a dedicated Pure Land devotee. (Stevenson 1995, p. 594)

That is, "grace" or "other-power" worked when all other options had failed and the person was dying and had no time to amend his or her life or begin practice. In order to gain auspicious signs during one's lifetime that one would attain rebirth in the Pure Land, the tradition placed more emphasis on the devotee's own efforts in keeping precepts and cultivating practices.

In this connection, it is interesting to note that the deathbed testimonial of Lady Yueguo, which follows her dream trip to the Pure Land with her former servant, opens by severely criticizing those who deliberately wait until the last moment to begin practice, hoping that the compassion of the Buddha will save them from their fate. Echoing the thoughts of Tianru Weize, Huang Ce's interest in recording the life of this lady stems precisely from the fact that she did *not* act in this way but began Pure Land devotions while still young and healthy and lived a virtuous Buddhist life. By holding her up as an exemplar, Huang is saying to his readers that they should take this as their pattern and combine Pure Land devotion with diligent practice and virtuous behavior (Stevenson 1995, p. 598; see also T.1969.47:189c10–190a27). Lady Yueguo provides a suitable example of the "two powers of self and other" working together to produce the most ideal result.

Constructing Pure Land Ethics

Based on the above, the following picture emerges of human striving within the Pure Land path as interpreted by the Chinese tradition: New Mahayana Buddhist practitioners set out on the path in order to achieve buddhahood for the sake of saving all other sentient beings. This goal is important enough that it is worth considering how best to reach it in the shortest possible time. Taking a realistic look at their present situations, they see that, dwelling in this Sahā world and laden with heavy karmic burdens, they cannot count on having proper teachers or any other requisites for practice. They judge that their prospects for attaining the goal on their own in one lifetime are scant, and they cannot count on conserving their gains in future lives. However, Amitābha Buddha, through the power of his vows, has created an ideal land where they may make the speediest progress toward buddhahood, and so they resolve to gain rebirth there in order to make their way toward the final goal without risk of backsliding or failure.

Nevertheless, while Amitābha's vow-power is essential for reaching the Pure Land, they may still expedite the process of attaining buddhahood by making whatever progress in the Way they can in the present life. Achieving rebirth at a higher level in the Pure Land can still cut eons off the process and propel them to buddhahood faster. Thus, rather than relying exclusively on other-power, they begin a process in which self-power and other-power work together to get the very best and fastest results. The practice of *nianfo* will assure that they are reborn in Sukhāvatī, and all other practices will serve to gain the highest possible level of rebirth therein. This plan comports best with the compassionate motivation of the Mahayana.

While I have not yet located a premodern text that puts all the elements surveyed above together in just this manner, a modern Buddhist leader, Sheng Yen (*Shèngyán* 聖嚴, 1930–2009) did so as part of a series of dharma-talks given during a seven-day Buddha-recitation retreat (*fóqī* 佛七) in Taiwan. Here is how he put the matter to the participants:

> What we have practiced in the course of past lives is called good roots (*shàn'gēn* 善根). The wholesome conditions we gather widely, the living beings that we broadly strive to liberate, and the vigorous practice of reciting the name (*chímíng* 持名) that we undertake at present is called good circumstances and merit (*fúdé* 福德). Merit is what you have gained in your own mind; good circumstances are what benefit living beings. We practice every kind of wholesome karma in order to help ourselves to bring living beings to achievement quickly because in this way we deepen our good circumstances and merit a little. The more good circumstances and merit we have, the higher will be our lotus-ranking (*liánhuā pǐnwèi* 蓮花品位), the greater our lotus-blossom will be in the Western Land of Utmost Bliss, and the earlier we can return to the Sahā world to save living beings far and wide. (Sheng Yen 2010, p. 93)

An earlier historical text outlining the case for self-exertion may yet turn up, but it may also be the case that Sheng Yen is here articulating an understanding of human effort in the Way that had been implicit all along and went without saying.

We began by noting that Chinese Pure Land Buddhism never followed the path of disparaging human effort charted by the Kamakura Pure Land founders in Japan. Thus, it is now appropriate to ask: How do we understand why a figure such as Shinran never arose in China to propose utter dependence upon the other-power of Amitābha to the deprecation of moral effort? After all, the idea of Amitābha's other-power was present in both places; why was it carried to this extreme in only one? One plausible explanation emerges from the fact that there never existed a Pure Land "school" as such in China, at least not as demonstrated by the achievement of the institutional independence that the various Pure Land Schools enjoy in Japan. Sheng Yen points out that during the Song dynasty (960–1279) most of the developments in Pure Land took place within the Tiantai School and stressed a combination of meditation, Pure Land, and *vinaya*. By the end of the Ming dynasty (1368–1644), he says, there was no one Pure Land School that had exclusive propriety over a set of practices identified as "Pure Land practice." Rather, Pure Land became the common property of all schools (Sheng Yen 1992, p. 89, 102).

This means that a strictly Pure Land soteriology had no room to develop in isolation from other schools and strains of thought. What we call "the Pure Land tradition" in Chinese Buddhism could also be called the "Pure Land component" of the thought and practice of other schools or of Chinese Buddhism as an organic whole. Thus, the practice of *nianfo* and speculation on the efficacy of self-power and other-power generally took place among educated lay and clergy who were also Tiantai thinkers (such as Siming Zhili and others), *vinaya* masters and preceptors (such as the figures mentioned in Liu's study), or active in these and many other facets of Buddhist life and thought (such as the Ming dynasty polymath and ninth "patriarch" of the Pure Land tradition, Ouyi Zhixu). Ensconced as it was in the wider tradition, Pure Land thought could never dispense with, declare its independence from, or assert its opposition to the other concomitants of the Buddhist life, nor need it have felt a need to do so.

It may also be of some interest to note that such thought appears to be taking hold in Japanese Pure Land Buddhism in the modern world. In an essay published in 1993, the Japanese Pure Land thinker Tokunaga Michio called attention to the Mahayana Buddhist concept of "the return to this world" as a practical motivation for practice. Responding to Christian criticisms that Pure Land Buddhism represents a mere escape from suffering with no compassion for others, Tokunaga says, "The central purpose of my presentation is to claim that *shinjin* or *nembutsu* as revealed by Shinran is nothing but the Mahayana Bodhisattva path, and that it is the concept of 'return to this world' (*gensō ekō*) which fulfills the actual significance of the Mahayana *bodhisattva* path to its utmost. Seeking rebirth in the Pure Land in order to help other beings is the best way to fulfill the Mahayana ideal of 'benefitting self and other'" (Tokunaga 1993, p. 2, 5-6). Whether this represents a new trend in Japanese Pure Land thought or not, I leave to my colleagues in Japanese Buddhist studies to say.

As the last chapter showed, the Chinese Pure Land tradition always thought spiritual progress came about through collaboration between self-power and other-power. While one relied on the power of the Buddha to attain rebirth, one could still contribute to the process through one's own exertions. Here we see that if one takes into account the compassionate aspirations necessary for generating *bodhicitta* and understands that Chinese Pure Land practitioners are serious about fulfilling that aspiration, then it becomes clear that the practitioner is morally culpable if he or she chooses not to participate in the process of gaining the highest rebirth of which they are capable. They must take on precepts and keep to the highest moral standards to do this. In this light, choosing to engage the cooperation of self-power and other-power becomes an intelligible ethical decision in its own right.

Chapter 6

Defending Pure Land in Late Imperial China

> The Pure Land dharma-gate is a path of skillful means in Buddhist practice. Many parts of it seem to be in conflict with Buddhism or look like adulterations from other religions. It generates many qualms in and of itself because the sutras that introduce it contain many discrepancies and contradictions.
>
> Sheng Yen, *Master Sheng Yen Teaches the Pure Land Dharma-Gate*

With few exceptions, when western scholarship on Chinese Pure Land history has treated relationships between it and other sectors of Chinese Buddhism, it has focused on the resolution of conflicts and the emergence of schemas such as "the dual practice of Chan and Pure Land" (*chán-jìng shuāngxiū* 禪淨雙修; for examples, see Chappell 1986, Shih 1991, 1992, and Yü 1981). These studies give the impression that the way in which Pure Land authors or other Chinese Buddhist figures resolved their conflicts had lasting, pervasive, or normative effects and settled disputes once and for all. Movements toward the harmonization of Chan and Pure Land proposed in the Song dynasty (960–1279) and receiving greater definition in the Ming are prominent within this picture. The "dual practice of Chan and Pure Land" attributed to Yongming Yanshou and given further definition by Yunqi Zhuhong seems to have smoothed out the differences between these two approaches to Buddhist practice, eliminating their rivalry and averting mutual polemics.

The purpose of this chapter will be to trace the arguments between *some* Chan practitioners and *some* Pure Land authorities as they debated from the late Ming dynasty (1368–1644) down to the present day (those, that is, who did not buy into the "dual practice" model but wished to maintain a separate identity for Pure Land). After identifying the segment of the Pure Land tradition from which polemics emanated, I will concentrate on the works of Yuan Hongdao (*Yuán Hóngdào* 袁宏道,

1568–1610), Yiyuan Zongben (*Yīyuán Zōngběn* 一元宗本, sixteenth century), Jixing Chewu (*Jìxǐng Chèwù* 際醒徹悟, 1741–1810), and Yinguang (*Yìnguāng* 印光, 1861–1940), to provide examples from three historical periods: the late Ming, the mid-Qing, and the Republican eras, respectively. A survey of their works will yield patterns of response to Chan criticisms.

Identifying Pure Land's Defenders and Critics

The first order of business is to identify the two sides in this polemic. We have already seen that there is no discrete Pure Land "school" or "sect," and without a definite Pure Land School, it is difficult to identify the entities between which the "syncretism" of Chan and Pure Land would form (Sharf 2002). If the syncretism of the two is difficult to understand, though, the polemics that continued between them are most certainly not. Chan authors criticized Pure Land on several counts, and Pure Land defenders answered back. Still, the lack of any institution or school of Pure Land has a direct bearing on the question: In conflicts between Chan and Pure Land, who speaks for the Pure Land side, and what is their standing? That is to say, even if the two sides did not fit neatly into the category school or sect, polemicists were siding with *something* and claimed authority to speak for it. While I have identified what I take to be the Pure Land tradition in chapter 2, I must still specify here which figures entered into polemics to defend this tradition against detractors and on what basis.

As noted in chapter 3, in premodern times Pure Land thinkers came to name two distinct ways of explaining how Pure Land practice worked: The first was "mind-only Pure Land" (*wéixīn jìngtǔ* 唯心淨土), and the second was "western-direction Pure Land" (*xīfāng jìngtǔ* 西方淨土) or "other-direction Pure Land" (*tāfāng jìngtǔ* 他方淨土). The former mode of thought held that Amitābha Buddha is an image within the mind and that the Pure Land is nothing other than this Sahā world seen correctly by a purified consciousness. The most frequently quoted proof texts in this line of thinking were the dictum from the *Contemplation Sutra,* "This mind creates the Buddha, this mind is the Buddha" (T.365.12:343a21), and another from the *Vimalakīrti Sutra* that states, "If the bodhisattva wishes to acquire a pure land, he must purify his mind. When the mind is pure, the buddha-land will be pure" (T.475.14:538c4–c5; trans. Watson 1997, p. 29, adapted).

Such a point of view would stir little controversy within Chan circles, since it affirms many basic elements of Chinese Buddhist rhetoric: non-duality of subject and object, mind-only thought, buddha-nature, and the ultimate ungraspability of all distinctions and categories. If one understands the basis for practice as a fundamentally non-dual co-inherence of meditator and object of meditation (here understood as the Buddha Amitābha), then a form of dual practice such as the "*nianfo kōan*" (*niànfó gōng'àn* 念佛公案) makes perfect sense. As refined by Yunqi Zhuhong, this involved performing *nianfo,* stopping periodically to reflect back on oneself to ask "Who is reciting the Buddha's name?" (See his *Chánguān cè jìn* 禪關策進, T.2024.48:1102b18–b24; English in Yúnqī Zhūhóng 2015, p. 106. See the discussion in Yü 1981, p. 47–63.)

On the opposite side, however, those who affirmed the teaching of "western-direction Pure Land" and cultivated its associated practices found themselves subject to criticism, not only from self-identified Chan practitioners, but also from other Pure Land practitioners who hewed more to the standpoint of "mind-only Pure Land." Consider the offense these critics would have taken upon reading this passage from one of the letters of Yinguang, the Thirteenth Patriarch (*zǔ* 祖) of the Pure Land tradition:

> One must not give rise to deluded speculations according to the opinions of unenlightened people from the outer paths. They say that all of the inconceivable adornments [of the Pure Land] are ways of teaching by similes and metaphors, and have no basis in objective reality. If one holds to this foolish, heretical view, then one loses the benefit of rebirth in the Pure Land. What a great loss! One must be aware of this. (Yìnguāng 1991, p. 1:71)

Such statements would surely raise cries of "rank dualism!" from the Buddhist intelligentsia.

The core feature of "western-direction Pure Land," then, was its claim that the land of Sukhāvatī really exists in the objective world outside of the individual's mind. Turn west and one will face it; turn east and it will be at one's back. There once really had been a bodhisattva named Dharmākara who gained buddhahood in the past under the name Amitābha. The bodhisattva really had made a series of vows, whose real fulfillment meant that inhabitants of this defiled and uncertain world really could recite his name and he would really come for them at the time of death and escort them to this Pure Land. There they would really see him, hear him preach the dharma, and eventually attain full and perfect enlightenment.

This literal view was never part of the accommodation that led to "the dual practice of Chan and Pure Land." For many Buddhists in China, even after the development of dual cultivation, such a belief violated many of the unquestioned axioms of Buddhist philosophy as they understood them. It posited a dualism between buddhas and unenlightened beings and between purity and impurity. It negated the necessity of any practice and realization in the here and now. It appeared to deny that all beings possessed buddha-nature and were therefore fundamentally no different from Amitābha himself. Finally, it appeared to be a selfish practice aimed solely at escaping from this world of suffering to some Never-Never Land far away. Only the ignorant and deluded masses of illiterate peasants could possibly have any use for such nonsense!

Because of these widespread perceptions, the adherents of "western-direction Pure Land" had far greater need of the art of apologetics than did the advocates of "mind-only Pure Land," most of whom identified with Chan. The charges as listed above were all true on the face of things; it was up to the apologists to demonstrate that their more objective reading of Pure Land cosmology and soteriology still found support in the highest levels of Buddhist scripture and thought. From this necessity arose a rich and sophisticated account of Pure Land theory and practice that (1) positioned it within Tiantai 天台 and Huayan 華嚴 metaphysics, (2) listed the most advanced bodhisattvas among its practitioners and advocates, (3) showed that their position conformed to a basic understanding of mind-only, and (4) gave evidence that even the greatest teachers and texts of the Chan School itself agreed with the apologists' rather than their critics' reading of Pure Land practice. The remainder of this chapter, then, will briefly indicate the manner in which later Chinese Pure Land apologists utilized these four avenues of justification (among others) not only to defend their own practice, but to criticize their opponents as being the *real* detractors of the faith.

"Western-Direction Pure Land" Is Compatible with Buddhist Philosophy

One line of defense that the Pure Land apologists used was to demonstrate that their point of view, far from violating basic Buddhist metaphysical principles, actually honored them more than their opponents did. The strategy was simple: Since Chinese Buddhists widely regarded Tiantai and Huayan thought as the most advanced expressions of Buddhist metaphysics, they sought to position their own thought within these frameworks. Thus, they could show that Pure Land teachings did not violate or oversimplify their opponents' highest standards.

Pure Land Practice within a Tiantai Perspective

Since much Pure Land thought developed within the Tiantai School during the Song dynasty, placing Pure Land thought and practice within that school's perspective was not difficult. Indeed, the apologists made copious use of Tiantai categories in non-apologetic writings to expound and systematize Pure Land teachings. To give one example, Yuan Hongdao used the Tiantai schema of four distinct categories of Pure Lands in his *Xīfāng hélùn* (T.1976.47:391a23–c3; see also chapter 3). As Daniel Stevenson has pointed out, Tiantai Zhiyi's (*Tiāntái Zhìyǐ* 天台智顗, 538–597) massive work, the *Móhē zhǐguān* 摩訶止觀 (T.1911), taught the so-called Constantly Walking Samadhi (*cháng xíng sānmèi* 常行三昧) based on the buddha-recollection exercises recommended in the three-fascicle *Pratyutpanna-samādhi-sūtra* (*Bānzhōu sānmèi jīng* 般舟三昧經, T.418). In this practice, the practitioner constantly circumambulated an altar of Amitābha while visualizing the Buddha and his land for ninety consecutive days (Stevenson 1986, p. 58–61; Stevenson and Donner 1993, p. 27–28). Daniel Getz has extensively documented the pivotal role Tiantai monks played in the development of the Pure Land tradition, both as a system of thought and as a popular practice among clerics and laity. During the Song dynasty (960–1279), Tiantai monks brought the Pure Land tradition southward into Zhejiang and Jiangsu provinces and carried out many activities to promote its growth there. The monk Zongxiao (*Zōngxiǎo* 宗曉, 1151–1214) composed the *Lèbāng wénlèi* 樂邦文類 (Anthology of the Land of Bliss, T.1969A), and monks such as Shengchang (*Shěngcháng* 省常, 959–1020), Ciyun Zunshi (*Cíyún Zūnshì* 慈雲尊式, 964–1032), and Siming Zhili (*Sìmíng Zhīlǐ* 四明知禮, 960–1028), were instrumental in founding societies for pure conduct and vocal *nianfo* (Getz 1994, chap. 7–11).

Later Pure Land apologetic literature certainly made use of Tiantai's contributions to the formation of Pure Land thought as a way of validating their practice, but claiming such authority did not always help those who defended the "western-direction Pure Land" position. Their detractors could always claim that they had distorted the true teaching of the Tiantai School by violating the Three Truths in which, after passing through an understanding of emptiness and provisional truth, one came to a realization of the utter non-duality of the Middle. Did it not seem that to call this land "impure" and that land "pure" and to seek to abandon this land in favor of that land constituted an untenable dualism, even if phrased in Tiantai terms? Yuan Hongdao had these critics in mind when he quoted from the *Jìngtǔ shí yí lùn* 淨土十疑論 (Ten doubts about Pure Land, T.1961) attributed to Zhiyi:

> The wise zealously seek rebirth in the Pure Land, [but] the substance of what arrives for rebirth is ungraspable—this is true "non-birth." This is what we mean by "the mind is pure and therefore the buddha-land is pure." The foolish get entangled in [the word] "birth." Hearing "birth," they understand birth; hearing "non-birth," they understand non-birth. They do not know that birth *is* non-birth, and that non-birth *is* birth. Falling short of this principle, they are dominated by thoughts of "is" and "is not," and get angry at others who seek birth in the Pure Land, slandering them. (T.1976.47:403a18–a22; the text is quoted from T.1961.47:78a26–b1)

In other words, the critics falsely assert that Pure Land faith and practice, based on dualistic views, violate basic Buddhist philosophical principles. The above passage partly responds to this critique by pointing out that the critics themselves do not properly understand the meaning of non-duality: They interpret Pure Land language too concretely, taking "birth" and "non-birth" as mutually exclusive rather than mutually interpenetrating. That Yuan was quoting a text attributed to the very founder of the Tiantai School strengthened the argument's Tiantai *bona fides.*

Yuan finds a further response to this accusation in Tiantai's highest categories. Here, for example, he uses the Three Contemplations of Emptiness, the Provisional, and the Middle, to explain the exact relationship between the one who recites the Buddha's name and the Buddha himself:

> As to the saying that "the three contemplations subsist in *nian* (*Yán niàn cún sān guān zhě* 言念存三觀者)": one repetition of the Buddha's name leads to the penetration of the reciting subject's substance being empty and the recited object being without characteristics. This means that the recitation includes the "Contemplation of Emptiness." The Buddha that one recites is the transformation body, meaning that the mind breaks through the delusions of views and thoughts. Even though the substance of the reciting subject is empty and the object of recitation has no characteristics, this does not prevent the subject from discriminating the appearance of the object. Thus, recitation includes the "Contemplation of the Provisional." The Buddha being recited is a reward body, meaning that the mind has broken through the delusions of the manifold sense perceptions. Right in the instant that the subject and object are empty, the subject and object appear.

> Right in the instant that the subject and object appear, the subject and object are quiescent. Therefore, "emptiness" and "the provisional" mutually co-inhere, and recitation includes the "Contemplation of the Middle." The Buddha being recited is this very dharma body, the mind's breaking through the delusion of ignorance. This moreover is the cause of Buddha-recitation, penetrating the Three Truths and purifying the Four Lands. Like taking up a mote of dust and transforming the great earth into gold, this is the mutual interpenetration of the *dharmadhātu,* the gate of the inconceivable contemplation. (T.1976.47:405a15–a25)

This passage suggests that the critics, by one-sidedly holding on to the emptiness of the subject-object duality, have gotten stuck. In Tiantai terms, they themselves have not realized the truth of the Middle, in which provisionally appearing phenomena are revalorized as the very locus of the highest truth. The person who thinks that Amitābha and his Pure Land actually exist outside the boundaries of the Sahā world is not mistaken; this is as provisionally true as any other fact of our present existence. After practicing meditation and receiving teaching in the Pure Land, devotees will eventually come to see the truth of the Middle for themselves, but for now, "western-direction Pure Land" practice is enough to move them in the right direction.

In addition, Yuan made use of a teaching peculiar to the Tiantai School, namely that the One Mind pervading all reality includes afflicted as well as pure aspects. Indeed, according to Ng Yu-kwan, from the time of Zhiyi, Tiantai thought saw the mind's own defilements as a key ingredient in the achievement of nirvana; to extirpate the defilements would mean to extinguish the mind itself, leaving nothing to be either bound or liberated:

> Defilements, represented by evil and ignorance, are, together with good and Dharma Nature, what the mind embraces in nature. Their extirpation in an annihilative sense would indicate the extirpation of the mind as well. Such a condition would further result in the extirpation of good and Dharma Nature, rendering nirvana and liberation impossible. (Ng 1993, p. 176)

Such a view went far in indicating how impure minds could come to the Pure Land without despoiling it, and how even the ignorant mind of the lowly reciter of the Buddha's name could connect with the One Mind. Yuan explicitly cites the Ninth Tiantai patriarch Zhanran (*Zhànrán* 湛然, 711–782), who said that the mind *in its very delusion,* as it contemplates the Buddha Amitābha as if he were separate from the mind that contemplates him, can be the vehicle for liberation (T.1976.47:402a6–a9). If one understands that the One Mind in its afflicted aspect pervades all other minds, then such a viewpoint makes good sense.

With these arguments, Yuan sought to show that Pure Land practice accorded with Tiantai philosophy. However, most other Pure Land appeals to Tiantai took the form of quoting Tiantai sources on other topics, or of including famous Tiantai figures in lists of eminent practitioners of Pure Land in order to counter the charge that Pure Land practice was only for the vulgar. The apologists appealed more frequently to Huayan thought and scripture in order to provide a foundation for Pure Land's acceptance.

Pure Land Practice within a Huayan Perspective

A preliminary tactic in demonstrating the compatibility of Pure Land and Huayan teachings was to invoke the *Huayan Sutra* itself. This arose from a commonly held view that the *Huayan Sutra* was the paramount Mahayana scripture and that Huayan metaphysics was the most advanced form of Buddhist thought. Both Yuan Hongdao and Yinguang make this appeal explicitly and directly. Yinguang says, "Now the *Huayan Sutra* is the king of scriptures, reigning over the entire canon. One who does not believe the *Huayan Sutra* is an *icchantika*" (Yìnguāng 1991, p. 1:360; 2012, p. 34–35). Yuan Hongdao valorized Pure Land scriptures by utilizing pre-existing doctrinal classification (*pànjiào* 判教) schemas to place the *Amitābha Sutra* within the highest category of scripture alongside the *Huayan Sutra*. For instance, he quoted a commentary on this sutra by the Faxiang 法相 master Kuiji (*Kuījī* 窺基, 632–682), which used an eight-level classification scheme. Kuiji placed the *Amitābha Sutra* together with the *Lotus Sutra* and the *Huayan Sutra* as scriptures of the highest level, called "Perfect Truth Corresponding to Principle" (*yìnglǐ yuánshí zōng* 應理圓實宗; T.1976.47:400a23–a24; Kuiji's text is from his *Āmítuó jīng tōngzàn shū* 阿彌陀經通贊疏; see T.1758.37:329c13–c15). This tactic elevated the Pure Land scriptures to the level of the *Huayan Sutra* by association.

Apologists could make a stronger argument by locating support for Pure Land within the *Huayan Sutra* itself, as Yinguang did in his *Jìngtǔ juéyí lùn* 淨土決疑論 (Treatise resolving doubts about Pure Land). Using the eighty-fascicle translation by Śikṣānanda, he found the following passage near the end of the fortieth fascicle of the *Gaṇḍavyūha* section (*Rù fǎjiè pǐn* 入法界品), in which the great bodhisattva Samantabhadra counsels readers to seek rebirth in the Pure Land:

> O Son of a Good Family! If all sentient beings could hear this great king of vows, receive it, keep it, read it, recite it, and preach it widely to the people, then there would not be a buddha, a world-honored one in any of the other worlds who would not hear of their merit. Therefore, when you hear of this great king of vows, you should never have any doubt, but receive it in truth. Having received it, then one can read it; having read it, then one can recite it; having recited it, one can keep it, on up to being able to recopy it and preach it widely. The vows that these people keep for the span of a single moment will bring success; what they reap will be limitless, boundless fortune. They will be able to rescue all those in the sea of vexations and great sufferings, and let them out to where *they all gain rebirth in Amitābha's Land of Utmost Bliss.* (*Huáyán jīng hé lùn* 1977, p. 2:1468a–b)[1]

Yinguang was not the first apologist to notice this passage; earlier writers also cited it to show that Pure Land was not a vulgar practice reserved for the uneducated, since Samantabhadra and all the bodhisattvas of the Lotus Sea Assembly had aspirations for rebirth in Sukhāvatī (see, for example, Yunqi Zhuhong at CBETA X.424.22:611a2–a3).[2] Nevertheless, because Yinguang was the first author to see the implications of modern textual criticism for the apologetic use of sutra texts, he had to deal with the history of the sutra in order to maintain the relevance of this citation.

Yinguang's unnamed opponent in the *Treatise Resolving Doubts about Pure Land* points out that the above passage does not actually appear in Śikṣānanda's eighty-fascicle *Huayan Sutra.* Furthermore, an influential Tang dynasty commentator on the then newly translated text, Li Tongxuan (*Lǐ Tōngxuán* 李通玄, 635–730), made no comment regarding it, which for him establishes that the passage in question is an interpolation dating from after Li's time, and thus not part of the sutra itself. Furthermore, he says that Li Tongxuan, in other places in his commentary, actually disparaged the concept of a western Pure Land as an instance of worldlings grasping at characteristics. This, he says, should disqualify Yinguang's appeal to this spurious passage (Yìnguāng 1991, p. 1:361; 2012, p. 36).

This leads Yinguang into a lengthy exposition of the sutra's textual history. He begins by saying that Li, a figure revered as a manifestation of one of the bodhisattvas of the Lotus Sea Assembly, did not have the complete text in his hands, since the last section arrived in China only after 798, close to seventy years after his death. That is why he spoke of the western Pure Land in this way (Yìnguāng 1991, p. 1:361; 2012, p. 36). This is correct as far as modern scholars can reconstruct the transmission of the text.[3] Śikṣānanda's translation of the *Gaṇḍavyūha* section runs only to the end of the section corresponding to fascicle 39 of the later Prajñā translation. As preserved in the *Taishō Shinshū Daizōkyō,* the text ends where Yinguang's opponent says it does; the reader will not find the translated passage above in it.

However, Yinguang points out that the ending of this version does not conform to the standard pattern for most Mahayana sutras; no one asks the Buddha what the teaching ought to be called and how it is to be kept, and there is no statement that all the hearers rejoiced and went home. Armed with this literary-critical evidence, Yinguang says that the text "closes on an inconclusive note" (Yìnguāng 1991, p. 1:362; 2012, p. 37), and asserts that Elder Li had an incomplete translation. It should be obvious that Elder Li could not possibly comment on a passage that would not be available until many years after his death. It is not that he did not know the true ending; as an advanced bodhisattva, he must have known. Not having this section in hand to support this teaching, however, he skillfully chose not to reveal it and risk causing confusion by commenting on a scriptural passage that did not yet exist for his audience.

With the Pure Land teachings now endorsed by the *Huayan Sutra* itself, the apologists could move on to considerations of Huayan philosophy in relation to Pure Land. Yuan Hongdao points out that Chan masters in the past were aware of the compatibility of Pure Land and Huayan teachings. For example, he cites the *Zhēnxiē Qīngliǎo chánshī yǔlù* 真歇清了禪師語錄 (Recorded sayings of the Chan master Zhenxie Qingliao), which contains a chapter called "Essential Doctrines of Pure Land" (*Jìngtǔ zōngyào* 淨土宗要, CBETA X.1426.71:779b19–c7). In this work the Chan monk Zhenxie Qingliao (*Zhēnxiē Qīngliǎo* 真歇清了, 1089–1151) specifically used the parable of Indra's net to explicate the perfect interpenetration of Amitābha's Pure Land with all other buddha-lands and with all the impure lands (T.1976.47:400a24–b4). In addition, the Huayan concept of "the unobstructed interpenetration of principle and phenomena" (*lǐshì wúài* 理事無礙) provided an obvious source of help in establishing Pure Land teachings. Like the single moon reflected in its entirety on thousands of ponds and rivers, or like the single wind that sounds through a myriad of trees, the Amitābha who appears within the minds of countless practitioners is not an image created by those minds, as the proponents of the "mind-only Pure Land" position would have it; it really *is* Amitābha. The fact that thousands of people can be contemplating him at the same time disproves neither the oneness of Amitābha nor the reality of his presence within each individual's mental contemplation. Amitābha, like the moon, can reflect in a myriad of minds without losing his unity and wholeness. "If in the whole there are parts, then the whole will be partitioned. If in the parts the whole is not present, then the whole does not pervade the parts. The meaning of perfection cannot come to be if the parts and the whole are mutually opposed" (T.1976.47:400b2–b4). In this way, Huayan's unique take on the relationship between the parts and the whole, or the one and the many (Cook 1977, chap. 6), come into play in defense of *nianfo* practice by showing that the image of Amitābha in the practitioner's mind and the real Amitābha who dwells in his Pure Land perfectly interpenetrate. One need not deny the reality of Amitābha as an external and objectively real being to establish his real presence within the practitioner's mind; both are true. Pure Land practice and Huayan philosophy thus relate to one another in a seamless unity of practice and theory.

The High Caliber of Practitioners of "Western-Direction Pure Land"

One of the most commonly utilized criticisms of Pure Land practice was that it was an inferior path, fit only for the vulgar and ignorant who lacked the intellectual capability and firm resolve needed to pursue the threefold learning of morality, meditation, and wisdom. Yuan Hongdao caricatured this criticism as follows: "Look at today's Chan practitioners. [. . .] Upon seeing someone practicing Pure Land, they laugh and say, 'They are practicing something that is only for the ignorant masses'" (T.1976.47:394c9–c12). He responds to this charge with counterexamples, naming figures from Buddhist history and legend who taught the Pure Land dharma-gate that no one would dare call ignorant. He writes, "Let me try to talk to them about not looking down upon [all Pure Land practitioners as] ignorant men and women. To do so would be to look down as well upon Mañjuśrī, Samantabhadra, Nāgārjuna, Aśvaghoṣa, and so on" (T.1976.47:394c12–c13).

This defense draws upon many sources. As we have already seen, the "Chapter on Samantabhadra Carrying Out his Vows" that appears at the end of the *Huayan Sutra* depicts Samantabhadra and the entire "Lotus Sea Assembly" vowing together to seek rebirth in Amitābha's Pure Land. Yunqi Zhuhong pointed this out briefly in his *Āmítuó jīng shūchāo* (阿彌陀經疏鈔): "All the great bodhisattvas such as Mañjuśrī and Samantabhadra have made vows to seek rebirth [in the Pure Land] and none can excel them, so how much more should those at the novice level [follow suit]?" (CBETA X.424.22:611a2–a3).

Yinguang deploys the argument with more detail in this way:

> Your knowledge is limited to the ignorant men and women who can [only] recite the Buddha's name, and this leads you to denigrate the Pure Land. But why do you not look at the *Gaṇḍavyūha* section of the *Huayan Sutra,* where Sudhana, after attaining equality with all buddhas, is taught by Samantabhadra to generate the ten great vow-kings, and dedicate the merit of these acts to rebirth in the Western Paradise? There he will attain perfect buddhahood, and then urge [these vows on] all in the Lotus Sea Assembly.
>
> Now among the assembly of the Lotus Sea, there are no worldlings, nor are there the two vehicles [of Hinayana and *pratyekabuddhas*]. All the great *dharmakāya* masters at all forty-one stages have broken through ignorance, realized their dharma nature, and can ride the wheel of the Original Vow to manifest as a buddha in any world that lacks a buddha. Among this Lotus Sea Assembly, there are pure lands without number, and so it must be that those who dedicate merit toward attaining rebirth in the Western Land of Utmost Bliss can be assured that, having gained this rebirth, they have taken the hidden gate out of suffering and the short path to becoming a buddha. (Yìnguāng 1991, p. 1:360; 2012, p. 34)

In addition to this, the Pure Land tradition in China unquestioningly accepted passages in later treatises by acknowledged masters that upheld belief in Amitābha and recommended seeking rebirth in the Pure Land. These authors were added to the arsenal of the non-ignorant and non-vulgar who practiced Pure Land. Nāgārjuna was cited as the author of the *Daśabhūmika-vibhāṣā-śāstra* (*Shízhù pípóshā lùn* 十住毘婆沙論, T.1521), whose chapter "On Easy Practice" (*yìxíng pǐn* 易行品) praised the Pure Land. Vasubandhu, of course, was the putative author of the *Wǎngshēng lùn* 往生論 (Treatise on rebirth, T.1524; English translation in Vasubandhu 2015), a short classic on Pure Land practice. Aśvaghoṣa was the author of *Dàshèng qǐxìn lùn* 大乘起信論 (The awakening of faith in the Mahayana, T.1666, 1667), whose closing chapter includes a very brief exhortation to *nianfo* that most modern scholars believe to be a later interpolation. Who would dare to call such figures vulgar and unenlightened?

"Western-Direction Pure Land" Does Not Violate the Principle of Mind-Only

To my knowledge, no Pure Land apologist ever asserted that "western-direction Pure Land" was better than or exclusive of "mind-only Pure Land." That "the Triple World is mind-only" (*sānjiè wéixīn* 三界唯心) was a baseline belief; denying the truth of this put one outside of orthodox Buddhism and within the ranks of the worldlings who grasp at dualism. Thus, if one looks in their texts for a denial of "mind-only Pure Land," one will not find it. Instead, the writers appeal for acceptance of both concepts as necessary for balance.

According to the critics, "western-direction Pure Land" was an erroneous teaching because it clung to a Pure Land and a Buddha seemingly external to the mind, a premise they found inadmissible within standard Buddhist understandings of mind-only and the non-duality of subject and object. The apologists were quick to deny this, stating that the critics themselves were at fault for clinging to the ultimate aspect of the Pure Land to the exclusion of the provisional. Of course the Pure Land is mind-only, and of course Amitābha is a manifestation of one's own nature! Who would deny these statements? The critics erred in not seeing that all phenomena and beings, from Amitābha to rocks and trees, are like this, and yet we have to acknowledge that they are, provisionally at least, external to our consciousnesses.

Yuan Hongdao cast this argument in the mold of Mādhyamika Two Truths theory when he wrote,

> A *gāthā* says, "No phenomenon is self-produced; neither does it arise from something else, nor from both, nor causelessly. Thus we say, 'unproduced.'" And again [the *Vimalakīrti Sutra* says]: "It is like a man who builds a palace. In dependence upon both space and earth, he can follow his intention without obstruction. But if he depends [only] upon vacuous space, then he cannot complete it." The preaching of the Buddha always rests on the Two Truths—he proclaims the true characteristic of all phenomena without eliminating provisional names. (T.1976.47:403a13–a18)

In this way, Yuan pitches the criticism back at the critics. The very fact that they cling to the characterization of the Pure land as "unproduced" to the detriment of its conventionally "produced" character, and that they take "birth" there as excluding the truth of "non-birth" as shown in a previous quotation from Yuan's work, only demonstrates that *they* are the ones who have not grasped the depth of Buddhist analysis.

The Chan master turned Pure Land teacher Jixing Chewu was particularly fond of the mind-only line of argument. In one passage of his *Recorded Sayings,* he explains:

> There was a Chan [monk] who asked, "All dharmas are like a dream. The Sahā world is definitely a dream; the Pure Land is also a dream. Since they are both equally dreams, then what is the benefit in practicing [Pure Land]?"
>
> I said, "Not so. Prior to the seventh [bodhisattva] ground, one practices within dreams, the great dream of ignorance. [. . .] Before the eyes of the sleeper have opened, pain and pleasure will be vivid. In one's dream, one may receive the extreme suffering of the Sahā world, or one may receive the sublime pleasures of Sukhāvatī. Moreover, to be dreaming of the Sahā world is to go from one dream to another dream, dreams within dreams. One floats and turns about in delusion. But when one dreams of Sukhāvatī, one goes from dreaming to awakening, and from awakening to further awakening until gradually one comes to the great awakening. They are both dreams to be sure, but as dreams their content is very different." (CBETA X.1182.62:336c5–c12)

Thus, Chewu grants the opponent's point that this world and the Pure Land are both dreams but denies that all dreams are alike. If they were, then the buddhas would have no way to awaken slumbering beings!

In another passage, Chewu makes the important observation that mind-only philosophy has never denied the existence of consciousnesses outside of one's own; this would be solipsism. To say that Amitābha is an image in one's mind is not the end of the story; one is equally an image inside the Buddha's mind, and it is this *reciprocal model of mind-only* that makes Pure Land practice effective. Chewu writes:

> The monk Dharmākara uttered his 48 great vows before the Buddha Lokeśvararāja. In accordance with his vows he carried out his great practices for countless great *kalpas* and by the perfection of the causes and the fruition of the results, he became a Buddha. Dharmākara's name changed to Amitābha, and his world changed into the Pure Land. Now the reason that Amitābha can be Amitābha is that he deeply realized his self-nature as mind-only. However, this Amitābha and his Pure Land—are they not self-natured Amitābha [that is, of the nature of the practitioner's own self] and a mind-only Pure Land? This mind-nature is exactly the same in both sentient beings and buddhas; it does not belong more to buddhas and less to beings. (CBETA X.1182.62:336c24–337a5)

This passage is followed immediately by the quotation we saw in chapter 4, in which Chewu asserts that the practitioner who visualizes

Amitābha and the Buddha appear within each other's minds. Thus, sentient beings reciting the Buddha's name are just as much mental phenomena from the Buddha's perspective as *vice versa.* For this reason, even those still caught in the web of dreams may recite his name in their ignorance and get a response. The criticism that Pure Land thought violates the fundamental principle of mind-only falls.

Chan Method Is Unreliable, and Chan Critics of Pure Land Fail to Realize That Their Own Tradition Recognizes Pure Land Practice as a Valid Path

Not content merely to defend Pure Land thought and practice from detractors, the apologists often took the offensive, attacking Chan practice as unreliable and insufficient for liberation, and chastising its partisans for entertaining delusions of their own. The resource most commonly invoked for this purpose was a set of four verses attributed to Yongming Yanshou (*Yǒngmíng Yánshòu,* 永明延壽, 904–975) called the "Four Alternatives" (*sì liào jiǎn* 四料揀):

1. 有禪無淨土。十人九蹉路。陰境若現前。瞥爾隨他去。

   Having Chan but lacking the Pure Land, nine out of ten will stray from the path; when the realm of the aggregates appears before them, they will instantly follow it.

2. 無禪有淨土。萬修萬人去。但得見彌陀。何愁不開悟。

   Lacking Chan but having the Pure Land, ten thousand out of ten thousand who practice it will go [to rebirth]. Having seen Amitābha, why worry that one might not attain enlightenment?

3. 有禪有淨土。猶如戴角虎。現世為人師。來生作佛祖。

   Having both Chan and Pure Land, one is like a tiger with horns [i.e., doubly capable]. Such a person will be a teacher in the present life, and a buddha or patriarch in future lives.

4. 無禪無淨土。鐵床并銅柱。萬劫與千生。沒個人依怙。

   Lacking both Chan and the Pure Land, it will be the iron beds and bronze pillars [of hell] for ten thousand *kalpas* and a thousand lives with no one to turn to.[4]

While many traditional scholars and commentators have concentrated on verse three, extolling the virtue of one who masters both Chan and Pure Land, the apologists emphasized the contrast between verses one and two. The import of these verses, as they never tired of pointing out, was that Chan by itself was unreliable, while Pure Land was 100 percent effective with or without Chan. Another Chan master turned Pure Land advocate, Yiyuan Zongben (*Yīyuán Zōngběn* 一元宗本, sixteenth century), quoted the Chan master who first taught him the Pure Land way as saying, "For monks, [Pure Land] does not interfere with the practice of Chan" (*Guīyuán zhízhǐ jí* 歸元直指集, CBETA X.1156.61:428a17–a18; English from Cleary 1994, p. 124).

The real danger lay in relying *exclusively* on Chan without concurrently doing Pure Land practice. As the verse said, only one in ten could achieve liberation without the power of Amitābha's vows aiding their efforts. *Contra* much Chan rhetoric about sudden enlightenment, the Pure Land apologists stressed the difficulty of attaining an awakening so complete and profound that it sufficed to liberate one from samsara in this life, as well as the poor prospects for being able to continue making progress in future lives. Zongben said,

> People of sharp faculties and superior wisdom are capable of real Chan study and genuine awakening. But if there is the slightest error, [exclusive reliance on Chan] becomes a big mistake. *Question:* How do we know this is a mistake? *Answer:* The mistake comes in not awakening and going on as before revolving in the cycle of birth and death. [. . .] Haven't you heard the saying of the ancient worthy? "To study Chan it is necessary to completely comprehend birth and death, and not two or three in a hundred succeed. If they seek birth in the Pure Land by reciting the Buddha-name, not one in ten thousand fails." (CBETA X.1156.61:430a21–b3; Cleary 1994, p. 138; I have replaced Cleary's "Zen" with "Chan" for consistency)

However, Zongben still advocated the method of Chan-Pure Land dual cultivation called the "Pure Land *kōan*" ("Who is this that practices *nianfo?*" [*Niànfó shì shéi* 念佛是誰?]), and his teachings appear to have been directly aimed at convincing practicing Chan monks to supplement their practice with *nianfo*, not to abandon the former and commit themselves exclusively to the latter. (For example, see CBETA X.1156.61:b18–b19: "The *nianfo kōan* far surpasses any other *kōan*.")

Yuan Hongdao, in many places throughout the *Comprehensive Treatise on the West*, warns that many Chan practitioners believed their progress to be more advanced than it really was, and cautions that enlightenment must be absolutely complete before one is assured of not slipping back into samsara. To give one representative text, in a section called "The Pitfall of Sudden Enlightenment" (*dùnwù duò* 頓悟墮), he quotes Chan master Fenyang Wuye (*Fényáng Wúyè* 汾陽無業, Tang dynasty) as saying:

> These days, those in the world who understand Chan and understand the Way are like the sands of the river. Those who explain the Buddha and explain the mind number in the hundreds, thousands, tens of thousands, myriads of myriads. If one has not eliminated the very last mote of dust [i.e., worldly defilement], then one has not escaped samsara. (T.1976.47:413a21–a23)

The tactical objective here is to raise doubts about the sufficiency of Chan practice alone to liberate one. The language is deliberately alarmist: Even the slightest remaining obscuration will keep one in samsara, and one has no assurance that in the next life, one will have an opportunity to continue practice, or, having the opportunity, one will capitalize on it.

Yinguang goes to greater lengths in specifying how complete and unobstructed one's enlightenment must be if one's Chan practice is to be effective. He goes about this by stating just what the "four alternatives" attributed to Yongming Yanshou mean by *having* Chan:

> To "have Chan" is to practice and penetrate to the limits of your ability, with thoughts serene and passions stilled, and to see thoroughly your original face before your father and mother were born, to see one's own nature with a luminous mind. [. . .] If one practices Chan without reaching enlightenment, or is only partially enlightened, then one cannot call this "having Chan." [. . .] Most people in the world think that practicing Chan is "having Chan," and that practicing *nianfo* is "having the Pure Land." Not only do they not know "Chan" and "the Pure Land," they do not even know the meaning of these phrases. Failing to live up to the kind of compassionate mind of Yongming and the Buddhas of old, they cut off a shortcut out of suffering for later generations of practitioners. Deceiving themselves and others, what extreme damage they cause! As when people say, "to miss the balance-point of a steelyard," if there is even one hair's width of error, then it [might as well be] as far apart as Heaven and Earth. (Yìnguāng 1991, p. 1:366–367; 2012, p. 43–45)

Again, just as it only takes a "hair's width of error" to throw an entire steelyard out of balance, it only takes the smallest latent obscuration to keep one in samsara. Why not indeed practice Pure Land in addition to Chan so that one's next rebirth will be in the ideal *dàochǎng* 道場 of the Land of Bliss?

In addition, Pure Land apologists castigated Chan critics for not knowing their own tradition and literature. Yinguang at one point has his interlocutor say, "All the masters of the Chan School deny the Pure Land. What do you say to that?" (1991, 1:363; 2012, p. 38). Yinguang responds by rejecting this assertion in three ways: First, those apparently derogatory statements that certain Chan masters have made about Pure Land were skillful means set forth for specific listeners and circumstances; they did not utter them as systematic teachings. Second, many passages, while initially critical of Pure Land, then subvert themselves and support it. Third, many Chan masters and Chan texts express unadulterated praise for Pure Land, which leads Yinguang to wonder aloud why his Chan adversary does not know his own tradition better?

As an example of the first method of rebuttal, one of the most famous anti–Pure Land passages in any Chan text is the Sixth Patriarch Huineng's apparent derision found in the *Platform Sutra*. In Yampolsky's translation, it runs:

> The prefect [. . .] asked, "I notice that some monks and laymen always invoke the Buddha Amitābha and desire to be reborn in the West. I beg of you to explain whether one can be born there or not, and thus resolve my doubts."
>
> The Master said: "Prefect, [. . .] at Śrāvastī the World-honored One preached of the Western Land in order to convert people, and it is clearly stated in the sutra 'The Western [Land] is not far.' It was only for the sake of people of inferior capacity that the Buddha spoke of farness; to speak of nearness is only for those of superior attainments. [. . .] The deluded person concentrates on Buddha and wishes to be born in the other land; the awakened person makes pure his own mind. [. . .]
>
> "Prefect, people of the East, just by making the mind pure, are without crime; people of the West, if their minds are not pure, are guilty of a crime. The deluded person wishes to be born in the East or West, [for the enlightened person], any land is just the same. If only the mind has no impurity, the Western Land is not far. If the mind gives rise to impurities, even though you invoke the Buddha and seek to be reborn [in the West], if their minds are not pure, it will be difficult to reach." (Yampolsky 1967, p. 156–157)

Both Yunqi Zhuhong and Yuan Hongdao responded to this by saying that the Sixth Patriarch Huineng was simply ignorant. Zhuhong pointed out that the *Platform Sutra of the Sixth Patriarch* was incorrect in asserting that the Pure Land was only 108,000 buddha-lands to the west, because the *Amitābha Sutra* places it at an inconceivable distance from this world (CBETA X.424.22:633c13). Yuan, following up on this, says,

> The Pure Land is tens of myriads of millions of lands distant, but the *Platform Sutra* says 108,000. He is mistaking India for the Pure Land. [. . .] The Sixth Patriarch never [even] read the *Tripiṭaka*. He just heard someone say "western region" and thought it meant somewhere in India. The teachings very clearly state that the three poisons do not arise in the Pure Land and that one attains the stage of non-retrogression. To say "if those in the West commit a fault ['crime' in Yampolsky], in what land will they seek rebirth?" just proves it. (T.1976.47:410c2–c7)

Yiyuan Zongben and Yinguang were more charitable, explaining that Huineng simply seized the opportunity to open the prefect's mind through a skillful deployment of words. In an essay within his *Guīyuán zhízhǐ jí* 歸元直指集 (Direct pointing back to the source, CBETA X.1156) entitled "Clarifying the Great Master Sixth Patriarch [on] the Western Pure Land" (*Biànmíng liùzǔ dàshī xīfāng jìngtǔ* 辨明六祖大師西方淨土), Zongben says that the Sixth Patriarch "used principle to remove phenomena" (*yǐ lǐ duó shì* 以理奪事), whereas Zongben chose to use phenomena to manifest principle (*yǐ shì xiǎn lǐ* 以事顯理) (CBETA X.1156.61:436b14–b16). Yinguang asserted that to mistake Huineng's intention by taking these words as systematic teachings was, to use a Chan idiom, "mistaking the donkey's saddle-bone for your grandfather's jawbone." He goes on to say that all real Chan masters use such teaching devices as "the opportune moment" and "the turning word" (Yìnguāng 1991, p. 1:363; 2012, p. 38).

Yinguang's second method of refutation is to show that his opponent only knows part of a quotation from a Chan classic, and fails to follow the subsequent text to see how the Chan master continued the thought. In this case, the opponent quotes the eminent Tang dynasty Chan master Zhaozhou Congshen (*Zhàozhōu Cóngshěn* 趙州從諗, 778–897) as saying, "I do not like to hear the word 'Buddha,'" and "If a senior monk recites the name of the Buddha even once, he should rinse his mouth out for three days."[5] Yinguang reminds the monk that Zhaozhou did not stop there. After Zhaozhou said, "I do not like to hear the word 'Buddha,'" the *Zǔtáng jí* 祖堂集 (Patriarch's Hall anthology) has another monk ask, "Master, are you then only human?" Zhaozhou replies, "A buddha, a buddha" (*Zǔtáng jí*, 334b9–10). He also occasionally spoke in favor of Pure Land teachings, as when a monk asks, "If the master [Zhaozhou] were to receive a great king who came to make offerings, how would you respond to him?" Zhaozhou replied, "*Nianfo*" (Yìnguāng 1991, p. 1:363–364; 2012, p. 39; the story is found in *Zǔtáng jí*, 333b6; Zhaozhou goes on to say that he would give the same advice to a boy in the street). In another place the *Zǔtáng jí* reports: "Someone asked, 'Do the buddhas of the ten directions have a teacher or not?' The master said, 'They have.' The monk, surprised, asked, 'Who is the teacher of all the buddhas?' The master replied, 'Amitābha' " (Yìnguāng 1991, p. 1:364; 2012, p. 39–40; the original text is found in *Zǔtáng jí,* 335a4–5).

Yinguang's point is that even though Zhaozhou appeared in some places to belittle Pure Land practice, in others he supported it. It is not legitimate for his opponent to cite only the critical texts while ignoring the favorable ones.

Yinguang cited Chan passages and practices that unambiguously supported Pure Land as his third tactic. One of the most potent is the *Pure Rules* (*Bǎizhàng qīngguī* 百丈清規) traditionally attributed to Baizhang Huaihai (*Bǎizhàng Huáihǎi* 百丈懷海, 749–814), a disciple of Mazu Daoyi (*Mǎzǔ Dàoyī* 馬祖道一, 709–788). These rules set the standard for Chan monastic life. They specified that when a monk was sick, dying, or deceased, the other monks were to gather and chant Amitābha's name, dedicating the merit to the monk's rebirth in Sukhāvatī (Yìnguāng 1991, p. 1:364). (See also Yuan Hongdao at T.1976.47:411c–412a for other prooftexts from the *Pure Rules.* The passage from the *Pure Rules* is from T.2025.48:1147b.)

Finally, in case there remained any doubt as to whose textual citations carried more weight, almost all of the apologists reminded their Chan opponents that Chan teachings are contained only in treatises, biographies, and "Recorded Sayings," while Pure Land teachings come directly from sutras (which were by definition the word of the Buddha Śākyamuni himself) and treatises by highly enlightened Indian bodhisattvas such as Nāgārjuna, Vasubandhu, or Asaṅga. Thus, even if there are Chan texts that unequivocally disparage Pure Land practice, these texts are far less authoritative than scripture, and therefore far less persuasive. (For an example, see Yìnguāng 1991, 1:365; 2012, p. 42.)

Conclusions

The apologists who defended Pure Land practice during the Ming and Qing dynasties and the early Republican period sought to establish several points:

1. Recitation of Amitābha's name with a sincere vow to seek rebirth in the Pure Land ought to be *every* Buddhist's primary practice. If Yongming Yanshou's "Four Alternatives" taught anything, they taught this.

2. Although Pure Land practice was potentially sufficient for liberation all by itself, it did not exclude other practices. Their modest goal was not to supplant all other forms of study and practice, but to make sure everyone supplemented their practices with the infallible insurance policy of Pure Land. As noted in chapter 4, the ideal was a combination of self-power and other-power, and as chapter 5 demonstrated, practitioners were morally obligated to exert themselves to the utmost.
3. Pure Land did not violate any of the standard dogmas of Chinese Buddhism such as mind-only, buddha-nature, non-duality, the Two Truths, the Tiantai Three Contemplations, or the Huayan interpenetration of principle and phenomena.
4. At the same time, individual practitioners did not need to know Buddhist philosophy for *nianfo* to work. While the method in all its inconceivable power was understood only by buddhas and advanced bodhisattvas, ordinary people could still utilize it and gain safe passage to the Land of Utmost Bliss.
5. The masters never advocated abandoning the concept of "mind-only Pure Land" and the exclusive adoption of "western-direction Pure Land." Rather, they sought to hold both these points of view in tension, as one holds Conventional and Ultimate truth in Mādhyamika thought, or transcends both Emptiness and the Provisional to reach the Middle in Tiantai.

Finally, I should point out that the debates are still going on. In 1952, the disciples of the great Chinese Buddhist intellectual Yinshun (*Yìnshùn* 印順, 1906–2005) published a set of lecture notes under the title *A New Treatise on Pure Land* (*Jìngtǔ xīn lùn* 淨土新論) and leveled a new set of criticisms against the practice, going so far as to call the Pure Land a "Marxist Paradise" (Yìnshùn 1992, p. 115–133). The book caused a controversy that contributed to his ouster as the "guiding master" (*dǎoshī* 導師) of the politically important Shandao Temple 善導寺 in Taipei (Jones 1999, p. 115–133; Ritzinger 2017, p. 317–341). The monks and nuns at the Xilian Temple are still busy justifying their devotion to Pure Land Buddhism and exhorting people to follow it in this modern world. The quotation at the head of this chapter from Sheng Yen and the defense of Pure Land that follows it in his 2010 book show that the controversy continues in the twenty-first century. The smooth integration of Pure Land thought and practice with the rest of Chinese Buddhism, particularly Chan, remains a goal yet to be fully realized.

Chapter 7

Methods of *Nianfo* in Chinese Pure Land Buddhism

One fact that every scholar knows about the Pure Land tradition is that its main practice, called *nianfo* (*niànfó* 念佛) in Chinese and *nembutsu* in Japanese, consists of the oral invocation of the Buddha Amitābha's name, in response to which the Buddha will bring the reciter to his western Land of Utmost Bliss at the time of death. One can learn and practice *nianfo* effectively without adding much nuance, variety, or philosophical depth. Over time, however, a steadily accumulating body of specialized research has called the hegemony of this understanding of Pure Land into doubt, particularly in the case of its Chinese manifestations. Several scholars have directed attention to a variety of conceptions of Pure Land practice beyond simple oral *nianfo/nembutsu* (see Payne 2015, Chappell 1996, Corless 1996, and Yü 1981, chap. 3). Our picture of Chinese Pure Land thought and practice is becoming more complex with time, but we have not effectively communicated this complexity to the wider field of Buddhist studies, and it seems our understanding of the core practice of *nianfo* still requires some fine-tuning.

One scholarly work provides a model for our way forward. Many years ago, Ichirō Hori published an article entitled "Nembutsu as Folk Religion," which pointed out, among other things, that within the generally simpler world of Japanese Pure Land Buddhism, people could and did perform *nembutsu* for a variety of reasons, not all of which had to do with gaining rebirth (Hori 1968). As I have spent much time over several years reading through a wide variety of Chinese Pure Land materials, I have also noticed significant variations in the way individual authors, both in and out of the Pure Land tradition, discuss the practice of *nianfo*. While all accept this as the fundamental practice of the "easy path," their expositions of the nature and methods of the practice show that the term, in fact, is quite elastic. In these texts, one finds many different answers to the following questions: (1) In what does the practice of *nianfo* consist? (2) Is there one or are there many ways to *nianfo?* (3) If many, are they random (the "84,000 medicines" model), or do they form a graded path (the *mārga* model)? (4) What results should one expect from one's chosen method(s) of *nianfo,* either in this life or after death? (5) How does (do) the chosen method(s) of *nianfo* work to bring about their results? It is not realistic to expect a full rehearsal of all the answers to all of these questions regarding Chinese Pure Land Buddhism in one brief chapter, so I will limit myself to the relatively simple question of how different practices relate to each other. This breaks down into two subsidiary questions: First, how does *nianfo* relate to other practices within Buddhism? Second, if there is a variety of ways in which to perform *nianfo* itself, how do these methods relate to each other as well as to non-*nianfo* practices?

The purpose of this chapter is not to lay out a table of methods in which any one way of positioning and doing *nianfo* occupies a discrete place within an overall structure. As the reader will see, the material does not lend itself to such neat organization. Rather, I wish to pose the following analysis as a way of querying the material to see relationships with other practices that cut across the spectrum of Chinese Buddhist praxis in a number of directions at once. One may ask a series of questions of the materials at hand; the answer to one question may position the practice of *nianfo* in one way for a particular authority, but in another way when a different question is asked of that same authority. We should not deem such an investigation unsuccessful if it fails to yield a rigorous and consistent taxonomy of practices; it is simply a way to stimulate new curiosity about the variety of *nianfo* methods that have appeared in the history of Chinese Pure Land Buddhism. Such a way of viewing the historical materials will, I hope, enable the reader to ask fruitful questions upon encountering material not covered here.

When *Nianfo* Is One Practice among Many

Early Buddhist teachers based their understanding of *nianfo* on the *Pratyutpanna-samādhi-sūtra* (*Bānzhōu sānmèi jīng* 般舟三昧經, T.416, 417, 418, and 419) rather than the "Three Pure Land Sutras" (*jìngtǔ sānbù* 淨土三部), so they situated the practice of *nianfo* among many other practices. Lushan Huiyuan is a case in point. If we look into the *Jiūmóluóshí fǎshī dàyì* (鳩摩羅什法師大義, T.1856), a compilation of correspondence between Huiyuan and Kumārajīva, we find that Huiyuan, having read the *Pratyutpanna-samādhi-sūtra,* asks Kumārajīva to explain its teaching that a buddha seen in dreams can teach things the practitioner did not already know. Since Huiyuan regarded a visualized buddha as an image manufactured by the practitioner's own mind, he did not see how this is possible. The specifics of the question and answer will be the subject of the next chapter. Here we need only observe that Huiyuan (1) bases his practice on a scripture outside of the usual "Three Pure Land Sutras," (2) he intended the practice to lead only to the *nianfo* samadhi and a vision of the Buddha Amitābha in the present life rather than rebirth in Sukhāvatī after death, and (3) part of the purpose of this visualization-leading-to-vision is to have the Buddha bestow teachings on the practitioner. In addition, this is only one of a number of concerns Huiyuan raised with Kumārajīva. Like the sutra itself, his range of learning and practice included many other elements in addition to those centering on Amitābha. All of these factors present a significant contrast to future traditional methods of *nianfo.* Later Chinese Pure Land thinkers tended to ignore or gloss over this aspect of his teaching even as they elevated him to the status of first "patriarch" (*zǔ* 祖) of the Pure Land tradition.

Tiantai founder Zhiyi (*Tiāntái Zhìyǐ* 天台智顗, 538–597) taught *nianfo* in the context of his "constantly walking samadhi" (*chángxíng sānmèi* 常行三昧), discussed in his *Móhē zhǐguān* 摩訶止觀 (Great calming and contemplation, T.1911.46:12a19–13a23). Like Lushan Huiyuan, he based this practice on the *Pratyutpanna-samādhi-sūtra* (T.1911.46:12a20–a21). As described by Daniel Stevenson, this practice was a complicated and difficult one, attempted only by clergy who had already demonstrated great tenacity, devotion, and adherence to the disciplinary and procedural precepts of the monastic order. In this case, the term *niàn* 念 denotes both visualization and oral invocation, as Zhiyi directs the meditator to construct a highly detailed eidetic image of the Buddha Amitābha (and *only* Amitābha; see T.1911.46:12b19–b24) while slowly and sonorously reciting the name. At the same time, the meditator is to realize the empty nature of the visualized Buddha as a manifestation of his or her own mind (see T.1911.46:c12–c14, where Zhiyi cites an episode from the *Pratyutpanna-samādhi-sūtra* found at T.418.13:905b27–c3; trans. Harrison 1998, p. 20). Thus, the purpose of *nianfo* here is not only to gain a vision of the buddha(s), but also to realize wisdom. Finally, we should note that the "constantly walking samadhi" is only one of four different modes of practice contained in the *Great Calming and Contemplation.* Some of these others encompass further subtypes, creating a broad palette of possible practices.

Thus, both Huiyuan and Zhiyi saw *nianfo* as a very challenging practice derived from the *Pratyutpanna-samādhi-sūtra,* not as the stripped-down *nianfo* practice of other teachers. In addition, they saw it as only one mode of practice among many. In this way, they taught a method of *nianfo* integrated with other Buddhist methods of cultivation not as an "easy path" or a single, self-sufficient practice.

In these two examples, the practice of *nianfo* serves as one practice with one goal among other practices and goals. There is another way of presenting the practice, however, and that is to see *nianfo* as one practice among others that share the common goal of achieving rebirth in Sukhāvatī. This is the approach that the Yuan dynasty monk Tianru Weize (*Tiānrú Wéizé* 天如惟則, 1286?–1354) formalized in his *Jìngtǔ huòwèn* 淨土或問 (Questions about Pure Land, T.1972). In response to a question about the "Pure Land method" (*jìngtǔ xiūfǎ* 淨土修法), Tianru says that there are three main approaches: visualization (*guānxiǎng* 觀想), recollection and invocation (*yìniàn* 意念), and "various practices" (*zhòngxíng* 眾行; see T.1972.47:295a24–a27). Under the third heading, Tianru calls attention to passages from several sutras in which a buddha or celestial bodhisattva describes a practice other than *nianfo* and declares that the merit of the practice leads to rebirth in the Pure Land (or in buddha-lands generally). He also calls attention to some practices of virtue that the *Contemplation Sutra* says constitute causes of rebirth, such as filial piety, taking the Three Refuges, and so on. Finally, he notes that any Buddhist method of cultivation can serve as a cause of rebirth if one so dedicates its merit (T.1972.47:296b29–297a2; see also Sutra Translation Committee of the United States and Canada 1991, p. 55–66). This way of organizing practices, not unique to Tianru, makes *nianfo* one among many practices that lead to rebirth in the western Pure Land.

When *Nianfo* Is the Only Practice, but Takes Many Forms

Another approach was to recommend *nianfo* as the only practice, but to present this single practice as itself multiform. In other words, some masters promoted a sole focus on *nianfo,* but analyzed the practice into several varieties. This approach further branched in two directions. (1) Some described the varieties of *nianfo* simply as different modes of practice suited to the needs and capacities of different practitioners, an approach that resonates with traditional Buddhist presentations of methods of cultivations as "medicines" directed toward the treatment of distinct "ailments." (2) Alternatively, one might arrange various types of *nianfo* into a graded path, in which case a practitioner would begin with the simplest form and progress through the more advanced levels.

Nianfo as Medicine Cabinet

As an example of the "medicine cabinet" approach, I have chosen the eminent modern Buddhist figure Yinguang (*Yìnguāng* 印光, 1861–1940). Revered since his death as the thirteenth "patriarch" of the Pure Land tradition, Yinguang dedicated his entire monastic career to defending and advancing Pure Land practice. Hundreds of devotees were deeply affected by personal interviews at his cell at the Lingyan Shan Temple (*Língyán shān sì* 靈巖山寺) in Suzhou, and thousands of others were (and are) moved and inspired by his writings, collected and published as the *Complete Works of the Great Master Yinguang* (*Yìnguāng dàshī quánjí* 印光大師全集). Within this collection, one finds a few systematic expositions of Pure Land thought and practice, but his writing appears to have been driven by practical rather than theoretical concerns. One sees him engaging in apologetics or pastoral work in his writings (the former in his treatises, the latter in letters to his disciples). Thus, it would seem that he never set out Pure Land practice as a graded path, but recommended practices for individuals to suit their needs and capacities.

To give an example, among the memorial essays written after Yinguang's death, we find one entitled "The Great Master Taught Me the Method of *Nianfo*" (*Dàshī jiào wǒ niànfó fāngfǎ* 大師教我念佛方法), in which a disciple named Cizhou (*Cízhōu* 慈舟) describes a particular method that Yinguang recommended to him. The master told him to recite the name of Amitābha ten times mentally, but without actually counting from one to ten. In other words, Cizhou was simply to be aware of his oral recitation and, without counting or using a rosary, know when he had reached ten repetitions. This method served not only to gain Cizhou rebirth in Sukhāvatī, but increased his concentration in the process (Yìnguāng 1991, p. 7:471–472).

In a letter to another disciple, Yinguang defined *nianfo* as both recitation and visualization, and stressed the need for constancy in practice. One's *nianfo,* he said, had to involve faith in Amitābha's primal vows, one's own vows to be reborn in Sukhāvatī, and an intention to return the merit of one's practice to all living beings. He described the practice in quasi-esoteric terms as consisting of acts of body, speech, and mind, and gave advice to this disciple on factors of practice that would affect the quality of the samadhi he would attain. Thus, Yinguang considered *nianfo* a serious practice that, as with the other discipline mentioned above, would produce benefits even prior to gaining rebirth. At the end of the letter, he denies that mere oral invocation will produce any benefit in this life or after death if one lacks sincere and constant aspiration for rebirth and does not put forth genuine effort (Yìnguāng 1991, p. 1:39–43). Done within this framework, however, *nianfo* can produce marvelous results; Yinguang even credited the practice with curing him of conjunctivitis (Shì Jiànzhèng 釋見正 1989, p. 20), and he recommended *nianfo* to others to cure illnesses; as seen in his letter to "a certain layman" (Yìnguāng 1991, p. 1:327–328).

One could spend a great deal of time gathering the scattered fragments of Yinguang's teachings and recommendations to try to impose some order on to them. The point here is that Yinguang himself did not do so, and it appears that, while he had some basic ideas about *nianfo* that held in all cases (such as the need for aspiration and constancy of practice), he also did not hesitate to vary the practice for different people (as seen in the variety of recommendations that appear in his letters), and to vary it for different purposes (e.g., achieving rebirth, attaining samadhi, or curing illness). The fact that Yinguang never tried to systematize the practice, or put his various methods into any kind of order, demonstrates that, for him, it was like medicine to be administered for specific purposes, and not a graded path where one moved from easier to more difficult practices. This contrasts with the progressive systems to which we now turn.

Nianfo as Graded Path

Guifeng Zongmi's Fourfold Typology

As my first example of the "graded path" approach, I have chosen a fourfold schema described by Guifeng Zongmi (*Guīfēng Zōngmì* 圭峰宗密, 780–841), even though I am aware that this choice raises difficulties. As a Huayan patriarch and Chan master, it may seem more logical to include him in the section above, among the teachers who saw *nianfo* as one practice among many. According to Mochizuki Shinkō's *Chūgoku jōdokyōri shi*, in the fourth fascicle of his *Huáyán jīng Pǔxián xíngyuàn pǐn shū chǎo* 華嚴經普賢行願品疏鈔 (Subcommentary on [Chengguan's] commentary on the "Chapter of Samantabhadra's practice of his vows," XZJ 7:773ff.),[1] Zongmi defined four types of *nianfo,* each with its own scriptural support. While I would not place Zongmi within the Chinese Pure Land tradition, his fourfold typology exerted some influence on later Pure Land figures such as Yunqi Zhuhong.

1. The first type of *nianfo* is "contemplation of the name" (*chēngmíng niàn* 稱名念), based on a passage relating to the "single-practice samadhi" (*yīxíng sānmèi* 一行三昧) found in the *Wénshūshīlì suǒshuō móhēbōrě bōluómì jīng* 文殊師利所說摩訶般若波羅蜜經 (The Perfection of Wisdom Sutra preached by Mañjuśrī, T.232). This sutra recommends selecting a particular buddha (not necessarily Amitābha), facing that buddha's direction, and focusing upon his name (*zhuān chēng míngzì* 專稱名字) until one achieves a vision of all buddhas of the past, present, and future (T.232.8:731b1–b5). This, of course, is reminiscent of the practice outlined in the *Pratyutpanna-samādhi-sūtra,* except that it does not involve visualization, only oral recitation of the name. Zongmi presented this method as sufficient to gain the vision of the buddhas (CBETA X.229.5:280c9–c16).

I must note that, although later thinkers within the Chinese Pure Land tradition took the term *chēngmíng* 稱名 to refer to oral invocation, it is not at all clear that this is what either Zongmi or the sutra meant by the term. In this context, it appears to be a meditative practice in which the disciple fastens his or her mind on a buddha (*xìxīn yī fó* 繫心一佛) and then holds his name as a sound image (as opposed to a visual image) while seated properly and facing that buddha's direction. Chen Chienhuang points out that the term *chēngmíng* in early Chinese sutra translations as well as those by Chinese authors such as Tanluan often corresponds to words in Sanskrit texts that indicated a process of holding a meditative object firmly in mind without distraction. In this usage, it was synonymous with the word *chí* 持, meaning to "hold" something in one's mind. In fact, in different translations of the same sutra, *chēng* and *chí* may appear in the equivalent position (Chen Chienhuang 2009, p. 46, 148–155). Later the term comes more and more to mean only oral invocation of the name, and so future authors will use Zongmi's scheme but impute a different meaning to this particular term.

2. "Contemplating an image" (*guānxiàng niàn* 觀像念) involves contemplating a physical image or picture of a buddha. Zongmi took this from the *Dà bǎojī jīng* 大寶積經 (Great Jewel Collection Sutra, T.310), which says that in contemplating an image of a buddha, one realizes the non-duality of the image with the buddha. In this way, one achieves the five powers (*wǔ tōng* 五通) and the samadhi of universal light (*pǔguāng*

sānmèi 普光三昧; the relevant passage is T.310.11:513b28–c27; see Zongmi's text at CBETA X.229.5:280c16–c20).

3. "Contemplating the visualization" (*guānxiǎng niàn* 觀想念) means to contemplate the major and minor marks of a buddha's body without the aid of a physical image. One may select one feature upon which to focus or contemplate them all simultaneously. The first option is based on the *Fó shuō guānfó sānmèihǎi jīng* 佛說觀佛三昧海經 (Sutra on the samadhi-ocean of the contemplation of the Buddha, T.643), which speaks of gazing at the tuft of white hair between the buddha's eyes (see T.643.15:648a7–a8 on the white tuft specifically and 15:687b14–b18 on the benefit of picking one feature to contemplate). The second comes from the *Zuòchán sānmèi jīng* 坐禪三昧經 (Sutra on the samadhi of seated meditation, T.614), which recommends constant contemplation of the buddha's body as a means of "entering the buddha-way." If one can do this, and not set one's mind on "earth, wind, fire, water, or any dharma," then one will gain a vision of all the buddhas of the ten directions and the three times, and will eliminate countless *kalpas* of karmic guilt (see CBETA X.229.5:280c20–a7).[2]

4. "Contemplating the true mark" (*shíxiàng niàn* 實相念) is a method for advanced practitioners with an enlightened vision of the world. In this, one contemplates the buddha's dharma body, which is also the contemplation of one's own true self and the true nature of all phenomena. This is also based on *The Perfection of Wisdom Sutra Preached by Mañjuśrī*, which describes the true nature of the buddha as "unproduced and unextinguished, neither going nor coming, without name and without feature. That alone is called 'buddha'" (CBETA X.229.5:281a19). The scripture also calls this the "single-practice samadhi," and Zongmi cites other perfection of wisdom literature, such as the *Da zhidu lun* in support of this view of the buddha (CBETA X.229.5:281a7–a15).

Mochizuki Shinkō says that Zongmi presented these four methods of *nianfo* as a graded path going from easiest/shallowest to most difficult/most profound (Mochizuki 1942, p. 311). For our purposes, we can observe several relevant features of his program. First, his outline rests on different scriptural bases than traditional Pure Land practice. Second, it is aimed at gaining a vision of one buddha or all buddhas in this life and on attainment of wisdom and enlightenment (as opposed to rebirth in the Pure Land after death). Third, and perhaps most problematically, he does not use the term *nianfo* to describe these practices, but only the single word *nian*. This calls into question the identification of Zongmi as a Pure Land figure, and indeed, he is not treated as such in the literature of the tradition. Whatever his own intentions may have been, however, later Pure Land teachers in need of a graded curriculum of practice adopted his typology. For example, I first ran across it in an essay entitled "Four Types of *Nianfo*" (*Sì zhǒng niànfó* 四種念佛) by the contemporary Taiwan-based Pure Land master Zhiyu (*Zhìyù* 智諭, 1924–2000), in which he offers it as a set of techniques for his own disciples to use (Shì Zhìyù 1986, p. 71–80). The eighth patriarch Zhuhong also used it, as we will now see.

Yunqi Zhuhong's Deepening Realization

We find a second example of a master who saw Pure Land and *nianfo* as an ascending path of practice in the Ming dynasty monk-reformer Yunqi Zhuhong (*Yúnqī Zhūhóng* 雲棲袾宏, 1535–1615). One may find an extended statement of his vision of Pure Land practice in the first fascicle of his *Āmítuó jīng shūchǎo* 阿彌陀經疏鈔 (Commentary and notes on the Amitābha Sūtra, CBETA X.424)

At the outset, Zhuhong states that the purpose of *nianfo* (which he also calls *chēngmíng* 稱名 and *chímíng* 持名) is to achieve the "single, unperturbed mind" (*yīxīn búluàn* 一心不亂) or the *nianfo* samadhi (*niànfó sānmèi* 念佛三昧), both of which he equates with single-practice samadhi (*yīxíng sānmèi* 一行三昧; see CBETA X.424.22:614c9). He then makes a strong statement about the nature of the Buddha Amitābha and his Pure Land, and the way in which *nianfo* works. Building on the teachings of the second chapter of the *Vimalakīrti Sutra,* he states,

> Now to contemplate (*niàn* 念) emptiness is true *nian,* and production enters into non-production [or, birth enters into non-birth], and to *nian* the Buddha (*nianfo*) is to *nian* the mind. Birth there (i.e., in the Pure Land) does not mean leaving birth here (the present defiled world). Mind, Buddha, and sentient beings are of one substance, the middle stream does not abide on [either of] the two banks. Therefore, we say "the Amitābha of one's own nature; the Pure Land of mind-only." (CBETA X.424.606b8–b10)

Based on this, one might think that Zhuhong is espousing "mind-only Pure Land" (*wéixīn jìngtǔ* 唯心淨土), and that he was putting forward a path of practice aimed at an elite audience of religious virtuosi. However, he also included oral invocation under the rubric *nianfo,* making way for an easier form of practice. This apparent contradiction resolves itself somewhat when he brings in the vocabulary of principle (*lǐ* 理) and phenomena (*shì* 事) a bit further on. In a subsequent section entitled "Broadly Demonstrating What *Chiming* Covers" (*Guǎng xiǎn chímíng suǒ bèi*

廣顯持名所被), he says that the "one mind" divides into two types, the "one mind of principle" (*lǐ zhi yīxīn* 理之一心) and the "one mind of phenomena" (*shì yīxīn* 事一心). Here he clarifies that he used the vocabulary of mind-only Pure Land to point to the "one mind of principle," and that it represents only one side of a dyad that one must fuse with the other in order to achieve the highest wisdom.

> This, then, is the one mind of principle (*lǐ zhi yīxīn* 理之一心), which reverts entirely to superior wisdom while also connecting with phenomenal characteristics. It bends to those of dull roots. [. . .] Thus, this one mind does not specifically emphasize principle, but also connects with phenomena. By means of the phenomenal one mind (*shì yīxīn* 事一心) all people can practice. It does not mitigate the foolishness of [ordinary] men and women, yet it connects them with knowledge and ability as heaven overspreads all and the earth supports everything. (CBETA X.424.606c1–c7)

In fact, he does not approve of those who one-sidedly claim that Amitābha is *only* a manifestation of one's own nature, or that the Pure Land is *only* this world as seen by a purified consciousness. At the level of the "one mind of phenomena," Amitābha and his Pure Land are separate and distinct from the practitioner and exist countless buddha-lands off to the west. Only a truly enlightened being can see both of these truths at once.

The ordinary practitioner of the Pure Land path, alas, is stuck at a lower level of realization, and here Zhuhong makes a crucial recommendation. Since unenlightened beings can only hold one end of the principle/phenomena dyad at a time, it is actually better to lean toward phenomena than toward principle. He decries those who, based on "crazy wisdom" (*kuánghuì* 狂慧) assert a bland monism that collapses all distinctions and undermines religious practice and achievement. Better, he says, to be an ignorant peasant ardently reciting the Buddha's name in hopes of rebirth in the Pure Land than an educated monk with a little realization who thinks that he has already run the race and attained the vision of non-duality. At least the foolish practitioner will recite the name continuously and keep the precepts. They will achieve rebirth in the Pure Land and attain a purified body (*jìngshēn* 淨身; CBETA X.424.22:607a1–a13).

In a later passage, Zhuhong lists ten advantages of the Pure Land path. While the first nine are general and serve a hortatory function, the tenth contains concrete instructions for practice, which Zhuhong relates directly to the teachings of the *Amitābha Sutra*. After praising the superiority of *nianfo* over all other practices, Zhuhong states that there are many "gates" to *nianfo* itself (CBETA X.424.22:612a15–b21). When he lists the four types, one finds that he uses Guifeng Zongmi's typology as given above, but in reverse order, and with the caveat that ordinary practitioners will find Zongmi's numbers two through four too difficult and uncertain. His final recommendation is that everyone begin with the easiest practice, that of *chiming* or "holding the name," as it is the simplest and the quickest. One cannot expect to "begin to contemplate the true mark and grasp the true mark" (CBETA X.424.22:612b7). Just as *nianfo* is the "shortcut among shortcuts" (*jìng zhōng zhi jìng* 徑中之徑), so *chiming nianfo* is the "further shortcut among shortcuts" (*jìng ér yòu jìng* 徑而又徑; CBETA X.424.22:612a15–a18, 612b20–b21) with respect to the varieties of *nianfo*. This is why both the *Larger Sutra* and the *Amitābha Sutra* take the teaching of "holding the Buddha's name" (*chí fó mínghào* 持佛名號) as their main import.

Chün-fang Yü discovered other recommendations in the third fascicle of this text. For instance, depending upon the situation, "holding the name" could indicate audible recitation of the name (*míngchí* 明持), silent contemplation of the name (*mòchí* 默持), or contemplation accompanied by barely audible whispering of the name (*bànmíng bànmò chí* 半明半默持; Yü 1981, p. 59; see CBETA X.424.22:659c10–c12). She also notes that, further on in the commentary, Zhuhong details two specific ways of performing *nianfo*, or, more accurately, two different states of mind within which one performs the practice. One leads to the attainment of the "one mind of phenomena," and the other leads to the "one mind of principle." The first, called "phenomenal holding of the name" (*shì chí* 事持), consists of mental/oral invocation of the name while one remains concentrated on its individual syllables. This creates the "one mind of phenomena," which means a mind calm, focused, and free of defilements. It creates concentration, not wisdom, and so corresponds to the "calming" (*zhǐ* 止) phase of the two-part "calming and contemplation" (*zhǐguān* 止觀) meditation. The second, called "noumenal holding of the name" (*lǐ chí* 理持), moves the focus from the name to the mind that holds it, realizing the non-duality of practitioner and Buddha. This leads to the attainment of wisdom in the "one mind of principle" that Zhuhong had earlier identified with the higher attainment (Yü 1981, p. 59–60; see CBETA X.424.22:659c14–c16). However, as we saw earlier, this was a dangerous practice. It entailed the risk of becoming fixated on principle and non-duality to the denigration of phenomenal reality.

The foregoing represents nothing more than a very brief summary of a long and intricate argument in favor of Pure Land practice. However, we can note at least this much with regard to Zhuhong's thought: First, while he recognized a variety of methods of *nianfo* derived mainly from Zongmi's typology, he turned Zongmi's list backwards and asserted the superiority of the most basic form of practice, that of "holding the name." Second, he nevertheless maintained a graded hierarchy of practice, even if he was less optimistic than Zongmi about the possibility that beings could progress past the first of the four stages in this life. Third, he built upon this multiplicity of methods subsumed under the term *nianfo* and turned it into a complete system of practice that could potentially allow any practitioner to accomplish any Buddhist objective, from rebirth in the Pure Land to the completion of the Six Perfections to the realization of the highest wisdom. Finally, he recognized several levels of attainment that accrue from completion of the various stages: from rebirth in the Pure Land as a result of "holding the name" to the attainment of samadhi and the realization of the perfect interpenetration of principle and phenomena with the arising of the "single, unperturbed mind."

When *Nianfo* Is a Single Practice: Jixing Chewu

Not all Pure Land masters viewed *nianfo* as a graded path, and among these, we can take as an example another figure from the list of Pure Land "patriarchs," the former Chan master Jixing Chewu (*Jìxǐng Chèwù* 際醒徹悟, 1741–1810). He had abandoned the practice of Chan somewhere in mid-life, perhaps due to illness or some other circumstance that led him to question the real benefit of Chan enlightenment. While he practiced "dual cultivation" for a while, he came in the end to abandon Chan and advocate only the practice of *nianfo*. Chewu's literary remains are rather sparse, and so it is difficult to know whether we have access to the entire range of his thought, but within his *Chèwù chánshī yǔlù* 徹悟禪師語錄 (Recorded sayings of Chan Master Chewu, CBETA X.1182), we find only a single idea about how one ought to practice *nianfo*.

Chewu advised that one not begin practice until one had fulfilled several prerequisites. The practitioner needed to have first generated *bodhicitta,* the altruistic resolve to attain enlightenment for the sake of all sentient beings. He or she also needed to generate faith in the Pure Land path and a genuine aspiration to achieve rebirth in Sukhāvatī. In addition, one needed four other "minds": a sense of shame at past wrongdoing, joy at having learned of the Pure Land path, sorrow at the weight of one's karmic obstructions, and gratitude to the Buddha for having taught this path (CBETA X.1182.62:342c11–c14). Elsewhere, he laid out these eight factors of practice:

> First, in the face of samsara, one must truly generate *bodhicitta;* this is the highway leading into study of the Way. Second, one takes deep faith, vows, and holding the Buddha's name (*chí fó mínghào* 持佛名號) as the proper core of Pure Land. Third, focused and concentrated invocation (*niàn* 念) is the skillful means for beginning practice. Fourth, the quelling of present defilements is the main outcome of mind-cultivation. Fifth, by resolutely observing the four grave prohibitions, one enters into the very source of the Way. Sixth, by means of various austerities, one cultivates the auxiliary conditions (*zhùyuán* 助緣) of the Way. Seventh, one takes the single, unperturbed mind as the principle aim of Pure Land cultivation. Eighth, one takes the various kinds of auspicious omens (*língruì* 靈瑞) as proof of the attainment of rebirth. (CBETA X.1182.62:339b13–b18)

Like Zhuhong, Chewu used the term *chímíng* 持名 to indicate both audible recitation and silent internal contemplation of the Buddha's name. Chewu specifically recommended keeping Amitābha's name in one's mind at all times to purify it. Whereas Zhuhong used the image of a lion emerging from its den, whose roar silences all the other beasts, to indicate the power of the name held in the mind to clear other thoughts (CBETA X.424.22:606a18–a20), Chewu compared the name to a *maṇi* gem, which, when dropped into turbid water, clarifies it instantly. It is also important to note that Chewu only made use of the name and eschewed visualization of the Buddha's form. Indeed, for him the two were equivalent. He argued that the Buddha would not even merit the name "buddha" if he were not already fully endowed with all the virtues, merits, and bodily adornments of a buddha. Thus, the name could serve as a placeholder for the full image, rendering complex and difficult visualization exercises unnecessary (CBETA X.1182.62:337c11, 340b1). While he seemed indifferent as to whether one's *nianfo* were audible or silent, he was quite clear that to *nianfo* meant to "hold the name" and nothing else.

Even though he reduced Zongmi's and Zhuhong's typology of *nianfo* from a four-stage graded path to this single practice, he still held that this one practice brought both this-worldly and postmortem benefits. That the practice led to rebirth in the Pure Land after death seemed obvious, but he also echoed Zhuhong's assertions that the very process of performing *nianfo* led to a purification of the mind and the attainment of wisdom. However, Zhuhong had separated "holding the name" into phenomenal and noumenal aspects, one leading to purification and the other leading to wisdom. Chewu, in contrast, said that one could gain both results from this one practice, and did not require his students to contemplate their own state of mind and its non-duality with the Buddha. Instead, he asserted that the non-duality was simply given, and that the very practice of *nianfo* caused the practitioner's innate buddha-wisdom to manifest spontaneously, without the student necessarily realizing that such a thing was happening.

This was because Chewu gave Amitābha a more active role in the process. Zhuhong seemed to think that realization of non-duality and manifestation of buddha-wisdom was the practitioner's responsibility. Chewu stated that, because in *nianfo* both the Buddha and the practitioner hold each other in a mutual gaze, the Buddha's wisdom automatically became part of the practitioner's purified mind, even if the practitioner was unaware of this happening:

> Now if at this present moment, my mind is focused on Amitābha, the western region, and on seeking rebirth in the Pure Land of Utmost Bliss, then at this very moment the proper and dependent [recompense] of the western region are within my mind, and my mind is within the proper and dependent [recompense] of the western region. They are like two mirrors exchanging light and mutually illuminating each other. This is the mark of horizontally pervading the ten directions. If it firmly exhausts the three margins of time, then the very moment of contemplating the Buddha is the very moment of seeing the Buddha and becoming the Buddha. The very moment of seeking rebirth is the very moment of attaining rebirth and the very moment of liberating all beings. The three margins of time are all a single, identical time; there is no before and after. [. . .] Awakening to this principle is most difficult; having faith in it is most easy. (CBETA X.1182.62:334b15–334b21)

Thus, in Chewu we have an example of a master who saw *nianfo* as a single practice, not a graded path or even a heterogeneous variety of practices, but a practice that nevertheless could fulfill all of the possible goals of Buddhist cultivation.

When *Nianfo* Is Subordinated to Other Practices

One should not consider all those who recommended a Pure Land practice to their followers to be "Pure Land masters." Others, particularly in the Chan School, sometimes taught some form of Pure Land practice as a subsidiary method within the way their own school understood its mechanics. I am making this a different category than those who teach Pure Land and *nianfo* as one path among many, because in this instance one sometimes finds Pure Land denigrated as a last resort or redefined so as to eliminate it as competition, not as one viable practice among others. Two examples of this kind of teaching will suffice.

Hanshan Deqing

The late Ming dynasty Buddhist reformer Hanshan Deqing (*Hānshān Déqīng* 憨山德清, 1546–1623) was very clear in his own mind that Chan meditation was much better than Pure Land practice, and he never hesitated to say so, even when speaking to gatherings of Pure Land devotees. Nevertheless, he did not dismiss the practice outright; instead, he assigned it a place within a progressive practice that culminated in Chan. His various talks and writings have been anthologized in the collection known as *Hānshān lǎorén mèngyóu jí* 憨山老人夢遊集 (A record of Elder Hanshan's dream travels, CBETA X.1456), from which the following is derived.

Deqing begins his essay entitled "Instructing Laymen to Form a *Nianfo* Society" (*Shì yōupósāi jié niànfó shè* 示優婆塞結念佛社) by extolling the rich variety of Buddhist practices, comparing it to the rain that falls on all plants alike without changing its nature while plants as different as grass and trees absorb only what they are able. He then relates the story of ten or more laymen who came to him once to receive the five lay precepts and some instruction in practice. He saw that they were sincere but unenlightened and incapable of much realization, at least in the near future. Thus, out of compassion, he instructed them in the Pure Land path, and directed them to perform oral invocation (*chēngmíng* 稱名) and repentance three times daily, and to meet together once a month. They were to generate a genuine aspiration for rebirth in Sukhāvatī. Deqing indicates that this is a low-level practice for beginners, but is a valid practice nonetheless. Since it will make their faith more steady and purify their minds, how could it be false? Nevertheless, he still expected them to outgrow the practice as soon as possible and move on to more productive methods of cultivation (CBETA X.1456.73:473c19–474b2).

In another talk entitled "Instructions in the Essentials of *Nianfo*" (*Shì niànfó qièyào* 示念佛切要, CBETA X.1456.73:505c16–506b1), Deqing gives a more theoretical treatment of the practice of *nianfo* in which the reasons for his low estimation of the practice become apparent. The problem for him lies not in *nianfo* itself, but in the fact that people use it as a stand-alone practice without contextualizing it in the larger picture of Buddhist thought. Precisely because people believe that the practice of *nianfo,* however conceived, works automatically without any understanding or other effort on their part, they gain nothing beyond what this bare practice delivers. They must always remember, he says, that the "great matter" is to "penetrate samsara" and liberate themselves from it. When practitioners fail even to acknowledge that they have this task, then *nianfo* in hopes of gaining rebirth in Sukhāvatī becomes just another form of clinging that obstructs progress. Here is how he puts the matter:

> The practice of *nianfo* seeking rebirth in the Pure Land aimed originally at penetrating the great matter of samsara. That is why it was phrased, "*nianfo* and penetrate samsara" (*niànfó liǎo shēngsǐ* 念佛了生死). People of today generate the mind to penetrate samsara, but they are only willing to *nianfo.* [They think that by] merely saying "buddha," they will penetrate samsara. If one does not know the roots of samsara, then in what direction can you *nian?* If the mind that engages in *nianfo* cannot cut off the roots of samsara, then how can it penetrate samsara? (CBETA X.1456.73:505c17–c20)

In other words, the phrase "*nianfo* and penetrate samsara" has been misconstrued at a basic, grammatical level. Whereas the original meaning was something like "perform *nianfo* and then go on to penetrate samsara," contemporary practitioners have interpreted the phrase to mean "perform *nianfo* by saying the word 'buddha' and you will penetrate samsara." This grammatical misreading, as well as the misunderstanding that *nianfo* entails nothing more than oral recitation of the buddha's name, have led to a serious distortion of the practice and the results one may reasonably expect from it.

Xuyun

The modern Chan master Xuyun (*Xūyún* 虛雲, 1840?–1959) was once proposed as a candidate for the title of thirteenth patriarch of Pure Land, an honor that went instead to Yinguang. When one looks through the thoughts and speeches recorded in his "Chronological Biography" (*niánpǔ* 年譜), one can indeed find approving and instructive speeches about the Pure Land dharma-gate. However, I wish to argue that, like Deqing, Xuyun was not among those presenting Pure Land as one valid path among many, because, like many Chan masters, he took a strict position of "mind-only Pure Land" (*wéixīn jìngtǔ* 唯心淨土). He subsumed it under a Chan framework and assumed that it aimed toward Chan-defined goals.

For example, in December 1952, he gave a dharma-talk before followers of Yinguang on the occasion of the latter's twelfth death-anniversary. In this speech, he charged those who chose the Pure Land path to keep to their original vow, firm in their faith. The worst mistake that one can make in Buddhist practice, he said, is to jump from one method to another indiscriminately. Therefore, he praised Yinguang's unremitting devotion to the practice of reciting Amitābha's name and commended it to those assembled. However, when he compared Pure Land and Chan, he found no difference in the results to which both methods lead. In this extract, it becomes clear that Xuyun saw *nianfo* and Chan "capping phrase" (*huàtóu* 話頭) practice as equivalent:

> Chan and Pure Land seem to be two different methods as seen by beginners, but are really one to experienced practitioners. The *hua-tou* [*sic*] technique in Chan meditation, which puts an end to the stream of birth and death, also requires a firm believing mind to be effective. If the *hua-tou* is not firmly held, Chan practice will fail. If the believing mind is strong and if the *hua-tou* is firmly held, the practitioner will be mindless of even eating and drinking and his training will take effect; when sense-organs disengage from sense data, his attainment will be similar to that achieved by a reciter of the Buddha's name when his training becomes effective and when the Pure Land manifests in front of him. In this state, noumenon and phenomenon intermingle, Mind and Buddha are not a duality and both are in the state of suchness, which is absolute and free from all contraries and relativities. Then what difference is there between Chan and Pure Land? (Xuyun 1988, p. 153–154)

That final rhetorical question gets its obvious answer (i.e., there is no difference) from the fact that Xuyun describes *nianfo* as just another kind of "capping phrase" practice. Nowhere does he indicate that reciting the Buddha's name could have any effect other than to produce a Chan-style enlightenment experience—no rebirth in the Pure Land even for the simplest practitioners, none of Chewu's ebullient confidence that *nianfo* puts one's mind into resonance with Amitābha's and thus guarantees rebirth, only a phrase to which one holds on with firm faith until it detaches one from the "dusts of this world" and leads one to realize the non-duality of principle and phenomena. For Xuyun, one penetrates the word "Amitābha" just as one penetrates Zhaozhou's "wu" (*wú* 無).

These two Chan figures represent what some (Yinguang included) have considered the illegitimate colonizing of Pure Land by those of other schools. This kind of praise for the Pure Land path is, for them, the more pernicious because it appears positive on the surface, but when one looks into the substance behind the praise, one finds Pure Land practice redefined in such a way as to render it indistinguishable from the methods and goals of the Chan School. Once this happens, then much that is special and distinctive about Pure Land disappears, having been absorbed into the framework of its rival. This represents, then, a form of teaching about *nianfo* in which the practice becomes a gateway *out* of the Pure Land tradition and into other understandings of Buddhist practice and attainment. For this reason, I have created this special category for teachings of *nianfo,* and not simply treated them as other examples of *nianfo* as one practice among many.

When *Nianfo* Is Not for Rebirth

As mentioned at the outset, Hori Ichirō noted some years ago that in Japan, the *nembutsu* became, at the level of folk religion, an incantation credited with the power to provide a variety of this-worldly benefits in addition to assuring rebirth in the Pure Land. Ogasawara Senshū 小笠原宣秀 also noted a recent tendency in China to credit this-worldly benefits to *nianfo* (Ogasawara 1951, p. 12), but the trend actually goes back at least to Song times. Daniel Getz has called attention to the fact that when the Song dynasty Tiantai reformer Siming Zhili (*Sìmíng Zhīlǐ* 四明知禮, 960–1028) organized his Pure Land society in the early eleventh century, one of the purposes he envisioned for the society's practice was to "extend the emperor's longevity and contribute to the prosperity of the people" (1999, p. 494–495). In addition, Getz reports that a layman who lost his sight recited the buddha's name 360,000 times, as a result of which his eyesight was miraculously restored (1999, p. 501). This story reminds one of the modern reformer Yinguang's use of *nianfo* to cure his conjunctivitis, as mentioned above. These examples call attention to the fact that not everyone who practiced *nianfo* in China did so for the sole purpose of gaining rebirth in the Pure Land, or to achieve the *nianfo* samadhi, or to establish the "single, unperturbed mind," or to attain a vision of the Buddha, or for any other specifically Buddhist purpose. It appears natural to regard a short, mantra-like invocation as having magical power to grant wishes in this life.

One sees this very clearly in a text called "Forty-Eight Ways to *Nianfo*" (*Niànfó sìshíbā fǎ* 念佛四十八法) by one Zhèng Wéiān 鄭韋庵. It has been reprinted many times in many formats, both as an independent treatise and in anthologies of Pure Land texts. The copy of the text used here is in Zhèng 1991, p. 54–71. Page numbers given in the text will all refer to this edition. It contains brief instructions for forty-eight different methods of performing *nianfo* and describes the situations for which each is suitable.

Even though we have seen that there are many ways to *nianfo,* this text does not describe any method of mental contemplation or visualization. Each technique falls under the category *chiming,* to "hold the name," and all of them involve some form of oral invocation of Amitābha's name. To give a few examples: When one is sleepy or one's thoughts are scattered, then one ought to recite the Buddha's name in a loud voice (p. 55). If one is tired, one may rest by reciting quietly for a time until one is again able to recite loudly (p. 55). If one is in a place unsuitable for audible practice, then one may try the "*vajra* recitation" (*jīn'gāng chífǎ* 金剛持法) in which one moves only the lips, or the "silent recitation" in which one keeps the mouth closed and moves only the tongue (p. 55). There are instructions for reciting the name in various other circumstances, such as when walking or sitting straight (p. 56), at fixed times of day (p. 57), or before a buddha-image (p. 57–58). In this last method, one faces the image and does not worry if one is not facing west, and seeks nothing more than a respectful realization of one's non-duality with the Buddha. There are other methods marked by certain moods or attitudes, such as extreme respect (p. 58), in grave misfortune (p. 59), or with utter sincerity (p. 59). Some are meant to accompany other Buddhist acts or liturgies, such as making offerings to buddhas or clergy (p. 61) or giving alms (p. 62). Some seem quasi-esoteric, such as the one called "Holding the name in the midst of light" (*guāngzhōng chímíng* 光中持名, p. 63), in which one lets the sound of one's recitation revolve around the space within the heart, visualizes the sound turning into light, and then dwells in the midst of this light, still reciting the name (or perhaps contemplating? the text shifts from the word *chiming* to *nianfo* here).

The text proceeds in this vein until near its end one finds ways to hold the name in dreams, in sickness, at the end of life, and finally, while making vows and performing repentances (p. 69–71). It may appear at first that this text really belongs in another section of this chapter, among those who hold to many methods of performing *nianfo* without organizing them into a graded path, and this text does indeed have that kind of *ad hoc,* "medicine chest" character about it. However, I include it here, not because the methods described are not aimed at rebirth in the Pure Land, but because, assuming this goal, it recommends different methods of *nianfo* or *chiming* for their "side effects." That is, while assuming that the practitioner would like to achieve rebirth in the Land of

Utmost Bliss, it seems to ask the question: As long as one plans to perform *nianfo* anyway, why not vary the practice to achieve other, more immediate goals, such as arousing the mind, cheering oneself up when feeling self-pity, or to return your parents' kindness?

One may also find more modern texts that express such concerns. For example, the Culture and Publication unit of Dharma Drum Mountain (*Fǎgǔ shān* 法鼓山) in Taiwan recently published a book called *50 Questions on the Buddha-name Recitation Practice* [*sic*] (*Niànfó 50 wèn* 念佛50問). It too provides basic information about the practice of *nianfo* such as the connection between the practice and rebirth in the Pure Land, the relationship between oral invocation and mental *nianfo,* the goals of rebirth in the Pure Land versus attainment of the *nianfo* samadhi, and so on. In places, however, it also describes various benefits that one may reap here and now. For instance, question 35 deals with the practice of *nianfo* while sick, and asserts that the practice alleviates mental stress and worry, and in so doing helps the healing process (Fǎgǔ wénhuà biānjí bù 法鼓文化編輯部 2016, p. 122). Question 47 asks how *nianfo* can help improve one's mood when sad or angry, and the editors answer by showing how the practice can pick up one's mood or help one cool down before venting one's anger at someone (p. 147). It seems *nianfo* will always be applicable to the vexations of daily life even as it resolves worries about one's ultimate fate.

Conclusions

This chapter began by noting the wide variety of methods of practice found throughout the long stream of Chinese Pure Land literature and wondering if there might be some way to organize them and understand them in terms of the technique presented, the goal it seeks to achieve, and the rationale by which the practitioner understands it to bring that goal about. This involved looking at authors and texts both inside and outside of the Pure Land tradition as I understand it in this book. Doing so helps to clarify that not every occurrence of the term *nianfo* in a Chinese Buddhist text indicates an affiliation with this tradition, and helps us to see why some authors are omitted from the roll of "patriarchs" and why some texts do not get much notice even though they may ostensibly be speaking of *nianfo* and rebirth in the Pure Land.

Having made this attempt at systematizing the profusion of methods that I found in this (admittedly incomplete) survey of the literature, it seems clear that much refinement is necessary, both in terms of determining what categories will prove useful and in the placement of various authors within these categories. Nevertheless, I find value in this attempt. In this first approach to the task of looking more systematically at a practice that is too easily seen as simple and homogeneous, I have found that, when authorities recommend that their followers engage in the practice of *nianfo,* they may in fact have very different ideas about what this means. Here I have only asked the single question of how *nianfo* relates to other practices, or, in cases where *nianfo* itself takes different forms, how these forms relate to each other. Many other analytic questions could be raised, as indicated in the opening, and I hope others may continue pursuing this line of investigation until scholars have a clearer idea of what, exactly, one does when one practices *nianfo.*

Chapter 8

Lushan Huiyuan

The Evolution of the First Pure Land Patriarch

Many lists of Pure Land patriarchs (*zǔ* 祖) have appeared from the Southern Song dynasty to the present. These lists have grown from six patriarchs to thirteen, and have included different sets of figures, but two names have been constant: the first patriarch, Huiyuan of Mount Lu (*Lúshān Huìyuǎn* 廬山慧遠, 334–416), and the second patriarch, Shandao (*Shàndǎo* 善導, 613–668; see appendix). Huiyuan has been universally accepted as the first patriarch of the tradition in every version of the list throughout history (Chen 2015, p. 22–33), and many modern scholars, especially in Japan, have accepted this ascription at face value. One may also take the opposite view and see this as an anachronistic status projected retrospectively onto Huiyuan by a later, more fully developed tradition beginning in the Tang dynasty (Lǐ 2007, p. 201). Both interpretations invite examination, so the provocative title of this chapter is meant to initiate an honest inquiry. After presenting my translation and analysis of doctrinal and epistemological issues raised in the Huiyuan-Kumārajīva correspondence, I will proceed to other sources to assay the extent to which the retrofitting of a Pure Land identity on Huiyuan fits with the documents that describe his actual beliefs and practices. Doing so will require teasing apart his views from Kumārajīva's in the main translation, and then looking at other sources on Huiyuan. Finally, I will examine later texts within the Pure Land tradition, specifically the "rebirth biography" genre (*wǎngshēng zhuàn* 往生傳) and texts dealing with the patriarchate directly. In the conclusion, I will consider the significance of Huiyuan's patriarchal status.

This inquiry matters a great deal for our understanding of the Chinese Pure Land tradition. Implicit in all the foregoing chapters has been my understanding that the line of patriarchs forms the armature around which the later tradition developed. When the tradition accepted a certain figure as a member of the list, then that figure's views and practices became normative, and their texts enjoyed increased attention and exegesis. Lushan Huiyuan presents an especially interesting case. As we shall see in this chapter, the historical Huiyuan, as best we can reconstruct his thought and practice, was not an obvious candidate for the list. However, his image evolved over time in the hands of various authors so that when we arrive at the later period, his life and practices become fully congruent with his patriarchal status. Thus, this concluding chapter takes us back from late imperial times to the very beginning of the tradition, but in the end covers the entire sweep of Chinese Pure Land history.

Correspondence with Kumārajīva

Background

Early in 406 CE, Huiyuan wrote a letter to Kumārajīva, then residing in the northern capital of Chang'an 長安 (Wagner 1971, p. 31–34). As the *Gāosēng zhuàn* 高僧傳 (Biographies of eminent monks, T.2059) records, Huiyuan had heard that Kumārajīva was considering leaving China, and he wanted to ask him about some perplexing doctrinal matters before it was too late (T.2059.50:359c28360a2; English in Zürcher 1959, p. 248). Accordingly, Huiyuan composed a series of questions and sent them to Kumārajīva. After receiving the latter's response, he sent a set of further questions, and by the end of 407, he received Kumārajīva's responses to these. With these two exchanges, their correspondence came to an end (Wagner 1971, p. 30–31). Later redactors rearranged these letters into eighteen sets of questions and answers and gathered them in the canon under the title *Topics on the Great Meaning of the Mahayana* (*Dàshèng dà yì zhāng* 大乘大義章). This text is also called *Jiūmólóushí fǎshī dà yì* 鳩摩羅什法師大義 (The great meaning of [the teachings of] the Dharma Master Kumārajīva, T.1856). We will look at the eleventh of its eighteen sections. According to the section heading, it contains questions about *nianfo* samadhi (*niànfó sānmèi* 念佛三昧; T.1856.45:134b4). Huiyuan asks Kumārajīva about the status of the buddhas seen as a result of meditating using the practices of the *Pratyutpanna-samādhi-sūtra* (*Bānzhōu sānmèi jīng* 般舟三昧經, T.418). Are they real, externally existent buddhas, or are they visions that appear solely within the practitioner's mind?

The following is a full translation and analysis of this exchange.

The Translation

The text appears in *Jiūmólóushí fǎshī dà yì* 鳩摩羅什法師大義, T.1856.45:134b–135a. As the text in the Taishō is significantly corrupt, this translation benefited greatly from the critical edition and modern Japanese rendering edited by Kimura Eiichi 木村英一 in *Eon Kenkyū*, 2 vols. (1960–1962). His reconstruction of the following passage is found in volume one, pages 34–36, while the modern Japanese rendition is found in volume one, pages 165–169. The passage was previously translated in Tsukamoto (1985, p. 2:851–854), but Huiyuan's questions appear here in German, while Kumārajīva's response appears in English but is not translated in full. I have placed my own commentary and critical notes on various passages in the endnotes.

[134b4] Next, a question about the *nianfo* samadhi and [Kumārajīva's] reply:

[134b5] [Hui]yuan asked: With regard to the *nianfo* samadhi, the sections on *nianfo* in the *Pratyutpanna-samādhi-sūtra* frequently use dreams as an explanatory simile. Dreams are objects of cognition for unenlightened beings. Whether one is deluded or enlightened, [dreams are] to be understood as restricted to the self.[1] However, the sutra says that one sees the buddhas in the *nianfo* samadhi. One asks them questions and they respond, thereby severing the snares of their doubts.[2]

[134b8] Now if the buddhas [so seen] are the same as what is seen in dreams, then this would be nothing more than a conceptualized "self" gazing at a conceptualized idea. When focused, one achieves samadhi, and in samadhi, one sees the buddhas. [But] the buddhas that one sees do not come in from outside, nor does one go out [to them]. It is a direct matter of one's focus on the image and reason coming together in the dream. If I do not go out of myself, and the buddhas do not come in, then how is there any dispelling (*jiě* 解) [of doubts]?[3] Where would this dispelling [of doubts] come from? [On the other hand,] if [the buddhas] really do come from without in response [to the meditation], then one should not use the simile of dreams. [Rather,] the meeting would be through [the buddhas'] spiritual power (*shéntōng* 神通). Because it is not the true character, there could therefore be "going" and "coming."[4] Thus, the sutra [uses the word] "going" to express the surface meaning and does not indicate the real aim of the samadhi. In the end, what connects [meditator and buddha]?

[134b14] Again, the *Pratyutpanna-samādhi-sūtra* says that when one has three things, one attains the samadhi: first, keeping the precepts without violation; second, great merit; and third, the numinous power of the buddha.[5] I would ask about this "numinous power of the buddha."[6] Is this understood to mean a buddha [visualized] while in samadhi, or a buddha that comes from outside? If it is a buddha [seen in the] midst of this sama-

dhi, then it is established by my own thoughts and emerges from myself. If this buddha is external to the samadhi, then it is a sage (*shèngrén* 聖人) shown in a dream. However, to have the full meaning of "to meet with," then it cannot be both "concentrated within" and "getting to hear [the buddha's teaching]," nor can it be elucidated [by the simile of] a dream.[7] Is the method of *nianfo* samadhi like this? Of these two or three explanations, which should I follow?

[134b22] Kumārajīva's answer: There are three types of samadhi for seeing the buddhas (*jiànfó sānmèi* 見佛三昧): First, a bodhisattva might attain the divine eye or the divine ear, fly throughout the ten directions to where the buddhas reside, see them, ask questions about their difficulties, and have their snare of doubts severed. Second, even without spiritual powers, they can contemplate (*niàn* 念) Amitābha and all the buddhas of the present, and with their minds focused on this object, they can attain a vision of the buddhas and ask about their doubts. Third, they can study and practice *nianfo* whether or not they have abandoned their desires. Alternatively, they may gaze at a buddha image, or contemplate his earthly buddha-body, or see all of the buddhas of the past, present, and future. All three of these are called "*nianfo* samadhi."

[134b28] Nevertheless, they are not the same. The highest [i.e., the first method] is the ability to see all of the buddhas through one's own spiritual powers. The second, even though it does not give one spiritual powers, still enables one to see the buddhas of the ten directions, because it is based on the power of the *pratyutpanna*-samadhi.[8] The rest are lower down. All are called *nianfo* samadhi.[9]

[134b29] Also, if one constantly contemplates the world's repugnant character, one will have difficulty practicing compassion among living beings. For the sake of bodhisattvas who have yet to abandon desires, [the buddhas] praise the *pratyutpanna*-samadhi in many and various ways. By the power of this samadhi, one can focus the mind on a single object and see all of the buddhas even without abandoning [desires]. Thus, this provides a foundation for seeking the buddha-way.

[134c4] In addition, one who studies the *pratyutpanna*-samadhi abandons words and discriminations, and is not deluded.[10] Why is this? Because all the sutras preached by Śākyamuni illuminate the Buddha Amitābha's physical features completely. These are the perfect words of a Tathāgata.

[134c7] Again, the *Pratyutpanna-samādhi-sūtra* teaches in various ways that, even as [the practitioner] contemplates the discriminated Buddha Amitābha in his Pure Land more than 100,000 buddha-lands to the west, that buddha is constantly illuminating all the worlds of the ten directions with his immeasurable light.[11] If the practitioner can see the buddha in accordance with the sutra, then both root and branch are there [i.e., his or her own practice and the buddha's illumination][12]; it is not just a delusive

conceptual discrimination. Because they lack faith, people do not know how to practice this method of meditative samadhi. They wonder how performing this contemplation without having yet attained spiritual powers can enable one to see all the buddhas from afar?[13]

[134c12] This is the reason the Buddha used the simile of dreams, is it not? Through the power of dreams, people can go forth and see things that are far away. In just the same way, the bodhisattva [who practices] the *pratyutpanna*-samadhi sees all the distant buddhas by the power of the samadhi, unimpeded by mountains or forests. Because people believe in dreams, it serves as a simile. Moreover, dreams occur naturally[14] and do this without effort. How could one make effort and not achieve the vision?

[134c17] As for [the idea that] the bodies of all buddhas have set features, [some say] these are mere thoughts and discriminations (*yìxiǎng fēnbié* 憶想分別), and are thus false. However, the sutras explain that all buddhas' bodies are produced from the aggregation of conditions. They have no self-nature and are ultimately empty and quiescent, like dreams and magical illusions. If this is the case, then the bodies of buddhas seen by practicing in accordance with the [sutras'] teachings should not be the only things that are delusions. If [the vision of the buddhas] is a delusion, then everything must be a delusion. If it is not a delusion, then nothing else is a delusion either.

[134c21] Why is this? Because it leads all sentient beings to reap their own benefits and plant good roots.[15] One who attains the vision of the buddhas in accordance with the *Pratyutpanna-samādhi-sūtra* can produce good roots and become an arhat or non-returner. By this, you should know that nothing about the Tathāgata's body is unreal.

[134c24] Next: Thoughts and discriminations are sometimes real. If we follow the sutra's teaching, then often, in accordance with [our] thoughts and discriminations, [we] can reach actual realities. For example, when constantly practicing [the samadhi that takes as its objects][16] the light of lamps, candles, the sun, or the moon, then whenever one thinks of a hidden object, then one attains the divine eye and grasps its reality.

[134c27] Again, someone at the inferior level [of the three given above] who keeps the precepts purely, and whose faith and reverence are profound and weighty, brings together the buddha's numinous power and the power of the samadhi, knits these conditions together, and is able to see the buddha as a person sees [his or her own] image in a mirror.

[134c29] Again, a worldling who [at some point] in beginningless [time] has seen [the buddha][17] should abandon desires and attain the divine eye and divine ear. Yet he returns to cycle around the five paths. However, since beginningless birth and death, practitioners of the two vehicles [of voice-hearers and *pratyekabuddhas*] have never been able to attain the *pratyutpanna*-

samadhi; how much less could the worldlings? For this reason, one should not regard what one sees in this samadhi as false.

[135a4] Furthermore, all the bodhisattvas [who] attain this samadhi see the buddhas, ask their questions, and have all their doubts resolved. After they arise from this samadhi, they abide in their coarse minds. Taking deep pleasure in this samadhi, they give rise to grasping thoughts. For this reason, the buddha taught that the practitioner should form this thought: "I do not go to that [buddha], nor does that buddha come [to me], and yet I see the buddha and hear the dharma. This is only my mind's own thoughts and discriminations. All the things in the Triple World have their being as thoughts and discriminations, or as the karmic results of thoughts in past lives, or as that which thoughts in the present life have produced." Having heard this teaching, the mind is repulsed by the Triple World and increases in faith and reverence. Well did the buddha explain such a subtle and wonderful principle. The practitioner immediately abandons the desires of the Triple World, deeply enters into concentration, and attains the *pratyutpanna*-samadhi.

Huiyuan's Difficulty and Kumārajīva's Response

As many scholars have noted, Huiyuan was quite keen on meditation and sought the advice of many masters on the topic, and so it should not surprise us that he goes into the matter with Kumārajīva. The inquiry appears quite straightforward, but an analysis of his question and Kumārajīva's answer reveals an ongoing misunderstanding between Chinese and Indian/Central Asian conceptions of mental activity and cognition. Huiyuan wonders why the *Pratyutpanna-samādhi-sūtra* often uses dreams to illustrate its main method of meditation, one in which the practitioner sees all the buddhas of the present world, including Amitābha. Having attained the vision, one can ask them about one's perplexities and receive their explanations. However, Huiyuan believes that dreams are entirely self-generated; they are phantasms of the mind and include nothing that comes in from the external world. How could such a vision tell one anything one did not already know?

Furthermore, the sutra says that one meets the buddhas through their supernatural power. However, if the buddha is merely a visualization produced by one's own mind, then such an image cannot have supernatural power. Indeed, since the buddha would not be coming in from anywhere, he would have no need to travel through space and time. On the other hand, if the buddha so seen is real and does indeed come in from outside through his power, then it is not right to use the metaphor of dreams to explain it.

Huiyuan's question revolves around one basic issue: Is the buddha seen in the samadhi real or not? The very concreteness of the question points to a certain naive realism on Huiyuan's part that scholars have explained in a couple of ways. Walter Liebenthal averred that Huiyuan was incapable of thinking in psychological terms (1950, p. 249a). As he explains it, while the Chinese always had some notion of an "inner" and "outer" world, prior to Huiyuan's time, they had not thought about psychological states as such. Building on Liebenthal's observation, we may note that Indian Buddhist psychology made the mind a sixth sense organ and thus considered mental phenomena sense-objects. At this point in history, the Chinese only acknowledged the traditional five senses, as when Xunzi 荀子 (298–238 BCE) lists only the five sense organs: eye, ear, nose, mouth, and body in his essay "On the Rectification of Names." Although the list ends with the mind, he makes it clear that the mind does not perceive objects, but produces only emotional reactions to things and situations (Chan 1963, p. 125). Thus, for Kumārajīva, a buddha visualized in the mind would be a sense-object to the mind and thus would have more reality than the Chinese were able to accord it. Conversely, for Huiyuan, to use dreams to describe the visualized buddha was to deny its objective reality, while to say that the buddha comes into one's mind through his supernatural power made the dream simile inappropriate. In Indian Buddhist psychology, such problems would not arise.

Richard H. Robinson put the matter somewhat differently. Instead of psychology, he believed what Huiyuan lacked was epistemology (Robinson 1967, p. 109). That is to say, Huiyuan displayed a naive realism or objectivism when considering how the mind knows things in the world. That the mind itself plays a role in the construction of knowledge does not seem to have occurred to him, and thus he had to assume that the buddha visualized in *nianfo* meditation was either objectively real (i.e., entering in from the outside by the buddhas' supernatural power), or merely a mentally generated image (i.e., like a dream). To assert that something dreamed actually has something new to say to the dreamer makes no sense from this epistemological perspective.

Robinson's diagnosis of Huiyuan's perplexity might be more useful here because it makes more sense of Kumārajīva's response. Recall that, in the passage beginning at 45:134c17, Kumārajīva stated, "If this is the case, then the bodies of buddhas seen by practicing in accordance with the [sutras'] teachings should not be the only things that are delusions. If [the vision of the buddhas] is a delusion, then everything must be a delusion. If it is not a delusion, then nothing else is a delusion either." The presupposition behind this statement is that an image visualized in the meditation is no different from any other image that appears in the mind. That is, the buddha that one visualizes in samadhi is not different in kind from the image of a rock or a tree that appears in the mind when one looks at it. All perceptions of things involve mental construction, and thus the visualization of a buddha is an experience of the same kind as actually seeing a buddha standing before one.

This explains the disjunction between Huiyuan's question and Kumārajīva's answer. Huiyuan assumes that a dream-image is unreal, a mere mental construction without an object; that is why the statement in the *Pratyutpanna-samādhi-sūtra* that one can question the buddha seen in samadhi and receive answers puzzles him. Kumārajīva, in contrast, assumes the samadhi connects one with a real buddha. Thus, for him the real danger is that practitioners will become enamored of the ability gained in the meditation to converse with a buddha at will. For him, then, the sutra's comparison of the visualized buddha with a dream serves to denigrate the visualization in order to neutralize a potential source of attachment. While Huiyuan takes the dream-simile at face value and thus begins with the assumption that the visualized image is unreal, Kumārajīva begins with the opposite assumption, namely that the image is *too* real, and that the text uses a simile that lessens its reality to avert unwholesome attachment to the samadhi.

Was Huiyuan a Pure Land Master?

My interest in the passage above arose from the widely held belief that Lushan Huiyuan was a seminal figure in the development of Pure Land Buddhism in China. Not only does the Chinese tradition itself esteem Huiyuan as the first patriarch (*zǔ* 祖; Tsukamoto 1985, p. 763; see appendix), but many scholars accept the idea that he was an early devotee of the cult of Amitābha and aspired to rebirth in the western Pure Land (Robinson 1967, p. 88, 90; Liebenthal 1955, p. 71). Since this part of the correspondence dealt with the practice of *nianfo,* it seemed reasonable that it would display this devotional aspect of Huiyuan's interests.

After studying the passage, however, I could find no real evidence of interest in anything resembling Pure Land practice as it developed later. There is no mention of rebirth in Sukhāvatī and no hint of a need for the

Buddha's other-power to help one achieve that goal. All ideas that presage future developments appear in Kumārajīva's response, not in Huiyuan's question. It is Kumārajīva that hints that the Buddha might use his "numinous power" to enter into one's visualization, and it is Kumārajīva who mentions Amitābha by name. The possibility that Kumārajīva would have more devotion to Amitābha and interest in seeking rebirth in the Pure Land than Huiyuan would not be surprising at all. He translated the *Amitābha Sutra* while residing in Chang'an. Kumārajīva was also busy translating the *Dà zhìdù lùn* 大智度論 during the time of this correspondence, and this text has a great deal to say about Amitābha, Sukhāvatī, and the goal of rebirth. As Gregory Schopen demonstrated, rebirth in Sukhāvatī had become a normal goal for Mahayana Buddhists throughout North India by Kumārajīva's lifetime (2005). Strictly speaking, the portion of this passage written by Huiyuan himself merely raises a question about the practice of *buddha-anusmṛti;* it is a technical question about meditation, nothing more. This casts some doubt on Huiyuan's status as a founding master of Pure Land Buddhism.

Other scholars have questioned the ascription of Amitābha devotionalism to Huiyuan. Erik Zürcher, for instance, claims that Huiyuan was more interested in "Hinayanistic" meditations and only allowed the practice of devotion to Amitābha as a concession to the needs of his lay followers (1959, p. 222–223). Kenneth Ch'en echoes this doubt (1964, p. 108), and Li Xingling 李幸玲 affirms that, when teaching his lay followers, Huiyuan would accommodate their educational and cultural level. When speaking to Kumārajīva or other highly educated Buddhists, his tone would be different. He would be strictly Buddhist, use much technical vocabulary, and observe great precision (Lǐ 2007, p. 255). From the work of previous scholars, then, two possibilities emerge. Either Huiyuan was an active participant in the cult of Amitābha and in practices directed at rebirth in the Pure Land, or he was mostly uninterested in this and merely allowed such practices for the sake of his lay followers. In order to determine which of these (if either) is correct, one must consult other literary evidence for Huiyuan's religious activities.

One might easily conclude from various passages in the Taishō canon that the second hypothesis is right. As we have already seen, Huiyuan's correspondence with Kumārajīva regarding the practice of *nianfo* is really directed at the achievement of *nianfo* samadhi (*niànfó sānmèi* 念佛三昧), and has nothing to do with devotion to Amitābha or to rebirth in Sukhāvatī. Four other passages from two additional sources also bear on the question, so let us examine them in turn.

First and most importantly, Huiyuan's reputation as the founder of the Pure Land movement rests on his biography in the *Gāo sēng zhuàn* 高僧傳 (Biographies of eminent monks, T.2059), compiled in 519. This is the *locus classicus* for the story of the "White Lotus Society" (*Báilián shè* 白蓮社), an assembly of 123 of his followers that convened late in the year 402 to take a collective vow to seek rebirth in "the west" (T.2059.50:357–361; English translation in Zürcher 1959, p. 240–253). The wording implies that Huiyuan took the initiative, as he "organized a fast and established a vow that all would strive together for the western region" (T.2059.50:358c21–c22).[18] Therefore, it appears that Huiyuan was indeed the instigator of this gathering. However, Huiyuan asked a lay follower named Liu Yimin 劉遺民 (or Liu Chengzhi 劉程之, 354–410) to compose the text. This leads one to suspect that the Society may indeed have been convened for the sake of lay followers, though in itself it does not establish a disinterest on Huiyuan's part. The evidence from this passage remains inconclusive on that point.

Another detail of great interest appears upon examination of the text of the vows that Liu wrote. When describing the goal of their joint practice, he indicates that it is for the sake of rebirth in a place simply designated "the west" (*xīfāng* 西方 or *xījīng* 西境; see T.2059.50:358c22, 359a5) or the "spirit realm" (*shénjiè* 神界; T.2059.50:359a13). Liu's subsequent description of "the west" bears no resemblance to any canonical description of Sukhāvatī. Liu says that those who rise to this realm will abide on cloudy peaks (*yúnjiào* 雲嶠), their bodies and minds will be transformed, and they will sit in the shade of jade *ke*-trees (*qióngkē* 瓊柯; a term Zürcher says is associated with ancient legends of Kunlun; Zürcher 1959, p. 406n57). They will float to the eight corners of the world in cloud-garments and ride the wind until the end of their lives (T.2059.50:359a17). As Zürcher writes, this vow is a curious mixture of Buddhist and Daoist concepts, though it may be even more Daoist than he acknowledged given that the only references to "Amitābha" and "Sukhāvatī" appear in emendations that he inserted without justification (1959, p. 219, 245). Liu Yimin seems not to have written an orthodox picture of the Pure Land, and Huiyuan seems not to have corrected him. We must conclude, therefore, that the community on Mt. Lu, including Huiyuan and the members of the White Lotus Society, had only the vaguest and most rudimentary understanding of the land of Amitābha.

Next, we will consider Huiyuan's preface to a collection of poems praising the practice of *nianfo* samadhi composed by various lay followers. The anthology itself, called *Collected Poems on the Nianfo Samadhi*

(*Niànfó sānmèi shī jí* 念佛三昧詩集) is no longer extant, but Huiyuan's preface appears in the *Guǎng hóngmíng jí* 廣弘明集, (T.2103.52:351b10–351c7; also *Eon kenkyū*, 2:78–79). The impression one gets from this preface is similar to that conveyed by the questions to Kumārajīva translated above. That is, it is primarily about a particular kind of samadhi, not any recognizable Pure Land practice. The term *nianfo* occurs only once (at T.2103.52:351b21), but only to specify one type of samadhi among many. For the most part, the preface praises the practice of samadhi for its benefits in "focusing and stilling thoughts" (*zhuān sī jì xiǎng* 專思寂想, T.2103.52:351b12), thus calming and clarifying the mind. This text, therefore, provides no more support for considering Huiyuan a Pure Land master than does the passage from his letters to Kumārajīva. In addition, as in the passage from the *Biographies of Eminent Monks,* it appears that Huiyuan wrote on the topic of the *nianfo* samadhi in response to his lay followers' interest. There is one line of this preface, however, that contributed to his status as a patriarch of the Pure Land tradition in later texts. It says. "Moreover, there are many [kinds of] samadhi; their names are legion. [Among them,] the *nianfo* samadhi is preeminent for height of merit and ease of practice." (又諸三昧。其名甚眾。功高易進念佛為先。 T.2103.52:351b20–b21). This statement, or at least its sentiment, will be reproduced many times over the centuries.

The third passage, also from the *Biographies of Eminent Monks,* presents a different picture. This is a brief biography of one of Huiyuan's monastic disciples, Sengji (*Sēngjì* 僧濟; T.2059.50:362b12–b27). Here is an abridged translation of the passage:

> Afterward, [Sengji] stopped at the mountain [i.e., Mt. Lu] for a short while when he suddenly felt critically ill. Therefore, he wanted sincerely [to seek] the Western Country (*xī guó* 西國) and visualized an image (*xiǎngxiàng* 想像) of the Buddha Amitāyus. Huiyuan presented Sengji a candle and said "By setting your mind on [the land of] peace and sustenance [*ānyǎng* 安養; i.e., Sukhāvatī], you may strive against the defilements for a while." Grasping the candle as a support, Sengji stilled his thoughts and was unperturbed, and he asked the monks to assemble during the night in order to rotate [in reciting] the *Larger Sutra*. In the fifth watch, Sengji gave the candle to his fellow students and asked them to pass it among the monks. Thus, he lay down for a while. In a dream, he saw himself holding a candle and riding in space to see the Buddha Amitāyus [. . .] Suddenly he woke up and told the attendant at his sickbed about it, who was both grieved and comforted. [. . .] He looked for his shoes and stood up, and his eyes looked out into space as if he saw

> something. The next moment he lay down again with a look of delight and said to his companions, "I am going!" He turned on his right side, and his breath left him. He was 45 years old. (T.2059.50:362b16–b27)[19]

Two features of this passage are of interest. First, the subject of the story is not a lay follower, but one of Huiyuan's monastic disciples, and, to judge from the text preceding the death narrative, a highly respected one. This would seem to cast doubt on Ch'en's and Zürcher's contention that Huiyuan's Pure Land practice was primarily for the benefit of lay followers, and leads us to consider the possibility that it was an integral component of the life of his monastic community.

Second, unlike all of the other passages, we see a fully developed Pure Land theology and soteriology at work here. The story itself follows the pattern of countless deathbed rebirth stories found in the literature. More than that, it displays all the features normally associated with Pure Land practice: It centers on the Buddha Amitābha (under his other name Amitāyus); the monk seeks rebirth in the Pure Land; the scriptural support is the *Larger Sutra;* most importantly, the goal of the night vigil is to help the monk attain his stated goal of rebirth in Sukhāvatī, described as being in the west. Also of significance for our purposes, Huiyuan himself is there to sanction Sengji's desire and assist him in achieving it.

The last passage we will consider describes Huiyuan's death and comes from the *Biographies of Eminent Monks.* Here we might expect Huiyuan to express concern with attaining birth in the West when faced with his own imminent passing, especially given his willingness to assist others to achieve this in their last hours. However, in this account we find that as he lay dying at the age of 83, he was only concerned with observing the monastic rules and expressed no desire at all for the Pure Land. Since he was in pain, his disciples and fellow-monks tried to get him to drink first bean wine and then fermented rice juice. He refused both because the *vinaya* did not allow the consumption of alcohol. When they suggested a mixture of water and honey, he asked a *vinaya*-master to see if that were allowed, but before the master could locate the appropriate rule, Huiyuan died (Zürcher 1959, p. 253; T.2059.50:361b1–b10). Thus, this early biography does not portray Huiyuan doing any of the things that became typical of the "good death" as recorded in countless other stories. He expresses no desire for rebirth in Amitābha's Pure Land, he does not ask monks and disciples to gather around and help him stay focused by chanting, and no one reports any signs of successful rebirth.

In what sense, then, could we consider Lushan Huiyuan a Pure Land Buddhist? There is very little basis for such a characterization. As a meditator devoted to the *dhyāna* methods found in the *Pratyutpanna-samādhi-sūtra*, he was an advocate of the *nianfo* samadhi and was aware of the central role the Buddha Amitābha plays in it. He understood that followers worried about their postmortem fates and was willing to help them seek rebirth in "the west" by presiding over the White Lotus Society or facilitating Sengji's deathbed practice. In his *Preface to the Collected Poems on the Nianfo Samadhi,* he contributed a phrase that would become a cliché in Pure Land apologetic literature to the effect that the *nianfo* samadhi is the easiest to put into practice and the most efficient for accumulating merit (T.2103.52:351b20–b21). Thus, while we might consider some of his lay followers and fellow monastics early adherents of Pure Land, Huiyuan himself was not.

Nor did any early Buddhist tradition consider him such. His extensive notice in the *Biographies of Eminent Monks* calls attention to the wide range of activities in which he involved himself. Its final judgment, expressed at the end of his biography, holds him to be a well-rounded monk, erudite in literature and doctrine, and politically canny in dealing with the ever-changing political and military landscape of the moribund Eastern Jin. He was a literary giant, a deft debater, an imposing presence, a masterful teacher, and a virtuous monk of solid reputation and standing. It notes that his legacy to Chinese Buddhism consisted in his collected works in ten fascicles. He was "highly esteemed by his generation" (Zürcher 1959, p. 253; T.2059.50:361b9–b13). However, as we survey the literature of the Pure Land tradition, we find that it is not the historical Huiyuan who became the first patriarch; rather, it was a reimagined Huiyuan who ascended to that position, and so we must conclude by looking at the evolution of Huiyuan from a polymath monk to a Pure Land master.

Huiyuan's Evolution from Scholar and Meditator to Pure Land Patriarch

Huiyuan was not always regarded as a significant Pure Land figure. As already noted, his notice in the *Biographies of Eminent Monks* presents him as a multifaceted and accomplished monk, whose Pure Land–related activities account for only a minor part of his life story. During the Tang dynasty (618–907), when much of what we now regard as the Chinese Pure Land tradition began to take shape, Jiacai (*Jiācái* 迦才, seventh century) even criticized Huiyuan in harsh terms: "[T]he teachers of high antiquity, men such as the Dharma-master [Hui-]yuan and Hsieh Lingyün [*Xiè Língyùn* 謝靈運, one of Huiyuan's lay followers], though all hoped for the Western region, were ultimately perfecting only themselves. Of students of later times, there is not one who accepted or repeated what they did" (T.1963.47:83b12–b13; English in Tsukamoto 1985, p. 2:860). Jiacai's rough contemporary Daochuo (*Dàochuò* 道綽, 562–645) compiled what appears to be a list of patriarchs in his *Ānlè jí* 安樂集 that does not include Huiyuan (T.1958.47:14b11–c6; also Nogami 1962, p. 1:227). Nogami Shunjō 野上俊靜 has pointed out that, after the passing of Huiyuan's immediate circle of disciples, his Pure Land thought became so unknown that the Pure Land movement in North China under Tanluan and Daochuo betrayed no hint of familiarity with him, and their thought is at variance with his in many places (1962, p. 1:226–227). Thus, even though later Japanese scholarship follows Hōnen and treats Huiyuan as the founder of a particular "stream" (*ryū* 流) of Pure Land thought and practice, his near contemporaries in the early Tang dynasty either show no awareness of him or regard him as anything but.

Huiyuan's image began to change during the middle years of the Tang dynasty. As Nogami points out, a couple of figures began speaking positively of Huiyuan in connection with Pure Land. Zhulin Fazhao (*Zhúlín Fǎzhào* 竹林法照, ca. 740–838), a figure later honored as the Fourth Patriarch of Pure Land, went to Mt. Lu, and a stele inscription says that between 765 and 766 Fazhao went to Lushan specifically to look for Huiyuan's teachings (Nogami 1962, p. 1:241). Fazhao also mentions Huiyuan as someone who attained rebirth in the Pure Land in the middle fascicle of his *Jìngtǔ wǔhuì niànfó sòngjīng guānxíng yí* (淨土五會念佛誦經觀行儀, T.2827.85:1244b10–b12). Fazhao refers to Huiyuan once more near the end of the same work. In this passage, Fazhao mentions Huiyuan immediately after stating that the Pure Land teaching came from India to China, and goes on to tell the story of the White Lotus Society. It ends by saying that Huiyuan and his lay followers "all saw the western land of Utmost Bliss" (T.2827.85:1255b11–b13).

Directly following the first reference to Huiyuan, Fazhao reports on another figure from the Chen dynasty (*Chén cháo* 陳朝, 557–589) named "Chan master Zhen" (*Zhēn chánshī* 珍禪師), also of Mt. Lu.[20] While in meditation one day, Zhen saw a man riding a ship to the west, and asked if he could go with him. The man answered, "The dharma-master has not yet recited the *Amitābha Sutra,* and so you cannot go." Chan master Zhen recited the sutra 20,000 times, and toward the end of his life, a "holy man" or "spirit man" (*shénrén* 神人) sent him a silver dais and told him he could ride it to rebirth in Amitābha's land. The light of the dais filled the sky and was brighter than the sun, and this sign assured Zhen that he would attain rebirth. When his death came, those gathered around him noticed an unusual fragrance that lasted for some days, and many saw a number of transformation buddhas (*huàfó* 化佛) come to greet him (T.2827.85:1244b12–b22). Perhaps because this story follows immediately upon that of Huiyuan, later accounts of Huiyuan will incorporate many details of this episode.

The *Niànfó sānmèi bǎowáng lùn* 念佛三昧寶王論 (T.1967) by Feixi (*Fēixī* 飛錫, d.u.), written between 785 and 805, contains another mention of Huiyuan as a Pure Land master. As before, it refers to Huiyuan as the first figure in China to receive and transmit the Pure Land way from an Indian master, and it recounts the story of the White Lotus Society. Notably, this is the first text to describe the goal of their practice as rebirth in the "Pure Land" (*jìngtǔ* 淨土) rather than simply "the west" (*xīfāng* 西方; see T.1967.47:140b6). Feixi clearly considered Huiyuan to be a pioneer of Pure Land.

During the Sui and Tang dynasties, a new genre of literature called "biographies of those who achieved rebirth [in the Pure Land]" (*wǎngshēng zhuàn* 往生傳) came into being. The earliest is the *Wǎngshēng xīfāng jìngtǔ ruìyìng shānzhuàn* 往生西方淨土瑞應刪傳 (T.2070) by Shaokang (*Shǎokāng* 少康, d. 805) from the mid-Tang. According to Shaokang, although Huiyuan "was expert in all the sutras, he inclined toward the propagation of the west." He built a "Pure Land Hall" (*jìngtǔ táng* 淨土堂) below a cliff and practiced worship and repentance in it night and day. Many eminent laymen gathered around, and they all practiced Pure Land together (*tóng xiū jìngtǔ* 同修淨土). Directly after reporting Liu Yimin's leadership in the gathering of the White Lotus Society, Shaokang says that a voice of "an immortal riding the clouds" sounded; whether all the members of the Society heard it or just Huiyuan is not clear. Also noteworthy is the fact that the biography of Tanluan follows directly upon that of Huiyuan, and those of Daochuo and Shandao come soon after. Thus, this text places Huiyuan within a more unified Pure Land tradition that included other future patriarchs.

The final evolution of Huiyuan's story occurs in the Song dynasty. We will consider two texts in the "rebirth biography" genre, the *Xù jìngtǔ wǎngshēng zhuàn* 敘淨土往生傳 (T.2071) by Jiezhu (*Jièzhū* 戒珠, d.u.) and the *Xīnxiū wǎngshēng zhuàn* 新修往生傳 (CBETA X.1546) by Wang Gu (*Wáng Gǔ* 王古, d.u.). These two texts introduce a new element into the story of Huiyuan's life and practice. For the most part, Jiezhu's text recapitulates Huiyuan's entry in the original *Biographies of Eminent Monks,* and up to the death scene, the text conveys the impression of Huiyuan as a widely read, brilliant religious figure and shrewd political survivor whose Pure Land connection is tentative and peripheral. However, near the end Jiezhu shifts to an account from an otherwise unknown "supplementary" or "alternative biography" (*biézhuàn* 別傳). According to this source, Huiyuan exerted himself in Pure Land cultivation (*jìngtǔ zhi xiū* 淨土之修). During his first eleven years at Mt. Lu, he settled his mind and focused his thoughts, and thrice saw the superior characteristics (*shèngxiàng* 勝相), but did not report these visions to anyone. Then we read:

> Nineteen years later, in the evening of the last day of the seventh month, [Hui]yuan was in the Eastern Shrine of the Wisdom Hall. He had just arisen from his meditation when he saw Amitābha Buddha's body filling all of space. All the transformation-buddhas appeared in his nimbus, and the Bodhisattvas Avalokiteśvara and Mahāsthāmaprāpta attended him on the left and right. He also saw water flowing and light breaking into fourteen streams, each one of which flowed upward and downward proclaiming suffering, emptiness, impermanence, and selflessness. The Buddha said to him, "By the power of my Original Vow I have come to give you comfort. In seven days you will achieve rebirth in my land." He also saw Buddhayaśas, along with [his younger brother] Huichi and Tanshun at the Buddha's side. They assembled before Huiyuan and said, "Master, you preceded us in intention [i.e., to gain rebirth], why are you late in coming?" [Hui]yuan saw this clearly with his own eyes while observing it with an unperturbed mind. He thereupon told his disciples Fajing (*Fǎjìng* 法淨), Huibao (*Huìbǎo* 慧寶), and others what he had just seen. He said to [Fa]jing, "During my first eleven years living here I was fortunate to have three visions of the superior characteristics of the Pure Land. Now I have seen them once again, and so my rebirth in the Pure Land is assured." The next day he felt ill and took to his bed. [. . .] When the time came, he passed away. (T.2071.51:110b18–c2)

As Nogami Shunjō notes, we do not know the provenance of this "supplementary biography," and the story told here is completely new (1962, p. 1:238). It is interesting that Jiezhu retains the other version of Huiyuan's death narrative from the *Biographies of Eminent Monks,* and the new story seems to contain elements of the story of Chan master Zhen as recounted in Fazhao's text. Jiezhu's text is thus a little disjointed, with a first half that repeats the older version of Huiyuan's life and a second half that depicts him much more as a Pure Land master.

Wang Gu's biography of Huiyuan (which he writes 惠遠), with a preface dated 1084, builds upon Jiezhu's but is more concise. Wang truncated most of the material dealing with Huiyuan's early life, which makes his text a good bit shorter while shifting the emphasis much more to Huiyuan's Pure Land activities. The latter half repeats Jiezhu's text almost verbatim (CBETA X.1546.7:148a15–148c9). The overall effect of Wang's deletions is to give a stronger impression than previous biographies that Pure Land was the focus of Huiyuan's life and practice.

The first literary attempts to establish a line of Pure Land patriarchs (*zǔ* 祖) appeared during the Southern Song dynasty (1127–1270). Two texts from this period propose slightly variant lists, but both place Huiyuan first in the line. This is their most salient innovation in terms of the evolution of his image. These texts are the *Lèbāng wénlèi* 樂邦文類 (T.1969A) compiled by Zongxiao (*Zōngxiǎo* 宗曉, 1151–1214) in 1199 and the *Fózǔ tǒngjì* 佛祖統紀 (T.2035) composed by Zhipan (*Zhìpán* 志磐, 1220–1275) in 1269. Both of these texts provide extensive material on Huiyuan, reproducing the entry from the *Biographies of Eminent Monks* in its entirety with the addition of the new material found in the early Song texts just examined. Both retain the two versions of Huiyuan's death and the account of his three visions of the Pure Land during his first eleven years at Mt. Lu. (See *Fózǔ tǒngjì* T.2035.49:262c17–c18; *Lèbāng wénlèi* T.1969A.47:192b29–c1.)

The next list of Pure Land patriarchs appeared in the *Jìngtǔ zhǐguī jí* 淨土指歸集 (CBETA X.1154), by Anqu Dayou (*Ānqú Dàyòu* 庵蘧大佑, 1334–1407), with a preface dated 1383. Dayou's account of Huiyuan's life presents many of the main reference points in summary fashion: his early brilliance, mastery of Daoist texts, his enlightenment under Daoan's preaching, his ordination, and his journey to Mt. Lu. It then presents a short version of the meeting of the White Lotus Society in 402, again with a more specific reference to the Pure Land than simply "the west" (in this case, *ānyǎng* 安養). It ends with the judgment: "Because of this, all who cultivate Pure Land practices (*jìngyè* 淨業) consider the Lotus Society of Donglin [Temple] the pattern (*shīfǎ* 師法) for ten thousand generations" (CBETA X.1154.61:389b12–b23). The next section again asserts that Huiyuan had three visions during his first eleven years on the mountain, but did not let anyone else know of them (CBETA X.1154.61:389b24–c2). It then goes on to narrate Huiyuan's death, repeating all the same details of his premonitory vision of Amitābha and his retinue as given above (CBETA X.1154.61:389c2–c9).

Late in the Ming dynasty, the monk Zhengji (*Zhèngjì* 正寂, d.u.) composed the *Jìngtǔ shēng wúshēng lùn zhù* 淨土生無生論註 (CBETA X.1167), and Shoujiao (*Shòujiào* 受教, d.u.) wrote the *Shēng wúshēng lùn qīnwén jì* 生無生論親聞記 (CBETA X.1168). Both texts contain somewhat different lists of Pure Land patriarchs (see appendix), and both merely reproduce Dayou's biography of Huiyuan, but with one interesting variation. Whereas Dayou indicated that the White Lotus Society itself provided a template for all future Pure Land practice, Zhengji and Shoujiao phrase the matter in this way: "In this land (*cǐtǔ* 此土), [the practice of] *nianfo* truly begins with [Hui]yuan, and thus he is styled the first patriarch" (CBETA X.1167.61:834a24–b1, X.1168.61:851c22). Thus, what was termed Huiyuan's "*nianfo* samadhi" in earlier texts became "Pure Land practice" (*jìngyè* 淨業) for Dayou and simply *nianfo* for Zhengji and Shoujiao, and the latter two shifted the focus from the lay members of the White Lotus Society to Huiyuan himself. He now looks even more like a Pure Land adherent.

In the early Qing dynasty, Ruizhang (*Ruìzhāng* 瑞璋, d.u.) published his *Xīfāng huìzhēng* 西舫彙征 (CBETA X.1551), for which he formulated a new list of patriarchs that included late Ming dynasty figures for the first time. Ruizhang gives a more extensive biography of Huiyuan, bringing back much of the material found in the *Biographies of Eminent Monks* and reinstating the image of Huiyuan as a renaissance monk with many accomplishments. Regarding Pure Land, Ruizhang quotes Huiyuan's statement that the *nianfo* samadhi is the easiest to implement and the most effective (CBETA X.1551.78:357b2–b3) though without citing its source. In recounting the story of the White Lotus Society, Ruizhang adds a new detail: Rather than saying that the 123 participants gathered in front of an image of Amitābha, he says they fashioned images of the "three holy ones of the west" (*xīfāng sānshèng xiàng* 西方三聖像; CBETA X.1551.78:357b9), that is, the Buddha and his two bodhisattva-attendants. He repeats the claim that Huiyuan put all his effort solely into Pure Land practice (CBETA X.1551.78:357b15), that Huiyuan had three visions of the Buddha during his early years on the mountain, which he kept to himself (CBETA X.1551.78:357b15–b16), and recounts the vision in which the Buddha Amitābha appears and predicts his death in seven days' time. In this instance, a new list of friends and followers who have gone before appear with the Buddha: Buddhayaśas, his brother Huichi, his fellow disciple Huiyong, and his lay follower Liu Yimin. Ruizhang concludes with this appraisal of Huiyuan:

> When one investigates the Pure Land dharma-gate, [one finds that] although it was transmitted into the eastern (or stately) court (*zhèncháo* 震朝) and came to Fotucheng, from [Fotu]cheng to Daoan, and among [Dao]an's disciples, it was Master [Hui]yuan who carried it forward and taught it. He expanded this holy Way, and monarchs revered his name. This dharma flowed out into the entire world. A hundred generations have praised him as the first patriarch of Pure Land practice (*jìngyè* 淨業). (CBETA X.1551.78:357c11–c14)

To conclude this survey, we will turn to the mid-Qing dynasty *Liánzōng jiǔ zǔ zhuànlüè* 蓮宗九祖傳略 (Brief biographies of the nine Patriarchs of the Lotus School, 1824) by Wukai (*Wùkāi* 悟開). The biography of Huiyuan has many of the same features and alterations seen so far, but adds a few new elements. First, it credits Huiyuan with all of the initiative in convening the White Lotus Society. In contrast to earlier accounts, which said that 123 literati and clerics joined together to create the society and asked Huiyuan to facilitate the event, Wukai says that 123 people of "pure faith" (*qīngxìn* 清信) came to the mountain, and after their arrival Huiyuan asked rhetorically, "Could all you gentlemen have arrived with no intention toward the Pure Land?" (Wùkāi 1824, p. 39:19345). He then assumes all of the responsibility for establishing the Society, directing Liu Yimin to compose the aspiration text. Huiyuan himself also arranges the hall and sets up the three images of Amitābha and the two bodhisattvas. Further on, Wukai says that in the thirty years Huiyuan lived on Mt. Lu, he was "entirely devoted to Pure Land" (*zhuān zhì jìngtǔ* 專志淨土; Wùkāi 1824, p. 39:19347). After the biography, Wukai added some personal comments in which he raises two important points about Huiyuan. First, he established the White Lotus Society and many worthy clergy and laymen came to it for refuge. Second, he wrote the four words "thoughts focused, imagination stilled" (*sīzhuān xiǎngjì* 思專想寂) in his "Preface" to the poems on the *nianfo* samadhi. These four words, says Wukai, are the "secret essence and primal border-crossing" (*mìyào yuánguān* 秘要元關) of *nianfo* (1824, p. 39:19348). In Wukai's text, Huiyuan's transformation into Pure Land's founding patriarch appears to be complete.

The foregoing demonstrates that the Huiyuan who became the first patriarch of the Pure Land tradition was not the historical Huiyuan portrayed in the earliest sources, but a literary Huiyuan whose image was constructed over several centuries. In the earliest sources, he is a scholar-monk and meditator, a patron of new translations, a master of the political parry, and a strict observer of discipline. He facilitates practices aimed at a vaguely defined "west" before images of Amitābha, but his main interest in this buddha arises from his practice and promotion of the meditation found in the *Pratyutpanna-samādhi-sūtra*. By the time his story reaches its full development in the Qing dynasty, he is a dedicated practitioner of Pure Land who has visions of the Buddha Amitābha and his Land of Bliss and ardently wishes to gain rebirth there. *This* is the Huiyuan who is a Pure Land Buddhist and patriarch.

Conclusions

This chapter posed the question whether Lushan Huiyuan is a Pure Land Buddhist. The process of answering that question has led us to discover that there are two Huiyuans. The first is the Huiyuan who studied Buddhist texts and doctrines, sponsored translation activities, corresponded with Kumārajīva about sutras and methods of religious cultivation, navigated treacherous political waters, kept the rules of the *vinaya* strictly even on his deathbed, attracted a substantial following among both monastics and literati, and avidly practiced the meditation of buddha-visualization or *nianfo* samadhi as prescribed by the *Pratyutpanna-samādhi-sūtra*. When his followers wished to perform rituals and set forth vows to seek rebirth in a "western region" that they only dimly understood, he accommodated them and provided facilities, sponsorship, and guidance. His own personal connection to anything that might be later understood as "Pure Land practice" lay in the *Pratyutpanna-samādhi-sūtra*'s recommendation that one who wished to see a vision of all the buddhas at once should begin by visualizing the Buddha Amitābha as an exemplar of all the rest. This first Huiyuan could not be considered a Pure Land Buddhist in any real sense, and in the centuries that lay between him and the mid–Tang dynasty, he exercised no real influence over the nascent Pure Land movement. Figures such as Tanluan, Daochuo, and Shandao show no sign that they knew of his teaching or were influenced by him, and Jiacai even criticized him.

The second Huiyuan is very different. Beginning in the mid-Tang with the writings of Fazhao, we begin to see the development of an alternative biography for Huiyuan. This new story developed while keeping some elements of the older biographies (as when two different death narratives appear one after the other), but as time went on a new picture emerged. This version of Huiyuan was solely devoted to Pure Land practice (either described as *nianfo* or *jìngyè* 淨業), eagerly sought rebirth in the Pure Land (now called *jìngtǔ* 淨土 or *ānyǎng* 安養, rather than "the west"), had three visions of the Pure Land during his early years on Mt. Lu, actively organized and participated in the White Lotus Society, and had an elaborate vision of the Buddha Amitābha that predicted his coming death and assured him of rebirth. When shorter versions of his life story appear in later texts such as those putting forward lists of Pure Land patriarchs or "rebirth biographies," these items become the essential elements: his three visions, his organization of the White Lotus Society, his assertion that *nianfo* samadhi is the easiest practice to implement and brings the quickest results, and his vision of the Buddha in his last week. *This* Huiyuan is the paradigmatic Pure Land Buddhist whose practice "established the pattern for ten thousand generations."

The answer to the question, then, is both yes and no. The historical Huiyuan was not a "Pure Land Buddhist," but the other Huiyuan, the one whose story came to dominate the later sources, surely was.

Chapter 9

Conclusions

Academic books comprised of previously published articles face the challenge of coherence. Many remain simple anthologies, convenient venues for assembling a scholar's *oeuvre* in one place for easy reference. In this volume, I have aspired to something more. As noted in the introduction, I saw in this project an opportunity to pull together several ideas that, taken together, might provide a much-needed orientation to the study of Chinese Pure Land Buddhism. The essays that I chose to include and the ones that appear here for the first time all tended toward macro-level studies of themes that have endured within the tradition across several centuries. Placing them all together in one volume allowed me to revise them in order to bring out a set of motifs that might help modern western readers understand the tradition as a whole. Now that we have come to the end of this study, the time has come to articulate these themes in order to see the arc of the argument.

The first task was to say with as much precision as possible just what this tradition is. Past studies argued that Pure Land is not Buddhist in any meaningful way, that it does not exist as a school or sect within Buddhism, or that it is so widely diffused throughout Chinese Buddhism that it has no independent standing as a separate topic of study. In contrast, I have argued that Chinese Pure Land Buddhism occupies a distinctive place within the panorama of Chinese Buddhism, and that the best way to understand that place is to define it as a "tradition of practice." This means that Chinese Pure Land Buddhism is a distinctive set of practices accompanied by a set of explanations and understandings within which the practices make sense. These explanations constituted a kind of "theology" of this tradition and provided resources for commending it to potential practitioners and defending it from detractors.

At this point, readers might suspect that I have merely identified one line of thought and practice among many within Chinese Buddhism and then simply designated it as "the Pure Land tradition." I would argue that the identification of this tradition happened within China itself, where arguments took place regarding the legitimacy of this tradition and regarding its proper delineation. For example, the formation of a line of thirteen "patriarchs" provided an armature around which the tradition could be sculpted. The patriarchs were chosen by influential figures and texts, and the inclusion of a given figure within this line followed principles that defined and gave shape to this tradition (see the appendix). It matters that Shandao is a patriarch while Kuiji is not, even though they both wrote a commentary on one of the central scriptures of the tradition.

I hope to have shown that the *sine qua non* of this tradition is the idea of non-elite and unearned achievement. While chapter 8 showed that Lushan Huiyuan took a significant step toward this paradigm by fostering the convocation of the first lay society devoted to *nianfo* practice, it was still rooted in the tradition of virtuoso practice, and the nature of the questions he put to Kumārajīva and the visionary experiences of his disciple Liu Yimin hardly point toward any future "path of easy practice." Tanluan and Daochuo, while crucial precursors to this position, tended to explain the surprising ability of *nianfo* to produce great effects by pointing to factors that made the practitioner's efforts work: roots of merit stored from previous lives, the unusual concentration of the mind at the moment of death, and so on. They also affirmed that the Pure Land into which one was reborn was a reward-land or a transformation-land in accordance with one's level of mental cultivation. It was Shandao who shifted the explanation over to the power of Amitābha and declared that even those who did not have the requisite accomplishment and merit still achieved rebirth into a reward-land. When Shandao severed the connection between a practitioner's level of purification and the kind of Pure Land she or he experienced after death, space finally appeared for popularization of the tradition as a live option for non-virtuoso Buddhists. It led to the possibility of salvation for the butchers and chicken-slaughterers who needed saving from their deathbed terrors, and made controversies inevitable with other Buddhists who still thought practice and achievement mattered. Their determined rejection of this idea necessitated the development of a line of apologetic texts that no other Buddhist teaching in China ever required, as seen in chapter 6.

In addition, we can trace arguments among Chinese Buddhists about the proper set of practices and accompanying explanations that ought to constitute the tradition. The most salient of these was, prior to modern times, the struggle for primacy between the "western-direction" and "mind-only" constructs, which respectively underwrote the practices of simple oral *nianfo* and the more virtuosic meditative practice of the *nianfo* samadhi. The stable endpoint of these arguments was a tradition that allowed for a variety of practices undertaken at a variety of levels of skill, moral self-regulation, and commitment, provided that the diversity include a lower end in which even a person of no skill, no prior practice, and no moral discipline could still achieve rebirth in the Pure Land, attain the stage of non-retrogression, and be forever free of samsara.

Opening up an "easy path" by crediting one's salvation to the "other-power" of Amitābha Buddha entailed the danger of antinomianism as the early Japanese Pure Land schools experienced. The Chinese tradition mitigated this peril by retaining a meaningful role for the practitioner's own efforts. As detailed in chapter 4, the Chinese tradition settled on a scheme whereby self-power and other-power worked together to create a synergy that maximized the benefits of practice. Chapter 5 demonstrated that this vision of the two powers working together prevented any antinomian tendencies from sprouting by insisting that while Amitābha can and will bring those with no contribution whatsoever to rebirth in Sukhāvatī, those who *could* accomplish something were obligated to do so to the best of their ability. With these moves, the tradition navigated a *via media* in which it could affirm both that the Pure Land was open even to the most wretched and evil of people and that one ought nevertheless to make as much progress as possible in this life. As a result of following this middle path, the Pure Land tradition could encompass the many forms of *nianfo* practice described in chapter 7.

While I assert that Chinese Pure Land subsists as a coherent tradition of practice with a unifying set of explanations, we should not assume that the tradition is monolithic. Variations in complexity and emphasis were inevitable given the tensions that its *via media* tried to straddle. These tensions disappear when one affirms one or the other horn of the dilemma to the exclusion of the other. If rebirth and buddhahood are to be attained solely through virtuoso accomplishments in the *nianfo* samadhi, or if the Buddha does all the hard work and one need only commit oneself to his compassion, then no tension need arise. However, the tradition saw the danger in the first (that only a very few practitioners will even attempt the practice while others remain without hope) and in the second (the specter of antinomianism) and so took the difficult step of affirming both. Various figures thus found themselves settling at different points along the continuum, some pushing followers to strenuous and sustained practice, others offering the comfort of trust in Amitābha.

This could also lead to a lack of systematicity in some authors, as when Daochuo in his *Anle ji* slides easily between counseling trust in the Buddha's other-power and pushing readers toward efforts in meditation. The literature of this tradition tends to be responsive rather than systematic; works in the question-and-answer (*wèndá* 問答) format and letters to followers predominate. Systematic treatments such as the first fascicles of Shandao's *Commentary on the Contemplation Sutra* and Zhuhong's *Commentary on the Amitābha Sutra* are the rare exceptions. Consequently, while it is quite possible to provide a reasonable resolution of the dilemma of effort versus entrusting, the scholar generally has to infer it from literature that is pastoral or apologetic in nature.

The resolution was not perfect, either. While the solution outlined in chapter 5 was elegant and allowed the tradition to steer clear of both excessive reliance on practitioner's wobbly abilities and the risk of antinomianism entailed by a complete entrusting to other-power, it never quite provided the certainty of salvation that many desired. Since some element of self-power, however small, remained, one could still fail in the end. This was amply demonstrated by the near-failure of the deathbed practice done on behalf of Yuan Hongdao's nephew cited in chapter 4: The mere presence of a ritually impure maidservant almost dashed his chance for rebirth in the Pure Land. More concerning was the invocation of *ganying* or "sympathetic resonance" as the mechanism whereby one attained rebirth. This brought with it the fear that one's mind might slip from its focus on Amitābha at the last moment of life, and one might not achieve rebirth after all. We saw this in the unsettling story of the man whose years of assiduous practice should have assured him of rebirth in the Pure Land, but who failed right at the finish line simply because a distressed wife worried about her upkeep distracted him.

Still, in the generations after Shandao first opened up the possibility for non-elite attainment of rebirth, the Chinese Pure Land tradition achieved a remarkably stable paradigm that has endured dynastic changes, cultural shifts, and the onset of the modern era. As a tradition embracing practices that range from the simplest to the most complex, it appeals to a wide variety of people and provides a level of practice and an assurance of success across the entire spectrum of human religious aspiration.

Appendix

The Thirteen Chinese Pure Land Patriarchs

As the second chapter has made clear, western scholars made much of the putative list of thirteen "patriarchs" in arguing against the existence of an independent Pure Land School in China. At the same time, I relied on this list along with other factors in determining what figures, texts, and practices are central to the Pure Land tradition, since the inclusion of a figure on this list indicates that a community has agreed to make their teachings and examples normative. I would contend that this is even true, or perhaps especially true, when the life and contributions of a figure like Lushan Huiyuan had to be reconfigured in order to provide a narrative suitable for the list makers' purposes. Given all this, it would be well to give the reader a synopsis of the development and significance of this list. I am heavily indebted to an article by Chen Chienhuang 陳劍鍠 on this subject for much of what follows (see Chen 2015, p. 22–33; an English version of this article may be found at Chen 2017).

While most scholars date the first appearance of such a list to the Northern Song dynasty, it is interesting to note that Daochuo (*Dàochuò* 道綽, 562–645) compiled what appears to be a list of patriarchs over five centuries earlier, though without using the term *zǔ*. In the second fascicle of his *Ānlè jí* 安樂集 (T.1958), he names six members of a master-disciple chain (*shīchéng* 師承) who contributed to the transmission of the Pure Land path (T.1958.47:14b11–c6):

1. Bodhiruci (*Pútíliúzhī* 菩提流支, d. 527)
2. Huichong (*Huìchóng* 慧寵, d.u.)
3. Daochang (*Dàochǎng* 道場, d.u.)

4. Tanluan (*Tánluán* 曇鸞, ca. 476–572)
5. Dahai (*Dàhǎi* 大海). According to Hisao Inagaki, this refers to Huihai (*Huìhǎi* 慧海, 541–609; see trans. Inagaki 2014, p. 157n7).
6. Fashang (*Fǎshàng* 法上, 495–580)

It seems Daochuo intended this list to reflect a series of master-disciple relationships. However, it should be readily apparent from the dates that Fashang's place is implausible. However, Daochuo's list never gained currency, and so we will simply note its existence and move to later, more authoritative lists.

Zongxiao (*Zōngxiǎo* 宗曉, 1151–1214) compiled the first list of patriarchs for the Pure Land tradition to gain wide recognition and adoption. In a section of his *Lèbāng wénlèi* 樂邦文類 (Anthology of the Land of Bliss, T.1969A) called "Biographies of the Additional Five Great Masters of the Lotus Society" (*Liánshè jìzǔ wǔ dàfǎshī zhuàn* 蓮社繼祖五大法師傳) he wrote:

> The Lotus Society was established with Master [Hui]yuan as its first patriarch. From his passing to the present 5th year of Qìngyuán 慶元 in the Song, a *jǐwèi* 己未 year [i.e., 1199], about 800 years have elapsed. During this time, five masters have transmitted his Way. The first is Shandao (*Shàndǎo* 善導), the second is Fazhao (*Fǎzhào* 法照), the third is Shaokang (*Shǎokāng* 少康), the fourth is Shengchang (*Shěngcháng* 省常), and the fifth is Zongze (*Zōngzé* 宗賾). (T.1969A.47:192c18–c22)

Since that time, several other authors put forward suggested lists of patriarchs of the Pure Land School, and while there is some variability, the names of the first six have remained stable. The following table shows how the list evolved through several publications.

	Lèbāng wénlèi 樂邦文類, 1199	*Fózǔ tǒngjì* 佛祖統紀, 1269	*Jìngtǔ zhǐguī jí* 淨土指歸集, 1383	*Jìngtǔ shēng wúshēng lùn zhù* 淨土生無生論註 by Zhèngjì 正寂, preface 1612	*Shēng wúshēng lùn qīnwén jì* 生無生論親聞記 by Shòujiào 受教, preface 1626	*Xīfāng huìzhēng* 西舫彙征 by Ruìzhāng 瑞璋, Qing dynasty	*Liánzōng jiǔ zǔ zhuànlüè* 蓮宗九祖傳略 by Shi Wùkāi 釋悟開, 1824	*Shízōng lüèshuō* 十宗略說 by Yáng Wénhuì 楊文會, late Qing	*Liánzōng shí èr zǔ zànsòng* 蓮宗十二祖讚頌, by Yìnguāng 印光, 1935	*Língyán shān sì niànsòng yíguī* 靈巖山寺念誦儀規, by Yìnguāng 印光, 1930–1932
1	Huìyuǎn 慧遠	Huìyuǎn 慧遠	Huìyuǎn 慧遠	Huìyuǎn 慧遠	Huìyuǎn 慧遠	Huìyuǎn 慧遠	Huìyuǎn 慧遠	Huìyuǎn 慧遠	Huìyuǎn 慧遠	Huìyuǎn 慧遠
2	Shàndǎo 善導	Shàndǎo 善導	Shàndǎo 善導	Shàndǎo 善導	Shàndǎo 善導	Shàndǎo 善導	Shàndǎo 善導	Tánluán曇鸞	Shàndǎo 善導	Shàndǎo 善導
3	Fǎzhào 法照	Chéngyuǎn 承遠	Chéngyuǎn 承遠	Chéngyuǎn 承遠	Chéngyuǎn 承遠	Chéngyuǎn 承遠	Chéngyuǎn 承遠	Dàochuò 道綽	Chéngyuǎn 承遠	Chéngyuǎn 承遠
4	Shǎokāng 少康	Fǎzhào 法照	Fǎzhào 法照	Fǎzhào 法照	Fǎzhào 法照	Fǎzhào 法照	Fǎzhào 法照	Shàndǎo 善導	Fǎzhào 法照	Fǎzhào 法照
5	Shěngcháng 省常	Shǎokāng 少康	Shǎokāng 少康	Shǎokāng 少康	Shǎokāng 少康	Shǎokāng 少康	Shǎokāng 少康	Yánshòu 延壽	Shǎokāng 少康	Shǎokāng 少康
6	Zōngzé 宗賾	Yánshòu 延壽	Yánshòu 延壽	Yánshòu 延壽	Yánshòu 延壽	Yánshòu 延壽	Yánshòu 延壽	Zhūhóng 袾宏	Yánshòu 延壽	Yánshòu 延壽
7		Shěngcháng 省常	Shěngcháng 省常	Shěngcháng 省常	Shěngcháng 省常	Shěngcháng 省常	Shěngcháng 省常		Shěngcháng 省常	Shěngcháng 省常
8			Zōngzé 宗賾	Zōngzé 宗賾		Zōngzé 宗賾	Zhūhóng 袾宏		Zhūhóng 袾宏	Zhūhóng 袾宏
9						Zhūhóng 袾宏	Shěng'ān 省庵		Zhìxù 智旭	Zhìxù 智旭
10									Xíngcè 行策	Xíngcè 行策
11									Shěng'ān 省庵	Shěng'ān 省庵
12									Chèwù 徹悟	Chèwù 徹悟
13										Yìnguāng 印光

Below is the list of thirteen patriarchs of the Pure Land School as constituted by Yinguang and finalized after his death by his followers with him as the thirteenth name:

1. 廬山慧遠 Lúshān Huìyuǎn (334–416)
2. 善導 Shàndǎo (613–681)
3. 承遠 Chéngyuǎn (712–802)
4. 法照 Fǎzhào (d.u.)
5. 少康 Shǎokāng (d. 805)
6. 永明延壽 Yǒngmíng Yánshòu (904–975)
7. 省常 Shěngcháng (858–1020)
8. 蓮池 Liánchí or 雲棲袾宏 Yúnqī Zhūhóng (1535–1615)
9. 蕅益智旭 Ǒuyì Zhìxù (1599–1655)
10. 行策 Xíngcè (1628–1682)
11. 實賢 Shíxián (1686–1734)
12. 際醒徹悟 Jìxǐng Chèwù (1741–1810)
13. 印光 Yìnguāng (1861–1941)

Note: Birth and death dates vary with sources.

As noted in chapter 2, this was never intended to represent a continuous lineage of masters and disciples. What is the lists' purpose, then? First and foremost, it represents an orthodox lineage of teachers whose centrality within the tradition exerts some control over its contents and interpretations. Zongxiao articulated this purpose in his *Lèbāng wénlèi* as seen in the quote given above (T.1969A.47:192c18–c21). Wukai echoed Zongxiao in his 1824 text *Liánzōng jiǔ zǔ zhuànlüè* 蓮宗九祖傳略:

> Master Shima [Zong]xiao of the Song dynasty established seven figures as patriarchal masters of the Lotus School (*liánzōng* 蓮宗). These patriarchs of the Lotus School signify the extension of the orthodox dharma-line from ancient times so that later generations could uphold the discipline of this household (*jiāfǎ* 家法) without mixing in extraneous elements or deviating into heterodoxies. (Wùkāi 1824, p. 39:19339)

Explaining why he compiled his own list of nine patriarchs in another work, he says: "These [patriarchs] are the pillars of this dharma-gate. Recently I humbly published my *Lianzong jiu zu zhuanlüe* out of a desire that the source and stream of the Lotus School's orthodox lineage may have something upon which to depend" (CBETA X.1184.361c24–362a2). Those who put forward lists of patriarchs, then, regard these figures as the "fathers" of a discrete tradition whose orthodoxies they defined, defended, and transmitted. The various rolls of patriarchs serve to articulate an understanding of the Pure Land tradition.

Once formulated, these lists then enter into the life of that tradition in various ways. For example, in his 2006 general introduction to Pure Land Buddhism, the modern proponent Daan (*Dàān* 大安, b. 1959) provides short biographies of the thirteen patriarchs as part of his presentation (2006, p. 127–222). He thus seems to believe that knowing about these men is essential to understanding the tradition. Other writers have circulated their own collected biographies of the patriarchs, making explicit their role in carrying forward what the authors consider the orthodox tradition. For example, the preface to Liang Yongkang's (Liáng Yǒngkāng 梁永康) collection of patriarchs' biographies defines the tradition as one in which ordinary people can purify themselves completely simply by holding the Buddha's name and attaining rebirth in his Pure Land. This teaching flourished in China because of the patriarchs from Huiyuan to Yinguang who kept it alive (Liáng 1979, p. 351).

In certain breviaries, one finds Pure Land liturgies that name the patriarchs for veneration. For example, a breviary called *Jìngzōng gòngxiū kèběn* 淨宗共修課本 contains a set of liturgies for a seven-day *nianfo* retreat (*fóqī* 佛七). The retreat's closing ceremony includes a litany to the thirteen patriarchs in which participants pay homage to each of them by name (Huázàng jìngzōng xuéhuì 華藏淨宗學會 2003, p. 25–27). Likewise, the more generally oriented breviary *Fómén bìbèi kèsòngběn* 佛門必備課誦本 has a ceremony for transferring the merit of participating in a seven-day *nianfo* retreat to the thirteen patriarchs (*Fómén bìbèi kèsòngběn* 1954, p. 117–119). Honoring these men in a ritual setting signals that they are of vital importance to the Pure Land tradition.

While various Buddhist authors through the centuries have had their own purposes in formulating lists of patriarchs and criteria for inclusion, these lists (especially the final list of thirteen) have gained wide acceptance among Chinese Buddhists. The patriarchs are no longer just a roster of paragons of the tradition as imagined by elite writers; they now provide ordinary devotees a central list of "fathers" who help them to understand the teachings and define the boundaries of the tradition in which they participate.

Notes

Chapter 2: What Is the Chinese Pure Land Tradition?

1 The parenthetical phrase is in the original text.

2 This is Professor Chen's preferred Romanization.

3 Two further observations are pertinent here: First, there is a passage at the beginning of the *Wangsheng lun zhu* that connects rebirth in the Pure Land to Amitābha's vow-power. However, this is a quotation from Nāgārjuna and is not of Tanluan's composition, and Tanluan does not refer to this statement in his comments. Second, as an example of the ways in which reliance on Japanese scholarship has sometimes misled us into thinking more is being said in such texts than is actually the case, Inagaki's translation renders *shí niàn niànfó* 十念念佛 as "call my Name even ten times," even though the passage does not contain any word corresponding to "name" and in a way that assumes that *niàn* 念 means oral invocation and not mental contemplation.

4 The Sutra Translation Committee of the United States and Canada published an English translation of Tianru's text in 1991. However, it is quite unsatisfactory and so while I have consulted it, I do not quote from it.

Chapter 3: The Development of the Concept of the Pure Land

This chapter is a significantly revised version of "The Pure Land in the History of Chinese Buddhism," in *The Buddhist World*, ed. John Powers (London: Routledge, 2015), p. 219–234.

1 The original text is ambiguous here. It might indicate that the various buddha-fields can be distinguished into the coarse (*cū* 粗) and the subtle or marvelous (*miào* 妙), which is the way Gómez translates the passage (1996, p. 165). It could also mean that the buddha described the coarser and

subtler aspects of each land, and Inagaki and Stewart follow this reading (2003, p. 13).

2 This means that translating *rénjiān jìngtǔ* as the "earthly Pure Land" or "Pure Land on Earth," as some authors do, is not accurate. See Ritzinger 2017, p. 119.

Chapter 4: Self-Power and Other-Power in Chinese Pure Land Buddhism

1 The term "Three Contemplations in One Mind" (*yīxīn sānguān* 一心三觀) generally refers to a Tiantai formulation in which a meditator in one thought simultaneously grasps the emptiness, provisionality, and mean of a phenomenon.

Chapter 5: Ethics and Precepts in Chinese Pure Land Buddhism

This chapter is a significantly revised version of "Foundations of Ethics and Practice in Chinese Pure Land Buddhism," *Journal of Buddhist Ethics* 10 (2003): 1–20.

1 This trend may be subsidiary to a larger trend noted by Jacqueline Stone wherein East Asian Buddhist history becomes a prologue to the "reform" movements of Kamakura-era Japan. In this view, not only Hōnen, Shinran, and Ippen but also Nichiren and Dōgen become *teloi* for the history that precedes them. See Stone 1999, p. 93–94.

2 In Pure Land texts, the term "pure karma" (*jìngyè* 淨業) is usually synonymous with Pure Land practice.

Chapter 6: Defending Pure Land in Late Imperial China

This chapter is a significantly revised version of "Apologetic Strategies in Late Imperial Chinese Pure Land Buddhism," *Journal of Chinese Religions*, no. 29 (2001): 69–90.

1 Although the *Huáyán jīng hé lùn* 華嚴經合論 is in the *Xùzàngjīng* 續藏經 (see CBETA X.223), that version does not contain this text, a fact that figures in the argument as seen below. However, the reprint I have cited contains it, and Yinguang clearly had this version in hand.

2 That Samantabhadra voices this vow is not accidental. Gregory Schopen has documented a connection between this bodhisattva and rebirth in Sukhāvatī that goes back to Indian Mahayana texts. See Schopen 2005, p. 179.

3 The most complete study of this question of which I am aware is the lengthy chapter in Gu 2000. See especially 181–183 for an account of the transmission of the last fascicle of the sutra into China.

4 Heng-ching Shih points out that this verse does not appear in any of Yanshou's extant works. Rather, it appears first in a 1393 work by Dayou (*Dàyòu* 大佑) called the *Jìngtǔ zhǐguī jí* 淨土指歸集, now found in XZJ 108.114–198 and CBETA X.1154. See CBETA X.1154.61:379b21–c9 for Dayou's text, and Shih 1992, p. 145, where they are called the "fourfold summary." The above is my own translation of the verses.

5 The first quote appears in the book *Zǔtáng jí* 祖堂集 (Patriarch's hall anthology), composed around 952 CE. The first quotation is found in the *Zu tang ji* 334b9. A variant of the second quotation appears in the *Chóngkè Zhàozhōu zǔshī yǔlù* 重刻趙州祖師語錄 (Newly engraved recorded sayings of Patriarchal master Zhaozhou) in CBETA at J24nB137_ p0357a15, but this is in the introduction rather than the main text. It appears in several other texts and contexts as well.

Chapter 7: Methods of *Nianfo* in Chinese Pure Land Buddhism

This chapter is a significantly revised version of "Toward a Typology of *Nien-fo*: A Study in Methods of Buddha-Invocation in Chinese Pure Land Buddhism," *Pacific World: Journal of the Institute of Buddhist Studies*, 3rd Series, no. 3 (2001): 219–239.

1 The following four types of *nianfo* are outlined in Mochizuki 1942, p. 309–311. The title is a variant of that given in Gregory 1991, p. 319, and I have to assume they both refer to the same work. The reference in the XZJ is also different, as I consulted the Xinwenfeng edition published in Taipei. In CBETA, this work is listed as *Dà fāngguǎng fó Huáyán jīng Pǔxián xíngyuàn pǐn biéxíng shūchǎo* 大方廣佛華嚴經普賢行願品別行疏鈔, CBETA X.229.

2 Zongmi's citation does not match the text as found in the Taishō beginning at T.614.15:281a22. His quotation appears first as an inexact quotation but it quickly deviates and becomes unrecognizable. The basic practice that Zongmi describes is present in this passage.

Chapter 8: Lushan Huiyuan

This chapter is a significantly revised version of "Was Lushan Huiyuan 盧山慧遠 a Pure Land Buddhist? Evidence from His Correspondence with Kumārajīva About *Nianfo* 念佛 Practice," *Chung-Hwa Buddhist Journal* 21 (July 2008): 175–191.

1 夢是凡夫之境。惑之與解皆自厓已還理了。My rendering follows Mochizuki Shinkō's Japanese paraphrase of this passage (1942, p. 25–26) and Kimura's modern Japanese rendering (1960–1962, *Eon Kenkyū*, p. 1:165).

2 Huiyuan is not quoting the sutra directly. The basic idea comes from T.418, p.13:905c25–c29. Paul Harrison translates this section, "When the forms

are clear, everything is clear. If one wishes to see the Buddha then one sees him. If one sees him then one asks questions. If one asks then one is answered. One hears the sūtras and rejoices greatly." See Harrison 1998, p. 21.

3 In other words, how could a buddha created by one's own mind preach the dharma that goes beyond one's own pre-existing understanding? Kimura suggests moving the repeated word *huò* 或 ("or perhaps") down below the word "buddha" in the next clause to create a parallelism that makes sense, and I follow his advice here. In addition, the Japanese paraphrase in Kimura 1960–1962, p. 1:166, glosses *jiě* 解 as *satori,* which normally means "enlightenment." However, Huiyuan is asking about a visualized buddha answering questions, and so I have used the word "dispelling" instead.

4 Most of the questions that Huiyuan puts to Kumārajīva in these letters have to do with the *dharmakāya* buddha that is free from all particular characteristics, including location in space. The meditation in the sutra has one visualize a buddha, which requires that the buddha have characteristics to visualize and be located in space. Under these circumstances, one may speak of the buddha coming to the meditator or the meditator going out to the buddha through supernatural power. This is why Huiyuan has to specify that he is not here talking about the "true character" of the *dharmakāya.*

5 Again, Huiyuan is not quoting directly, and so it is a little difficult to know exactly which part of the sutra he has in mind. In fascicle one, however, we find the following (T.418.13:905c16–c18): 於三昧中立者。有三事。持佛威神力。持佛三昧力。持本功德力。用是三事故。得見佛。Paul Harrison renders this passage as: "[Those] who are established in the meditation have three things: they possess the numinous power of the Buddha, they possess the power of the Buddha's meditation, and they possess the power of their former merit. Because of these three things they succeed in seeing the Buddha" (Harrison 1998, p. 21).

6 This sentence does not occur in the Taishō version of the text. Kimura explains that he added it to his critical text because it is in all other versions. See *Eon kenkyū,* p. 1:34 and 1:34n15.

7 This is a difficult passage, but after consulting Kimura's modern Japanese paraphrase (*Eon kenkyū,* p. 1:166) and Mochizuki's explanation (1942, p. 26), then we may perhaps paraphrase Huiyuan's difficulty with the dream metaphor as follows. If the buddha seen in the samadhi is internally generated, as a dream would be, then one cannot put questions to him and expect to learn anything new. On the other hand, if an external buddha comes in from outside, as the sutra seems to imply when it says one depends upon the buddha's "numinous power," then this violates the meaning of samadhi, which is a meditation wherein the practitioner is focused internally and external stimuli are shut out. The problem is in trying to square a state

of mind described by the words "samadhi" and "dream" with the idea that one sees a real being who can give one new teaching.

8 The phrase beginning "The second . . ." and ending with ". . . the *pratyutpanna-samādhi*" is missing from the Taishō edition, but appears in Kimura's critical edition from other sources. See *Eon kenkyū,* p. 1:35.

9 Many of the ideas, and much of the wording, in these two paragraphs reflect a discussion on the "divine eye" (*tiānyǎn* 天眼) and the "divine ear" (*tiān'ěr* 天耳) in fascicle 33 of the *Dà zhìdù lùn* 大智度論 (T.1509), which Kumārajīva was in the midst of translating during this exchange of letters. Beginning at T.1509.25:306a12, the *Dà zhìdù lùn* discusses the use of spiritual powers to fly throughout the ten directions to see all the buddhas. It even compares this specifically with the *nianfo* samadhi as explained in the *Pratyutpanna-samādhi-sūtra,* saying that those who have abandoned desires can achieve the divine eye and divine ear, while those who have not can still see the buddhas in samadhi. The *Dà zhìdù lùn* also agrees that the first is indeed superior and the second inferior. The first is like seeing all the buddhas in the clear light of day, while the second is like seeing them in the dark by lighting a lamp and seeing them only indistinctly (T.1509.25:306a22–23).

10 Other versions have *suī* 雖 ("although") instead of *lí* 離 ("abandon") in this sentence. If one adopts this version, the meaning becomes ". . . although they [use] words and conceptual distinctions, they are not deluded [*or* the visualization is not delusive]." See *Eon kenkyū,* p. 1:35n3.

11 Actually, the *Pratyutpanna-samādhi-sūtra* does not say this, but the *Dà zhìdù lùn* does in fascicle 29: "As explained in the middle of the *pratyutpanna* samadhi, a bodhisattva who enters this samadhi immediately sees the Buddha Amitābha and asks the buddha 'by what karma and cause-and-effect is one born in that land?' The buddha then answers, saying, 'Good son, by constantly cultivating the *nianfo* samadhi without respite, one obtains birth in my land.' Question: What is this *nianfo* samadhi and attaining birth in that land? Answer: *Nianfo* means recalling the buddha's 32 marks and 80 characteristics and his golden form-body. The body emits a light which illuminates and fills the ten directions." See T.1509.25:276a21–a25.

12 The text here has *běnmò* 本末, literally "root and branch," which Kimura paraphrases as *sujimichi* 筋道, "system or method." See *Eon kenkyū,* p. 1:167. Leon Hurvitz took the phrase to refer to the image of the Buddha seen in meditation as having a "top and bottom" (Tsukamoto 1985, p. 2:853). I am taking the phrase to indicate the confluence or the practice (root) and the Buddha Amitābha's outreach (branch), which creates an end-to-end connection. In this interpretation, Kumārajīva is explaining why the practice works even if the practitioner is not highly accomplished.

13 I have translated *chándìng* 禪定 as "meditative samadhi" and *niàn* 念 as "contemplation" because I believe Kumārajīva is talking about two very different practices here. The first refers to a very deep trance meditation, one that might well confer spiritual powers such as the divine eye, which would allow the practitioner to see buddhas from great distances. The other is a reflective contemplation or recollection involving no deep trance and so conferring no spiritual powers but only a settling of the mind. The point, therefore, is that people do not believe that a person who does not know how to perform the first practice and gain the power but only performs the second practice would ever be able to see a buddha 100,000 buddha-lands distant. Within the *Dà zhìdù lùn,* meditative samadhi is connected with the achievement of the divine eye in fascicle 2 (T.1509.25:684a4–a5). In fascicle 7, the commentator specifically states that the energetic practice of meditative samadhi along with keeping the precepts will lead to the attainment of the divine eye. See T.1509.25:112b25–b26.

14 The Taishō text has *bùrán* 不然 here, but other editions have *zìrán* 自然. See the critical text in *Eon kenkyū,* p. 1:35.

15 The argument here seems to be that the buddhas' bodies are just the same as any other phenomenon. They are quiescent and empty in themselves, while at the same time each mind that perceives them (through the *pratyutpanna*-samadhi) constructs them according to conditions, so that each attains his or her own proper benefit and puts down distinctive good roots according to their own individual conditions.

16 This is Kimura's emendation. See *Eon kunkyū,* p. 1:168.

17 Neither the Taishō text nor Kimura's critical text specifies that such a person has necessarily seen any buddha; the text at T.1856.45:135a ends with *jiàn* 見. Kimura adds the word "buddha" in his Japanese paraphrase with no justification. See *Eon kunkyū,* p. 1:168.

18 Zürcher's translation has "Huiyuan (and these lay devotees) held a fasting (ceremony) and made the vow together to strive for (rebirth in) the Western Region" (p. 244). I have translated it differently because the sentence structure clearly indicates that it was Huiyuan who held the fast and established the vow. The subsequent statement, which Zürcher translates correctly, indicates that Huiyuan ordered Liu to compose the vow. If read in the way that I have translated it, then this passage provides less support for Zürcher's downplaying of Huiyuan's interest in the affair.

19 Another version of this story with an extended commentary appears in fascicle 26 of the *Fózǔ tǒngjì* 佛祖統紀, T.2035.49:269a27–269c13. Another, somewhat different version is found in the *Dōnglín shíbā gāoxián zhuàn* 東林

十八高賢傳 (Biographies of eighteen high sages of the Donglin [Temple]), CBETA X.1543.78:119b9–b16.

20 A Tang dynasty text by Shaokang that we will consider next identifies this as Chan master Daozhen (*Dàozhēn* 道珍) and places him in the Liang dynasty (*Liáng cháo* 梁朝, 502–557) rather than the Chen. See T.2070.51:104b9–b19.

Bibliography

Primary Sources

Bǎizhàng qīngguī 百丈清規 (Pure rules of Baizhang), T.2025.

Bānzhōu sānmèi jīng 般舟三昧經 (*Pratyutpanna-samādhi-sūtra*), T.418.

Bingenheimer, Marcus, et al., trans. 2013. *The Madhyama Āgama* (Middle-length discourses). Vol. 1. Berkeley: Bukkyo Dendo Kyokai America, Inc.

Chewu 徹悟. 1993. *Chèwù chánshī yǔlù* 徹悟禪師語錄 (Recorded sayings of Chan Master Chewu). *Dai Nihon zoku zōkyō* 大日本續藏經. Kyoto: Zōkyō Shoin, 1905–1912. Rpt. Taipei: Xinwenfeng, 新文豐, vol. 109:750–790. Also CBETA X.1182.

Chóngkè Zhàozhōu zǔshī yǔlù 重刻趙州祖師語錄, CBETA J.B137.

Cleary J. C., trans. 1994. *Pure Land, Pure Mind.* New York: Sutra Translation Committee of the United States and Canada.

Corless, Roger, Takehiko Kameyama, and Richard K. Payne. 2015. "A Commentary on *The Upadeśa on the Sutras of Limitless Life with Gāthās on the Resolution to be Born* Composed by the Bodhisattva Vasubandhu." *Pacific World: Journal of the Institute of Buddhist Studies,* 3rd series, no. 17:69–233.

Dà bǎojī jīng 大寶積經, T.310.

Dà fāngděng dà jí jīng xián hù fēn 大方等大集經賢護分, T.416.

Dà zhìdù lùn 大智度論, T.1509.

Dàbān nièpán jīng 大般涅槃經, T.374.

Dàoaxuān 道宣. *Guǎng hóng míng jí* 廣弘明集, T.2103.

Dàochuò 道綽. *Ānlè jí* 安樂集 (Anthology of the Land of Bliss), T.1958.

Dàoshì 道世. *Fǎyuàn zhūlín* 法苑珠林, T.2122.

Dàshèng yì zhāng 大乘義章, T.1851.

Dàyòu 大佑. *Jìngtǔ zhǐguī jí* 淨土指歸集, XZJ 108.114–198. Also CBETA X.1154.

Dōnglín shíbā gāoxián zhuàn 東林十八高賢傳 (Biographies of eighteen high sages of the Donglin [Temple]), CBETA X.1543.

Fǎgǔ wénhuà biānjí bù 法鼓文化編輯部. 2016. *Niànfó 50 wèn* 念佛50問 (50 questions on the Buddha-Name recitation practice [*sic*]). Taipei: Fagu wenhua 法鼓文化.

Fǎhuá wénjù jì 法華文句記 (Notes on [Zhiyi's] Commentary on the text of the *Lotus Sutra*), T.1719.

Fó shuō Āmítuó jīng 佛說阿彌陀經 (Amitābha Sutra), T.366.

Fó shuō guān wúliàngshòu fó jīng 佛說觀無量壽佛經 (Contemplation Sutra), T.365.

Fó shuō guānfó sānmèihǎi jīng 佛說觀佛三昧海經, T.643.

Fó shuō wúliàngshòu jīng 佛說無量壽經 (Larger Sutra), T.360.

Fómén bìbèi kèsòngběn 佛門必備課誦本 (Essential lections for the Buddha Gate). 1954. Taipei: Fojiao Chubanshe 佛教出版社.

Gómez, Luis O., trans. 1996. *The Land of Bliss: The Paradise of the Buddha of Measureless Light.* Honolulu: University of Hawai'i Press.

Guīfēng Zōngmì 圭峰宗密. *Huáyán jīng Pǔxián xíngyuàn pǐn shū chǎo* 華嚴經普賢行願品疏鈔, CBETA X.229.

Hakeda, Yoshito S., trans. 1967. *The Awakening of Faith Attributed to Asvaghosha: Translation, with Commentary.* New York: Columbia University Press.

Hānshān Déqīng 憨山德清. 1992. *Hānshān lǎorén mèngyóu jí* 憨山老人夢遊集 (Record of Elder Hanshan's dream travels). Edited and compiled by Tóngjiǒng 通炯. 4 vols. Jiangbei: Jiangbei kejing chu, 1879. Rpt. Taipei: Xinwenfeng 新文豐.

Harrison, Paul, trans. 1998. *The Pratyutpanna Samadhi Sūtra.* BDK English Tripitaka, 25-II. Berkeley: Numata Center for Buddhist Translation and Research.

Huáigǎn 懷感. *Shì jìngtǔ qúnyí lùn* 釋淨土群疑論 (Treatise explaining a number of doubts about Pure Land), T.1960.

Huáyán jīng hé lùn 華嚴經合論. 1977. Compiled by Zhining 志寧. 2 vols. Undated print. Rpt. Taipei: Xinwenfeng 新文豐.

Huázàng jìngzōng xuéhuì 華藏淨宗學會. 2003. *Jìngzōng gòngxiū kèběn* 淨宗共修課本. Taipei: Huazang jingzong xuehui 華藏淨宗學會.

Huìjiǎo 慧皎. *Gāosēng zhuàn* 高僧傳, T.2059.

Inagaki Hisao, trans. 1998. *Ōjōronchū: T'an-luan's Commentary on Vasubandhu's Discourse on the Pure Land.* Tokyo: Nagata Bunshodo.

——, trans. 2014. *Collection of Passages on the Land of Peace and Bliss* 《安樂集》 *An Le Chi by Daochuo* 道綽. N.p.: Horai Association International.

Inagaki Hisao and Harold Stewart, trans. 2003. *The Three Pure Land Sutras.* 2nd rev. ed. BDK English Tripitaka 12-II, III, IV. Berkeley: Numata Center for Buddhist Translation and Research.

Jìngtǔ lùn 淨土論, T.1963.

Jìngtǔ shēng wúshēng lùn qīnwén jì 淨土生無生論親聞記, CBETA X.1168.

Jìngtǔ shēng wúshēng lùn zhù 淨土生無生論註, CBETA X.1167.

Jìngtǔ shí yí lùn 淨土十疑論, T.1961.

Jìngtǔ wǔhuì niànfó sòngjīng guānxíng yí 淨土五會念佛誦經觀行儀, T.2827.

Jìngtǔ zhǐguī jí 淨土指歸集, CBETA X.1154.

Jiūmóluóshí fǎshī dàyì 鳩摩羅什法師大義 (The great meaning of [the teachings of] the Dharma Master Kumārajīva), T.1856.

Kuījī 窺基. *Āmítuó jīng tōngzàn shū* 阿彌陀經通贊疏, T.1758.

Liáng Yǒngkāng 梁永康. 1979. "Liánzōng shísān zǔ chóngxíng jiāyán lù" 蓮宗十三祖崇行嘉言錄. In *Jìngtǔ zōng shǐ lùn* 淨土宗史論, edited by Zhāng Màntāo 張曼濤, p. 351–368. Xiàndài fójiào xuéshù cóngkān 現代佛教學術叢刊, 65. Taipei: Dasheng wenhua chubanshe 大乘文化出版社.

Liù zǔ dàshī fǎbǎo tán jīng 六祖大師法寶壇經, T.2008.

McRae, John, trans. 2000. *The Platform Sutra of the Sixth Patriarch.* BDK English Tripitaka, 73-II. Berkeley: Numata Center for Buddhist Translation and Research.

Móhē zhǐguān 摩訶止觀, T.1911.

Niànfó sānmèi bǎowáng lùn 念佛三昧寶王論, T.1967.

Ǒuyì Zhìxù 藕益智旭. 1989. *Fǎhǎi guānlán* 法海觀瀾. In *Ǒuyì dàshī quánjí* 藕益大師全集, p. 3:1877–2178. Taipei: Fojiao shuju 佛教書局.

Rúlái guǎngxiào shí zhǒng bào'ēn dàochǎng yí 如來廣孝十種報恩道場儀, CBETA ZW68.

Sēngzhào 僧肇. *Zhù Wéimójí jīng* 注維摩詰經, T.1775.

Shàndǎo 善導. *Guān wúliàngshòu fó jīng shū* 觀無量壽佛經疏 (Commentary on the *Contemplation Sutra*), T.1753.

——. *Guānniàn Āmítuófó xiànghǎi sānmèi gōngdé fǎmén* 觀念阿彌陀佛相海三昧功德法門 (The dharma-gate for the merit of the samadhi of contemplating Amitābha Buddha's ocean of marks), T.1959.

——. *Wǎngshēng lǐzàn jì* 往生禮讚偈 (Verses of obeisance and praise of rebirth), T.1980.

Shì Zhìyù 釋智諭. 1986. "Sì zhǒng niànfó" 四種念佛 ("Four kinds of *nianfo*"). In *Chípàn lián chāo* 池畔蓮鈔, vol. 2, p. 21–24. Sanxia: Xilian jingyuan 西蓮淨苑.

——. 1988. *Xiàyǔ qīngliáng* 夏雨清涼. Sanxia 三峽: Xilian jing yuan 西蓮淨苑.

——. 1992. *Shīfù de huà* 師父的話. Taipei: Xilian jingyuan 西蓮淨苑.

Shí zhù pípóshā lùn 十住毘婆沙論, T.1521.

Sutra Translation Committee of the United States and Canada. 1991. *Pure Land Buddhism: Dialogues with Ancient Masters.* New York: The Committee.

Tàixū 太虛. 1956. "Jiànshè rénjiān jìngtǔ lùn" 建設人間淨土論 ("On the establishment of the Pure Land in the human realm"). In *Tàixū dàshī quánshū* 太虛大師全書, p. 24:349–430. Taipei: Shandao Temple Sutra Distribution Center 善導寺佛經流通處. Downloaded from http://www.nanputuo.com/nptlib/html/200707/1812143485802.html.

Tánluán 曇鸞. *Lüèlùn ānlè jìngtǔ yì* 略論安樂淨土義, T.1957.

——. *Wúliángshòujīng yōupótíshè yuànshēngjié pósǒupántóu púsà zàobīng zhù* 無量壽經優婆提舍願生偈婆藪槃頭菩薩造并註 (Commentary on Vasubandhu's Treatise on the Pure Land), T.1819.

Thurman, Robert, trans. 1976. *The Holy Teaching of Vimalakīrti: A Mahayana Scripture.* University Park: The Pennsylvania State University Press.

Vasubandhu. 2015. "*Jōdoron* 淨土論: Discourse on the Pure Land." Translated by David Matsumoto. *Pacific World: Journal of the Institute of Buddhist Studies,* 3rd series, no. 17:23–42.

Walshe, Maurice, trans. 1987. *Thus Have I Heard: The Long Discourses of the Buddha.* London: Wisdom Publications.

Wáng Rìxuī 王日休. *Lóngshū zēngguǎng jìngtǔ wén* 龍舒增廣淨土文 (Longshu's augmented Pure Land essays), T.1970.

Wǎngshēng xīfāng jìngtǔ ruìyìng shānzhuàn 往生西方淨土瑞應刪傳, T.2070.

Wànshàn tóngguī jí 萬善同歸集, T.2017.

Watson, Burton, trans. 1997. *The Vimalakirti Sutra.* New York: Columbia University Press.

Wéimójí suǒshuō jīng 維摩詰所說經, T.475.

Wéizé Tiānrú 惟則天如. *Jìngtǔ huòwèn* 淨土或問 (Questions about Pure Land), T.1972.

Wénshūshīlì suǒshuō móhē bōrě bōluómì jīng 文殊師利所說摩訶般若波羅蜜經, T.232.

Wùkāi 悟開. 1824. *Liánzōng jiǔ zǔ zhuànlüè* 蓮宗九祖傳略. n.p.: n.p. Rpt. Zhōngguó guójiā túshūguǎn fēnguǎn 國家圖書館分館編, ed. 2005. *Zhōnghuá fójiào rénwù zhuànjì wénxiàn quánshū* 中華佛教人物傳記文獻全書, p. 39:19337–19398. Beijing: Xian zhuang shuju 綫裝書局.

——. 1825. *Niànfó bǎi wèn* 念佛百問, CBETA X.1184.

Wúliàng shòu jīng yōubōtíshè yuànshēng jì 無量壽經優波提舍願生偈, T.1524.

Xīnxiū wǎngshēng zhuàn 新修往生傳, CBETA X.1546.

Xù jìngtǔ wǎngshēng zhuàn 敘淨土往生傳, T.2071.

Xúnzǐ 荀子. 1999. *Xunzi.* Translated by John Knoblock and Zhang Jue 张觉. 2 vols. Changsha 长沙: Hunan People's Publishing House 湖南人民出版社.

Xuyun. 1988. *Empty Cloud: The Autobiography of the Chinese Zen Master Xuyun.* Translated by Charles Luk; revised and edited by Richard Hunn. Longmead: Element Books.

Yampolsky, Philip B., trans. 1967. *The Platform Sutra of the Sixth Patriarch.* New York: Columbia University Press.

Yìnguāng 印光. 1991. *Yìnguāng dàshī quánjí* 印光大師全集 (The collected works of Great Master Yinguang). Compiled and edited by Shi Guangding 釋廣定. 8 vols. Taipei: Fojiao Chubanshe 佛教出版社.

——. 2012. "Treatise Resolving Doubts about the Pure Land (*Jingtu jueyi lun* 淨土決疑論) by Master Yinguang 印光 (1861–1947)." Translated by Charles B. Jones. *Pacific World: Journal of the Institute of Buddhist Studies,* 3rd series, no. 14:27–61.

Yìnshùn 印順. 1992. *Jìngtǔ yǔ chán* 淨土與禪 (Pure Land and Chan). Rev. ed. Taipei: Zhengwen 正聞.

Yīyuán Zōngběn 一元宗本. *Guīyuán zhízhǐ jí* 歸元直指集 (Direct pointing back to the source), XZJ 108.221–356; also CBETA X.1156.

Yuán Hóngdào 袁宏道. 1978. *Pilgrim of the Clouds.* Translated by Jonathan Chaves. New York: Weatherhill.

——. *Xīfāng hélùn* 西方合論 (Comprehensive treatise on the West), T.1976.

——. 1981. *Yuán Hóngdào jí jiānjiào* 袁宏道集箋校. Edited and annotated by Qián Bóchéng 錢伯城. 3 vols. Shanghai: Shanghai guji chubanshe 上海古籍出版社.

Yúnqī Zhūhóng 雲棲袾宏. (1973) *Liánchí dàshī quánjí* 蓮池大師全集 (The collected works of the Great Master Lianchi [i.e., Zhuhong]). 8 vols. Taipei 臺北: Zhonghua fojiao wenhua guan 中華佛教文化館.

——. 2015. *The* Chan Whip *Anthology: A Companion to Zen Practice.* Translated by Jeffrey L. Broughton and Elise Yoko Watanabe. New York: Oxford University Press.

——. *Āmítuó jīng shū chǎo* 阿彌陀經疏鈔, CBETA X.424.

——. *Chánguān cè jìn* 禪關策進 (A whip through the barriers of Chan), T.2024.

——. *Dá jìngtǔ sìshíbā wèn* 答淨土四十八問, CBETA X.1158.

Zànníng 贊寧. *Sòng gāosēng zhuàn* 宋高僧傳 (Song biographies of eminent monks), T.2061.

Zhèng Wéiān 鄭韋庵. 1991. "Niànfó sìshíbā fǎ" 念佛四十八法 ("Forty-eight ways to nianfo"). In *Jìngzuò yàojué yǔ niànfó fǎ yào* 靜坐要訣與念佛法要 (Essential instructions for seated meditation and an outline of *nianfo*), edited by Yuán Liǎofán 袁了凡 and Máo Língyún 毛凌雲, p. 54–71. Taipei: Changchun shu shufang 常春樹書坊.

Zhēnxiē Qīngliǎo chánshī yǔlù 真歇清了禪師語錄, CBETA X.1426.

Zhìpán 志磐. *Fózǔ tǒngjì* 佛祖統紀 (Systematic record of Buddhas and Patriarchs), T.2035.

Zhōng āhán jīng 中阿含經, T.26.

Zōngxiǎo 宗曉. *Lèbāng wénlèi* 樂邦文類 (Anthology of the Land of Bliss), T.1969A.

——. *Sìmíng zūnzhě jiào xíng lù* 四明尊者教行錄 (Record of the Venerable Siming's teachings and practices), T.1937.

Zǔ táng jí 祖堂集 (Patriarch's Hall anthology). 1987. Kyōto: Chūbun shuppansha 中文出版社, 1972; Rpt. Taipei: Xinwenfeng 新文豐.

Zuòchán sānmèi jīng 坐禪三昧經, T.614.

Secondary Sources

Adamek, Wendi L. 2005. "The Impossibility of the Given: Representations of Merit and Emptiness in Medieval Chinese Buddhism." *History of Religions* 45, no. 2 (November): 135–180.

Atone, Joji. 1988. "Shan-tao: His Life and Thought." PhD diss., University of Wisconsin, Madison.

Bloom, Alfred. 1995. "The Western Pure Land." *Tricycle: The Buddhist Review* (Summer): 58–63.

Ch'en, Kenneth K. S. 1964. *Buddhism in China: A Historical Survey.* Princeton: Princeton University Press.

Chan, Wing-tsit. 1963. *A Source Book in Chinese Philosophy.* Princeton: Princeton University Press.

Chappell, David W. 1976. "Tao-ch'o (562–645): A Pioneer of Chinese Pure Land Buddhism." PhD diss., Yale University.

——. 1986. "From Dispute to Dual Cultivation: Pure Land Responses to Chan Critics." In *Traditions of Meditation in Chinese Buddhism,* edited by Peter Gregory. Studies in East Asian Buddhism, no. 4. Honolulu: University of Hawai'i Press.

——. 1996. "The Formation of the Pure Land Movement in China: Tao-ch'o and Shan-tao." In *The Pure Land Tradition: History and Development,* edited by James Foard, Michael Solomon, and Richard K. Payne, p. 138–171. Berkeley Buddhist Studies Series, 3. Berkeley: University of California Press.

Chen Chienhuang 陳劍鍠. 2009. *Xíngjiǎo zǒuguò jìngtǔ fǎmén: Tánluán, Dàochuò yǔ Shàndǎo kāizhǎn Mítuó jìngtǔ jiàomén zhī guǐzhé* 行腳走過淨土法門—曇鸞、道綽與善導開展彌陀淨土教門之軌轍 (Traveling along the Pure Land Dharmagate: Tanluan, Daochuo, and Shandao develop the path of Amitābha's Pure Land). Taipei: Shangzhou Publishing 商周出版.

——. 2015. *Wúshàng fāngbiàn yǔ xiànxíng fǎlè: Mítuó jìngtǔ yǔ rénjiān jìngtǔ de zhōubiān guānxī* 無上方便與現行法樂：彌陀淨土與人間淨土的周邊關係 (The highest expedient means and enacting of Dharma-joy: The common boundary of Amitābha's Pure Land and humanistic Pure Land). Taipei: Xianghai wenhua 香海文化.

——. 2017. "The Process of Establishing and Justifying the Thirteen Patriarchs of the Lotus School." Trans. Charles B. Jones. In *Pacific World: Journal of the Institute of Buddhist Studies* 19, 3rd ser.:129–148.

Chén Yángjiǒng 陈扬炯. 2008. *Zhōngguó jìngtǔzōng tōngshǐ* 中国净土宗通史 (A general history of the Pure Land School in China). Nanjing: Phoenix Publishing House 凤凰出版社.

Chéng Yíshān 程宜山. 1986. *Zhōngguó gǔdài yuánqì xuéshuō* 中國古代元氣學說 (Theories of primordial qi in Ancient China). Hubei 湖北: Hubei People's Press 湖北人民出版社.

Cook, Francis H. 1977. *Huayan Buddhism: The Realm of Indra's Net.* University Park: Pennsylvania State University Press.

Corless, Roger J. 1996. "T'an-luan: The First Systematizer of Pure Land Buddhism." In *The Pure Land Tradition: History and Development,* edited by James Foard, Michael Solomon, and Richard K. Payne, p. 107–137. Berkeley Buddhist Studies Series, 3. Berkeley: University of California Press.

Dàān 大安. 2006. *Jìngtǔ zōng jiàochéng* 淨土宗教程 (A course in Pure Land). Beijing: Zongjiao wenhua chubanshe 宗教文化出版社.

Dobbins, James. 1989. *Jōdo Shinshū: Shin Buddhism in Medieval Japan.* Bloomington: Indiana University Press.

Ducor, Jérôme. 2004. "Les Sources de la Sukhāvatī Autour d'une Étude Récente de G. Fussman." *Journal of the International Association of Buddhist Studies* 27, no. 2:357–410.

Eichman, Jennifer. 2016. *A Late Sixteenth-Century Chinese Buddhist Fellowship: Spiritual Ambitions, Intellectual Debates, and Epistolary Connections.* Sinica Leidensia, 127. Leiden: Brill.

Eiki Iwaki 岩城英規. 1998. "Chigyoku no kairitsu shisō" 智旭の戒律思想 ("Zhixu's vinaya thought"). *Tendai gakuhō* 天台学報, no. 40:77–80.

Fujita Kōtatsu 藤田宏達. 1970. *Genshi Jōdo shisō no kenkyū* 原始浄土思想の研究 (A study of early Pure Land thought). Tokyo: Iwanami Shoten 岩波書店.

——. 1996. "Pure Land Buddhism in India." Translated by Kenneth Tanaka. In *The Pure Land Tradition: History and Development,* edited by James Foard, Michael Solomon, and Richard K. Payne, p. 1–42. Berkeley Buddhist Studies Series, 3. Berkeley: University of California Press.

Getz, Daniel A. 1994. "Siming Zhili and Tiantai Pure Land in the Song Dynasty." PhD diss., Yale University.

——. 1999. "T'ien-t'ai Pure Land Societies and the Creation of the Pure Land Patriarchate," in *Buddhism in the Sung,* edited by Peter N. Gregory and Daniel A. Getz Jr., p. 477–523. Honolulu: University of Hawai'i Press.

——. 2003. “Shengchang’s Pure Conduct Society and the Chinese Pure Land Patriarchate.” In *Approaching the Land of Bliss: Religious Praxis in the Cult of Amitābha,* edited by Richard K. Payne and Kenneth K. Tanaka, p. 52–76. Honolulu: University of Hawai‘i Press.

Goodell, Eric. 2012. “Taixu’s (1890–1947) Creation of Humanistic Buddhism.” PhD diss., University of Virginia.

——. 2017. “Taixu’s Pure Land on Earth and the Vimalakīrti Sūtra.” *Foguang xuebao* 佛光學報, n.s., vol. 3, no. 1:171–200.

Gregory, Peter N. 1991. *Tsung-mi and the Sinification of Buddhism.* Princeton: Princeton University Press.

Gǔ Zhèngměi 古正美. 2000. “Cóng nántiān jí nánhǎi de 《*Huáyán jīng*》 fówáng chuántǒng yǔ mìjiào Guānyīn fówáng chuántǒng” 從南天及南海的《華嚴經》佛王傳統與密教觀音佛王傳統 (“The king of Orissa‘s donation of the *Huayan Sutra* to the Huayan Sutra Buddharāja and Esoteric Avalokiteśvara Buddharāja traditions of South India and Southeast Asia”). *Fóxué yánjiū zhōngxīn xuébào* 佛學研究中心學報, no. 5:159–201.

Guo, Hong Yue. 2007. “Rebirth and Karmic Retribution in Fifth-Century China: A Study of the Teachings of the Buddhist Monk Lu Shan Huiyuan 盧山慧遠.” PhD diss., Indiana University.

Guō Péng 郭朋. 1982. *Míng-Qīng fójiào* 明清佛教 (Buddhism in the Ming and Qing). Fuzhou 福州: Fujian Renmin chubanshe 福建人民出版社.

Hori, Ichirō. 1968. “Nembutsu as Folk Religion.” In *Folk Religion in Japan: Continuity and Change,* edited by Joseph M. Kitagawa and Alan L. Miller. Chicago: University of Chicago Press.

Huang Yi-hsun. 2001. “A Study of Yongming Yanshou’s The Profound Pivot of the Contemplation of Mind.” PhD diss., University of Virginia.

Jiāng Cànténg 江燦騰. 1998. “Lǐ Zhuōwú yǔ wǎn Míng fójiào sīxiǎng yǐ jí duì ‘kuáng chán’ de pīpíng” 李桌吾與晚明佛教思想以及對「狂禪」的批評 (“Li Zhuowu and late Ming Buddhist thought and a critique of ‘Crazy Chan’ ”). In *Zhōngguó jìndài fójiào sīxiǎng de zhèngbiàn yǔ fāzhǎn* 中國近代佛教思想的諍辯與發展, p. 323–399. Taipei: Nantian Shuju 南天書局.

Jiǎng Yìbīn 蔣義斌. 2000. “Dà zhìdù lùn *zhōng de jìngtǔ guān*” 《大智度論》中的淨土觀 (“The view of the Pure Land in the *Dà zhīdù lùn*”). In *Yìnshùn sīxiǎng: Yìnshùn dǎoshī jiǔ zhì jìn wǔ shòu qìnglùn wénjí* 《印順思想》—印順導師九秩晉五壽慶論文集 (Buddhist and Religious Studies, essays in honor of Venerable Yin-Shun on his 95th birthday), p. 221–244. Zhubei: Zhengwen Publishing Company 正聞出版社; Rpt. http://www.yinshun.org.tw/thesis/10.htm. Accessed December 6, 2010.

Jones, Charles B. 1997. “Stages in the Religious Life of Lay Buddhists in Taiwan.” *Journal of the International Association of Buddhist Studies* 20, no. 2:113–139.

——. 1999. *Buddhism in Taiwan: Religion and the State, 1660–1990.* Honolulu: University of Hawai'i Press.

——. 2000. "Mentally Constructing What Already Exists: The Pure Land Thought of Chan Master Jixing Chewu 際醒徹悟 (1741–1810)." *Journal of the International Association of Buddhist Studies* 23, no. 1:43–70.

——. 2001. "Toward a Typology of Nien-fo: A Study in Methods of Buddha-Invocation in Chinese Pure Land Buddhism." *Pacific World: Journal of the Institute of Buddhist Studies,* 3rd series, no. 3:219–239.

——. 2003. "Transitions in the Practice and Defense of Chinese Pure Land." In *Buddhism and the Modern World: Adaptations of an Ancient Tradition,* edited by Charles Prebish and Steven Heine, p. 125–142. New York: Oxford University Press.

——. 2008. "Was Lushan Huiyuan 盧山慧遠 a Pure Land Buddhist? Evidence from His Correspondence with Kumarajiva About *Nianfo* 念佛 Practice." *Chung-Hwa Buddhist Journal* 21:175–191.

——. 2009a. "Foundations of Ethics and Practice in Chinese Pure Land Buddhism." In *Destroying Mara Forever: Buddhist Ethics Essays in Honor of Damien Keown,* edited by John Powers and Charles Prebish, p. 237–259. Ithaca: Snow Lion.

——. 2009b. "Yuan Hongdao and the *Xifang helun:* Pure Land Theology in the Late Ming Dynasty." In *Path of No Path: Contemporary Studies in Pure Land Buddhism Honoring Roger Corless,* edited by Richard K. Payne, p. 89–126. Berkeley: Institute of Buddhist Studies and Numata Center for Buddhist Translation and Research.

Keenan, John P. 1987. "Pure Land Systematics in India: The Buddhabhūmisūtra and the Trikāya Doctrine." *Pacific World,* n.s., no. 3:29–35.

——. 1989. "Nien-fo (Buddha-Anusmṛti): The Shifting Structure of Remembrance." *Pacific World,* n.s., no. 5:40–52.

Kim, Jung-yeup. 2015. *Zhang Zai's Philosophy of Qi: A Practical Understanding.* Lanham: Lexington Books.

Kimura Eiichi 木村英一, ed. 1960–1962. *Eon Kenkyū* 慧遠研究 (Studies on Huiyuan [*sic*]). 2 vols. Tokyo: Sobunsha 創文社.

Kroll, Paul W. 2015. *A Student's Dictionary of Classical and Medieval Chinese.* Leiden: Brill.

Lǐ Xìnglíng 李幸玲. 2007. *Lúshān Huìyuǎn yánjiū* 盧山慧遠研究 (A study of Huiyuan of Mt. Lu). Taipei: Wanjuanlou 萬卷樓.

Liebenthal, Walter. 1950. "Shih Huiyuan's Buddhism as Set Forth in His Writings." *Journal of the American Oriental Society* 7, no. 4:243–259.

——. 1955. "Chinese Buddhism During the 4th and 5th Centuries." *Monumenta Nipponica* 11, no. 1:44–83.

Liú Chángdōng 刘长东. 2000. *Jìn Táng Mítuó jìngtǔ xīnyǎng yánjiū* 晋唐弥陀净土信仰研究 (Studies in Jin-Tang Amitābha belief). Chengdu: Bashu shushe 巴蜀书社.

Marchman, Kendall. 2015. "Huaigan and the Growth of Pure Land Buddhism During the Tang Era." PhD diss., University of Florida.

Mochizuki Shinkō 望月信亨. 1942. *Chūgoku jōdo kyōrishi* 中国浄土教理史 (Pure Land Buddhism in China: A doctrinal history). Tokyo: Hōzōkan 法藏館.

——. 2016. *Pure Land Buddhism in China: A Doctrinal History.* Translated by Leo Pruden, edited by Richard K. Payne and Natalie E. F. Quli. 2 vols. Berkeley: Institute of Buddhist Studies, BDK America.

Nagao, Gadjin. 1981. "The Bodhisattva Returns to This World." In *The Bodhisattva Doctrine in Buddhism,* edited by Leslie Kawamura, p. 61–79. SR Supplements, 10. Waterloo: Wilfrid Laurier University Press.

Nattier, Jan. 2000. "The Realm of Akṣobhya: A Missing Piece in the History of Pure Land Buddhism." *Journal of the International Association of Buddhist Studies* 23, no. 1:71–102.

Ng, Yu-kwan. 1993. *T'ien-t'ai Buddhism and Early Mādhyamika.* Honolulu: Tendai Institute of Hawaii, University of Hawai'i Press.

Nogami Shunjō 野上俊靜. 1962. "Eon to kōsei no chūgoku jōdokyō" 慧遠と後世の中國淨土教. In *Eon Kenkyū* 慧遠研究 (Studies on Huiyuan [*sic*]), edited by Kimura Eiichi 木村英一, p. 1:223–247. 2 vols. Tokyo: Sobunsha 創文社.

Ogasawara Senshū 小笠原宣秀. 1951. "Chūgoku kindai jōdokyō no ichi kōsatsu" 中国近代浄土教の一考察 ("An inquiry into the modern Chinese Pure Land School"). *Ryūkoku shidan* 竜谷史壇, no. 34:7–14.

Ono Gemmyō 小野玄妙. 1932–1936. *Bussho Kaisetsu Daijiten* 佛書解說大辞典 (Encyclopedia of Buddhist literature). 12 vols. Tokyo: Daitō Shuppansha 大東出版社. Rpt. Taipei: Xinwenfeng 新文豐, n.d.

Orzech, Charles D. 1998. *Politics and Transcendent Wisdom: The Scripture for Humane Kings in the Creation of Chinese Buddhism.* University Park: Pennsylvania State University Press.

Pas, Julian. 1995. *Visions of Sukhāvatī: Shandao's Commentary on the Kuan Wu-Liang-Shou-Fo Ching.* Albany: State University of New York Press.

Payne, Richard K. 2015. "The Five Contemplative Gates of Vasubandhu's *Rebirth Treatise* as a Ritualized Visualization Practice." *Pacific World: Journal of the Institute of Buddhist Studies,* 3rd series, no. 17:43–67.

Pruden, Leo. 1973. "The Ching-t'u Shih-i-lun." *The Eastern Buddhist* 6, no. 1:126–157.

Qiū Mǐnjié 邱敏捷. 1993. *Cān chán yǔ niànfó: wǎn Míng Yuán Hóngdào de fójiào sīxiǎng* 参禪與念佛: 晚明袁宏道的佛教思想 (Chan practice and Buddha-Recitation:

The Buddhist thought of Yuan Hongdao in the late Ming). *Zōngjiào Wénhuà Cóng Shū* 宗教文化叢書, 3. Taipei: Shang Ding 商鼎文化出版社.

Rambelli, Fabio. 2004. "'Just Behave as You Like; Prohibitions and Impurities Are Not a Problem': Radical Amida Cults and Popular Religiosity in Premodern Japan." In *Approaching the Land of Bliss: Religious Praxis in the Cult of Amitābha*, edited by Richard K. Payne and Kenneth K. Tanaka, p. 169–201. Kuroda Institute Studies in East Asian Buddhism, 17. Honolulu: University of Hawai'i Press.

Ritzinger, Justin R. 2017. *Anarchy in the Pure Land: Reinventing the Cult of Maitreya in Modern Chinese Buddhism.* New York: Oxford University Press.

Robinson, Richard H. 1967. *Early Mādhyamika in India and China.* Madison: University of Wisconsin Press.

Rowell, Teresina. 1934. "The Background and Early Use of the Buddha-Kṣetra Concept. Introduction and Chapter One." *The Eastern Buddhist (Original Series)* 6, no. 3:199–246.

——. 1935. "The Background and Early Use of the Buddha-Kṣetra Concept. Chapter Two and Three." *The Eastern Buddhist (Original Series)* 6, no. 4:379–431.

——. 1937. "The Background and Early Use of the Buddha-Kṣetra Concept. Chapter IV, with Appendices and Bibliography (Concluded)." *The Eastern Buddhist (Original Series)* 7, no. 3:132–176.

Salomon, Richard, and Gregory Schopen. 2002. "On an Alleged Reference to Amitābha in a Kharoṣṭhī Inscription on a Gandhāran Relief." *Journal of the International Association of Buddhist Studies* 25, no. 1–2:3–31.

Schopen, Gregory. 1997. *Bones, Stones, and Buddhist Monks: Collected Papers on the Archaeology, Epigraphy, and Texts of Monastic Buddhism in India.* Honolulu: University of Hawai'i Press.

——. 2005. "Sukhāvatī as a Generalized Religious Goal in Sanskrit Mahāyāna *Sūtra* Literature." In *Figments and Fragments of Mahayana Buddhism in India: More Collected Papers*, p. 154–189. Honolulu: University of Hawai'i Press.

Sharf, Robert H. 2002a. "On Pure Land Buddhism and Chan/Pure Land Syncretism in Medieval China." *T'oung Pao* 88, fasc. 4/5:282–331.

——. 2002b. *Coming to Terms with Chinese Buddhism: A Reading of the* Treasure Store Treatise. Kuroda Institute Studies in East Asian Buddhism, 14. Honolulu: University of Hawai'i Press.

Sheng Yen 聖嚴. 1965. *Jièlǜxué gāngyào* 戒律學綱要 (An outline of vinaya studies). Taipei: Dongchu Publishing 東初出版社.

——. 1992. *Míngmò fójiào yánjiū* 明末佛教研究 (Studies in late Ming Buddhism). Taipei: Dongchu 東初出版社.

——. 1997. *Rénjiān jìngtǔ* 人間淨土 (The Pure Land in the human realm). Taipei: Fagu 法鼓.

——. 2010. *Shèngyán fǎshī jiào jìngtǔ fǎmén* 聖嚴法師教淨土法門 (Master Sheng Yen teaches the Pure Land dharma-gate). Compiled and edited by Guǒxián 果賢. Shèngyán shūyuàn 聖嚴書院, 5. Taipei: Fagu wenhua 法鼓文化.

Shì Jiànzhèng 釋見正. 1989. *Yìnguāng dàshī de shēngpíng yǔ sīxiǎng* 印光大師的生平與思想 (The life and thought of the Great Master Yinguang). Taipei: Dongchu 東初.

Shih Heng-ching. 1991. "The Syncretism of Chinese Chan and Pure Land Buddhism." In *Buddhist Thought and Ritual,* edited by David Kalupahana, p. 69–84. New York: Paragon House.

——. 1992. *The Syncretism of Chan and Pure Land Buddhism.* Asian Thought and Culture, 9. New York: Peter Lang.

Steadman, James L. 1987. "Pure Land Buddhism and the Buddhist Historical Tradition." *Religious Studies* 23, no. 3:407–421.

Stevenson, Daniel B. 1986. "The Four Kinds of Samādhi in Early T'ien-t'ai Buddhism." In *Traditions of Meditation in Chinese Buddhism,* edited by Peter N. Gregory, p. 45–98. Kuroda Institute Studies in East Asian Buddhism, 4. Honolulu: University of Hawai'i Press.

——. 1995. "Death-bed Testimonials of the Pure Land Faithful." In *Buddhism in Practice,* edited by Donald S. Lopez, p. 592–602. Princeton: Princeton University Press.

Stevenson, Daniel B., and Neal Donner, trans. 1993. *The Great Calming and Contemplation: A Study and Annotated Translation of the First Chapter of Chih-i's Mo Ho Chih Kuan.* Honolulu: University of Hawai'i Press.

Stone, Jacqueline I. 1999. *Original Enlightenment and the Transformation of Medieval Japanese Buddhism.* Kuroda Institute Studies in East Asian Buddhism, 12. Honolulu: University of Hawai'i Press.

Tan, Bee Leng. 1979. "The Conception of 'Nien-fo' in the Ching-t'u-shih-i-lun (Treatise on the Ten Doubts Concerning the Pure Land)." MA thesis, McMaster University.

Tanaka, Kenneth K. 1990. *The Dawn of Chinese Pure Land Buddhist Doctrine: Ching-ying Hui-yüan's Commentary on the Visualization Sutra.* Albany: State University of New York Press.

Tokunaga Michio. 1993. "Mahayana Essence as Seen in the Concept of 'Return to this World.'" *Pacific World,* n.s., vol. 9:1–10.

Tsukamoto, Zenryū. 1985. *A History of Early Chinese Buddhism: From its Introduction to the Death of Hui-yüan.* Translated by Leon Hurvitz. 2 vols. Tokyo: Kodansha International.

Wagner, Rudolf G. 1971. "The Original Structure of the Correspondence Between Shih Huiyüan and Kumārajīva." *Harvard Journal of Asiatic Studies,* no. 31:28–48.

Welter, Albert. 1997. "Yung-ming Yen-shou: Chan Master, Pure Land Master, or What? Bodhisattva Practice and Pure Land Practice in the Writings of Yung-ming Yen-shou." Paper presented at the Third Chung-Hwa International Conference on Buddhism, Taipei, Taiwan, July 19–21.

Xiao Yue 肖越. 2009. "What Is the Difference between Sukhāvatī and *Jingtu* 淨土?" *Bukkyō Daigaku Sōgō Kenkyūsho Kiyō* 佛教大学総合研究所紀要, 16:265–280.

Yü, Chün-fang. 1981. *The Renewal of Buddhism in China: Chu-hung and the Late Ming Synthesis.* New York: Columbia University Press.

Yu, Jimmy. 2014. "Pure Land Devotion in East Asia." In *The Wiley Blackwell Companion to East and Inner Asian Buddhism*, edited by Mario Poceski, p. 201–220. New York: Wiley Blackwell.

Zhāng Màntāo 張曼濤, ed. 1979. *Jìngtǔzōng gàilùn* 淨土宗概論 (An introduction to the Pure Land School). Xiàndài fójiào xuéshù cóngkān 現代佛教學術叢刊, 64. Taipei: Dasheng wenhua 大乘文化.

Zürcher, Erik. 1959. *The Buddhist Conquest of China: The Spread and Adaptation of Buddhism in Early Medieval China.* Sinica Leidensia, 11. Leiden: Brill. Rpt. Taipei: Caves Books, n.d.

Index

About the Author

Charles B. Jones is associate professor and director of the religion and culture graduate program in the School of Theology and Religious Studies at the Catholic University of America, Washington, DC. He earned a PhD in History of Religions from the University of Virginia in 1996 with an emphasis on East Asian Buddhism. In 1999 he published his first book, *Buddhism in Taiwan: Religion and the State 1660–1990,* the first history of its type to be published in any language. Since then, he has focused primarily on the study of Chinese Pure Land Buddhism in the late imperial period. He has also published books and articles on the Jesuit missions in late Ming dynasty China, late Ming gentry Buddhism, and interreligious dialogue. He was a Fulbright scholar in Taiwan during the 2004–2005 academic year.